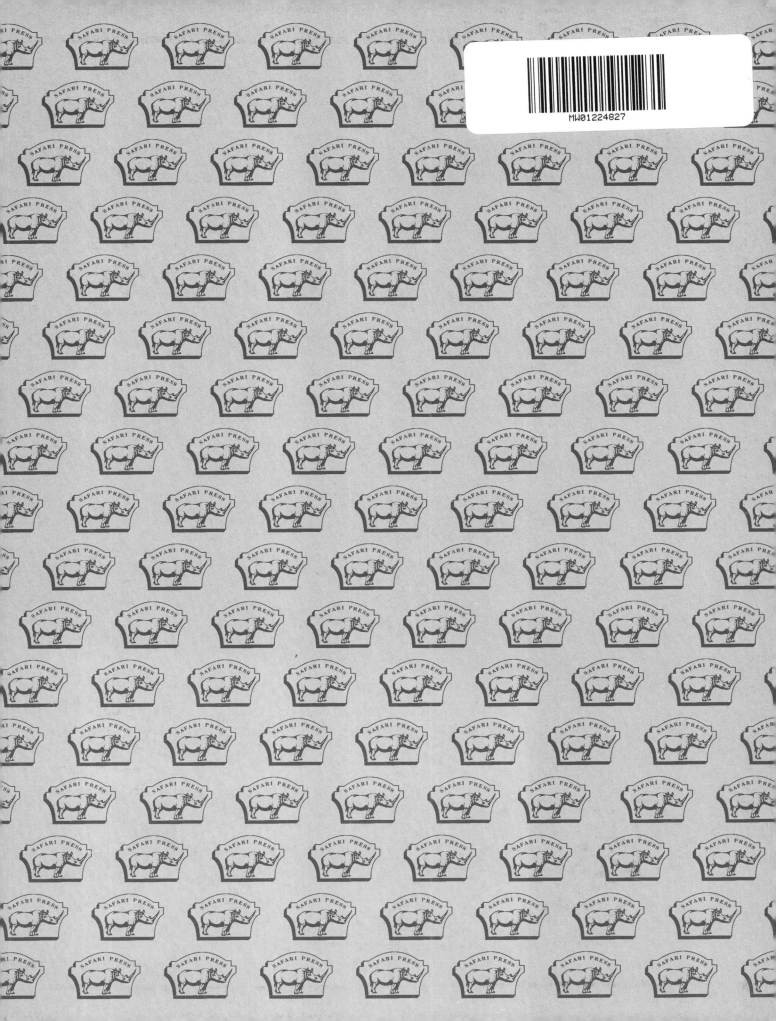

ON SAFARI WITH BWANA GAME

ON SAFARI WITH BWANA GAME

by

Eric Balson

SAFARI PRESS INC.

The trademark Safari Press ® is registered with the U.S. Patent and Trademark Office and in other countries.

Balson, Eric

Second edition

Safari Press Inc.

2003, Long Beach, California

ISBN 1-57157-301-1

Library of Congress Catalog Card Number: 2002112957

10 9 8 7 6 5 4 3 2 1

Printed in Singapore

Readers wishing to receive the Safari Press catalog, featuring many fine books on big-game hunting, wingshooting, and sporting firearms, should write to Safari Press Inc., P.O. Box 3095, Long Beach, CA 90803, USA. Tel: (714) 894-9080 or visit our Web site at www.safaripress.com.

DEDICATION

I dedicate this book to several people: First of all to my wonderful wife, Viva, and to our sons, Alan, Steven, and Kenneth, who were my companions on so many safaris and who made our lives such happy ones. My next dedication goes to my faithful and loyal staff, especially Rashidi Ramazani, Salum Kalangula, John Jonas, Elias Nampungu, and Lesenu Mungasi. And last, but not least, I dedicate this book to a very special person who has done so much for conservation, a fine sportsman, a keen naturalist, an excellent leader, who has given me his invaluable advice over many years, a real gentleman and a true friend—His Royal Highness Prince Bernhard of the Netherlands, who has honoured me by writing a greeting for this book.

IN APPRECIATION

I would like to express my deep thanks to an admirable lady who was always full of life and encouragement when I was down in the dumps, and who has stood by me for all these years, giving me advice and sometimes criticism when needed. To Viva, my wife, *asante sana* (thank you very much).

TABLE OF CONTENTS

FOREWORD

It is my privilege to introduce to you to the author.

I grew up in England, and during my teenage years I read every book about Africa that I could lay my hands on. Quite a number of them contained exciting stories of the lives of game wardens, and that became my ambition–to become a game warden in Africa.

Unfortunately, that did not come about. But after my period of conscription in the army and some years in the family merchanting business, I did travel to Tanganyika (now known as Tanzania) and bought a coffee plantation near the town of Arusha not far from the two highest mountains in that country–Mount Kilimanjaro and Mount Meru.

Shortly after taking up permanent resident in 1963, I was introduced to Eric Balson, a senior game warden in the Tanzanian Game Department, who happened to be stationed in Arusha. We struck up an immediate rapport and became firm friends–a friendship, I am proud to say, that continues to this day. I have the most profound respect and admiration for Eric Balson. He was everything I would have liked to have been.

Eric was born in Kenya and is fluent in the Swahili language, the lingua franca of Kenya, Uganda, and Tanzania and parts of the many surrounding countries. Growing up in East Africa and having an inborn love of nature and wildlife, it was a natural progression for Eric to make a dedicated career in the game department.

His complete mastery of Swahili made it easy for him to communicate with the indigenous people. He was a past-master in getting to know their modes and customs, which earned him great respect and liking amongst the tribal chiefs and elders. It also earned him the nickname of *Bwana Hakuna Matata*, meaning *Master without troubles.*

The purpose of my introducing Eric Balson to you, the readers, is to get you acquainted with the author. In his introduction, Eric's modesty led him to say little about himself, and those like me, who know him well, feel that people should get to know the depth and purity of his devotion, plus the intensity of his achievements and his aspirations as a senior game warden.

Many times I had the good fortune and privilege to go on safari with Eric into the bush. They were unforgettable experiences. He generously passed on to me his tremendous knowledge of the fauna and flora of the African bush. His remarkable energy, fantastic knowledge, interest in and experience with bushlore in all its phases (not forgetting his cool courage when confronted with immediate danger) really whetted my appetite to share with other hunters and conservationists the real outdoors. The information and guidance I gained from him stood me in good stead throughout the long years of my being a professional hunter and keen conservationist. Eric's remarkable achievements are many and diverse.

· He has conducted safaris with many famous people, e.g., H.R.H. Prince Bernhard of the Netherlands, President Marshal Tito from Yugoslavia, world-renowned wildlife artists David Shepherd and Guy Coheleach, and many more illustrious VIPs.

· He played a major role in creating the Ruaha and Katavi National Parks in Tanzania. He moved to Zambia where he created a national park in the Zambezi Valley on behalf of an American foundation, although his efforts there were sadly thwarted by the actions of the Rhodesian war. He traveled to Nepal as a member of a United Nations wildlife team to train and set up a thriving national park system in that kingdom.

· He received a special mandate from the Tanzanian president to stamp out commercial poaching, an activity that brought grave danger to Eric and his family, including several assassination attempts.

· Eric was then transferred to Papua New Guinea where he established one of the largest crocodile farming industries in the world in order to help the nationals of that country preserve the mighty saltwater crocodile from becoming extinct. He has demonstrated an ability to mediate and solve many problems with the local population.

· He managed and improved one of the largest game ranches in Namibia/South-West Africa, the Ohorongo Game Ranch. He also spent more than two years planning and starting the rehabilitation of the Niassa Game Reserve in the republic of Mozambique.

· Last but not least, Eric has been a guest speaker at many wildlife conventions worldwide.

His achievements, his vast knowledge, and his lifelong endeavors, therefore, make Eric Balson eminently suited to write a book on his experiences in the African bush. I am sure you will find Eric's stories intriguing and his book an exciting one to read.

Derek Evans
Eagles Rest
Nelspruit, Republic of South Africa
November 2002

INTRODUCTION

After considerable deliberation and hesitation, I have yielded to persuasion and put pen to paper. From my rather mixed random notes and records, I have endeavoured to relate some stories that I hope will be of interest to you, the reader. I have tried to depict, with pictures and words, actual events involving a member of royalty and other dignitaries whose entire public lives must be lived in front of crowds, cameras, and television. Everything they do is watched, imposing a tremendous strain on their responsible positions; consequently, it never ceased to amaze me how suddenly H. R. H. Prince Bernhard could switch from one mood to another. He has a terrific sense of humour just waiting to break through the required daily solemnity whenever opportunity arises (like being on safari in Africa with his favourite animal, the elephant).

During the past several decades, a great number of books have been published by hunters and naturalists as well as by scientists and ordinary novelists. Many of these books have been excellent, each in its own way, but to the best of my knowledge very few have been like this one. My book is about friends, true friends, who over many years, despite their varied backgrounds, enjoyed and experienced untamed nature at its best.

As you read these accounts, please keep in mind that in Victorian times, little pity was wasted on the poor beasts that died; they were the legitimate prey of humankind. Their extermination was never regretted, for they existed purely to furnish thrills and amusement for Homo sapiens.

Then came the change, primarily due, I believe, to people like Prince Bernhard, who dedicated a lot of his valuable time to the preservation of these admirable creatures, which he believed had an essential place in our modern world. Elephant, lion, buffalo, and even insects, big or small, were no longer regarded as insensate beasts but the very opposite—interesting, sagacious creatures whose conduct might, in many circumstances, be a source of beauty and delight to the beholder.

Finally, it has been a great joy and honour for me to have had the responsibility for and experiences with such a great man as Prince Bernhard on safari in Africa with its varied mysteries and enchantment. If I have been able to convey some of my enthusiasm and admiration for the prince through this book and its pictures, then my task will have been well worthwhile. For this, Sir, I thank you.

And last but not least, I should like to thank all my dear friends, past and present, for their support and encouragement, including Bill Moore-Gilbert, Myles Turner, Norman Carr, Dr. John Owen, Joe Newby, Colonel Coen Geertsema, Hans Teengs Gerritsen, and Doc Stan Furber, not forgetting some of my faithful game guards who are sadly no longer with us, though their memories and pictures are here to stay.

A very special mention must go to Mike and Debbie Ghaui for all their help and enthusiasm over the years and especially to Mike for the fantastic drawings he has done for my book. Mike, you are a star.

To another great and talented artist, David Shepherd, and his family, thanks for your friendship and efforts to save the wild animals on this planet. To Richard Allen, Paddy Curtis, Nick Klapprott, John Stewart-Smith, and Peter Jenkins for allowing me to use your photographs—thanks, Bwanas.

I am also deeply indebted to *Roget's Thesaurus* for helping me with my limited vocabulary. And to my special friends Derek and Susi Evans, Pat French, Gerard and Leenie Miller, Roy and Mike Carr-Hartley (plus their wives Judy and Sue), Gerhard and Belinda Ambrose, Ricky and Sally Mann, Ian and Jane Craig—not forgetting Susan Pirs, who spent many hours reading and correcting my first manuscript; Derek Evens, who kindly wrote the preamble; and, last but not least, a very special word of thanks to my son Alan Balson for reviewing the final proof at such short notice—a big THANK YOU to you all.

AUTHOR'S SPECIAL NOTE

Throughout my stories I have used a lot of Swahili words, simply because I love this Bantu language. I was born and brought up in Kenya and worked most of my life in eastern Africa, so I consider Swahili to be almost my mother tongue, despite being of English parentage, education, and upbringing.

The Swahili language is very expressive and has a fascinating euphonic type of tempo that makes it easy to follow. Many words are softened or emphasized, depending on their importance to the subject being discussed.

If you already know Swahili, then you will have no problems in understanding what I am trying to convey, but for many of you it will be a new language. My advice is to read it exactly as it is spelled, read it aloud (make sure that no one is listening, or they may think you are going crazy), and listen to what a melodious language it can be. Good luck with your first Swahili lesson below.

"Jambo, Bwana na Bibi, salamu nyingi sana na karibu kusoma kitabu yangu." Meaning: "Hello, Misters and Misses, many greetings and welcome to reading my book."

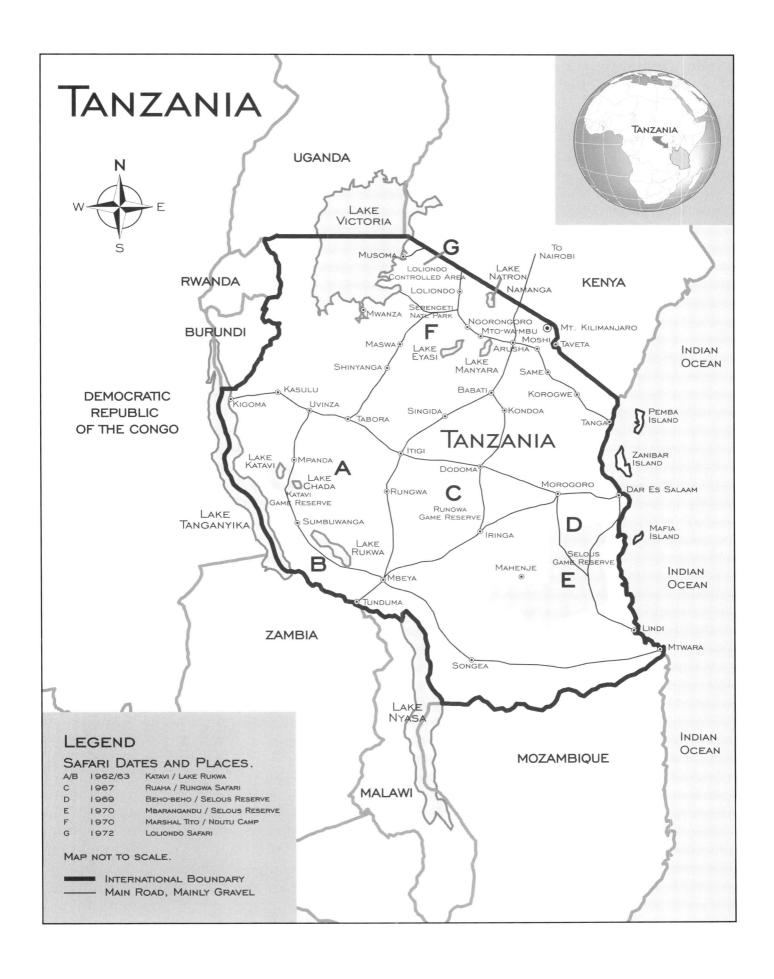

TANZANIA

N
W · E
S

UGANDA

LAKE VICTORIA

RWANDA

BURUNDI

DEMOCRATIC REPUBLIC OF THE CONGO

MUSOMA

G

LOLIONDO CONTROLLED AREA

LOLIONDO

MWANZA

SERENGETI NAT'L PARK

F

LAKE NATRON

NAMANGA

KENYA

To NAIROBI

NGORONGORO
MTO-WA-MBU
ARUSHA
MOSHI
Mt. KILIMANJARO
TAVETA

MASWA

LAKE EYASI

LAKE MANYARA

SHINYANGA

KASULU

KIGOMA

UVINZA

TABORA

SINGIDA

BABATI

KONDOA

SAME

KOROGWE

TANGA

INDIAN OCEAN

PEMBA ISLAND

ZANIBAR ISLAND

TANZANIA

LAKE KATAVI

MPANDA

A

LAKE CHADA

KATAVI GAME RESERVE

ITIGI

RUNGWA

DODOMA

C

MOROGORO

DAR ES SALAAM

RUNGWA GAME RESERVE

D

MAFIA ISLAND

LAKE TANGANYIKA

SUMBUWANGA

B

LAKE RUKWA

IRINGA

MAHENJE

SELOUS GAME RESERVE

E

INDIAN OCEAN

MBEYA

TUNDUMA

LINDI

MTWARA

ZAMBIA

SONGEA

LAKE NYASA

MOZAMBIQUE

INDIAN OCEAN

MALAWI

LEGEND
SAFARI DATES AND PLACES.

A/B	1962/63	KATAVI / LAKE RUKWA
C	1967	RUAHA / RUNGWA SAFARI
D	1969	BEHO-BEHO / SELOUS RESERVE
E	1970	MBARANGANDU / SELOUS RESERVE
F	1970	MARSHAL TITO / NDUTU CAMP
G	1972	LOLIONDO SAFARI

MAP NOT TO SCALE.

━━━ INTERNATIONAL BOUNDARY
─── MAIN ROAD, MAINLY GRAVEL

On a 1972 photograph, Prince Bernhard of the Netherlands inscribed, "To Eric—Thanks for a great safari."

SALAMU SANA!
(many good wishes)

from H. R. H. Prince Bernhard

I am happy to write an introduction to Eric's book. We have had a lot of good times together in Africa—shooting and filming, and talking about our experiences.

Of course, Eric had been in Africa a long time, and listening to him was also an experience for me. He describes our safaris very well indeed, and also his work when we were not together. I find this book fascinating, and I hope the reader will not think that the word "fascinating" is only my biased opinion.

Bernhard
Prince of the Netherlands
Soestdijk Palace
September 13, 2000

"Catching the Breeze" *by Mike Ghaui.*

CHAPTER ONE
On Safari with H. R. H. Prince Bernhard

The following stories are based on facts and actual incidents that took place during some of the hunting and photographic safaris to Tanganyika, later Tanzania, for which I had the honour to be the official guide and professional hunter for His Royal Highness Prince Bernhard of the Netherlands. Many years have gone by since my last safari with the prince, so I have decided to put pen to paper to create a record for my children and grandchildren and for many friends who have kept at me for years to write about the wonderful experiences we shared over some twenty-five years.

He is an outstanding man of our time, given his experience and his ceaseless efforts to protect for posterity both the fauna and the flora of the world. He was the president of the World Wildlife Fund (WWF) for many years and raised thousands of dollars for the benefit of wildlife. He also initiated the Thousand and One Club, the proceeds from which went directly for the betterment of wildlife all over the world. In those days, the early 1970s, it cost U.S. $10,000 to become a member. The club was a great success and had its full complement of 1001 members plus a

long waiting list of people from all walks of life eager to join. Only when an existing member passed away did a vacancy occur, and this was filled immediately. Both the club and the WWF performed gallant work for wildlife.

Prince Bernhard traveled all over the world seeking agreements from many nations to set aside areas for the protection of their fauna and flora. He conducted tours with other members of the Thousand and One Club, visiting national parks and game sanctuaries all around the globe. He loved his work and really enjoyed every minute he was in the bush, walking for many hours each day. He did not shoot much—only when camp food was needed—and indulged more in the hobby of shooting with a camera.

In 1973 the World Wildlife Fund launched Operation Tiger, a campaign to save this magnificent animal, which had been listed as an endangered species by the International Union for the Conservation of Nature (IUCN) based in Geneva, Switzerland. David Shepherd, a renowned wildlife artist and conservationist, came up with a brilliant idea. He would create an oil painting of an enraged tiger, call it *Tiger Fire*, have 850 prints made

1

from the original, and sell them for £150 each. David appeared on television and marketed his plan. He also signed each numbered print and donated all the proceeds from their sale, plus the original, to Operation Tiger, thereby raising £127,500 toward the target of £400,000—a great effort.

I happened to be staying with David and Avril at their beautiful sixteenth-century home called Winkworth Farm at about the time David came up with his brilliant idea. He asked me if I would invite Prince Bernhard to come to London for the special ceremony, which included a drawing to determine who would win the original painting. Each print had a number; all 850 numbers were put into a drum, and it would be Prince Bernhard's task to draw out the winning number. I jumped up and asked David to show me his phone, for I had PB's telephone number on hand.

The reply to my phone call was immediate: "Of course, my friend; tell David just to let me know the exact date and time, and I will make sure I am there. I will do all I can to see the tigers are safe and secure."

I thanked him and added, "Please make sure that you pick number seven, because that is my numbered print."

He responded, "I will do my level best for you," and he laughed. Unfortunately, he drew another number.

While Prince Bernhard was in London, he presented David with his personal and special award, the Order of the Golden Ark. David said afterward, "It was one of the greatest thrills of my life."

A couple of years later when I was visiting David and Avril at Winkworth, I walked into my bedroom, and there on the windowsill was a small painting of an elephant. Curiosity got the better of me, and I took a closer look. Yes, it was an original. I picked it up, and on the back I found two handwritten inscriptions. The first read, "To Eric, one of those truly dedicated few who over so many years have done so much for the wildlife of Africa, unsung and without the glamour of publicity—with warmest regards, David Shepherd." And the second read, "Well done, me old mate! And with love to Viva too," signed "David." Goose pimples appeared all over my body. I was touched by the words and proud to be the owner of a David Shepherd original.

There have been numerous occasions over the past half-century when Prince Bernhard went out of his way to work for the survival of wildlife and especially the endangered species. The prince always had a full calendar of engagements, attending many gatherings, functions, and meetings, but he always made the time and exerted the effort for those that concerned wildlife.

To help the prince exercise his passion for elephant, I always tried to place our campsites near or overlooking water holes where I knew elephant would come to drink. His summer resort at Porto Ercole in Italy was called *L'Elefante Felice,* the happy elephant, and on the side of his boat was painted *Budi,* a Swahili word for a tuskless elephant. He loved to get close to elephant so he could smell them, hear the special rumblings of their stomachs, marvel at the antics of the calves, and watch in amazement as tiny babies suckled milk from their mothers. Elephant are fascinating animals; no wonder they are admired and sometimes worshiped by so many people the world over.

Prince Bernhard was an easy person to please on safari. He was not afraid of hard work, even in the hot tropical sun. He would walk for miles in search of a chance for a perfect photograph. His ardor for that unique photo and his desire to get as close to the subject as possible placed me in tricky and often dangerous situations unbeknownst to him. Wild animals are just that, although they may appear tame or not alarmed by humans. Many people have misjudged or mistakenly trusted the behaviour of wild animals, only to end up being killed or badly injured. The prince always said to me, "Eric, I rely on you entirely, so don't be afraid to tell me when I am too close or when it is time to quit, OK?" I had to do this in several dangerous situations, especially with female elephant, which were only trying to protect their young from intruders. I will be telling you more about some of these adventures later on.

The prince had many "routines," even when on safari in the bush miles from nowhere. Whether we were driving or walking or just resting, he would ask me to please allow him a few minutes, usually around midday, so that he could drink a toast to his wife, Queen Juliana. I cannot recall that he ever missed this daily routine. I will always remember how he would write in his diary no matter how tired he was. Usually after dinner, he would light his cigar, sit down, and write the day's events in detail; then he would invariably produce a pack of

His Royal Highness Prince Bernhard (left) on his arrival in Tanzania, being greeted by President Julius Nyerere "Mwalimu" (right), with the Netherlands ambassador to Tanzania, Mr. A. M. E. Brink (center). Tanzania, 1970.

cards and challenge anyone to a game of gin rummy. He really enjoyed beating me; I don't think I ever won a game from him. Some of his close friends who accompanied him on our safaris used to win occasionally. The prince was an expert at gin rummy.

His closest friend was Colonel Coen Geertsema, who used to organize all his safaris. Sadly, Coen died suddenly a few years ago. He was a fine man, and we got on very well always. Another very close friend was Hans Teengs Gerritsen, who came on many a safari over the years. Sadly, they have all left us—only the prince and I remain of the "old gang." Together we enjoyed many interesting and exciting safaris in Tanzania and Zambia.

Let me begin my description of those times with our first safari, more than forty years ago in 1961. I was a district game warden in Tanzania when my boss, Bill Moore-Gilbert, a senior game warden, informed me that I was to accompany him on a hunting/photographic safari with His Royal Highness Prince Bernhard and party. Bill was a personal friend of the prince, having been on a few safaris with him before. Bill knew that I had some wonderful game areas under my control and that I knew where to find the best animals as well as some fantastic photographic opportunities.

Prince Bernhard always piloted his own plane to destinations around the world. He was an exceptional and reliable captain, never taking undue risks. I can well remember him arriving in his first plane, a trusty Dakota DC3. Later he switched to a Fokker Friendship F27, and for his last two safaris with me he used the Fokker Fellowship of the Dutch government, a lovely jet in which I had the privilege of traveling to Europe on two

occasions. Whenever the prince came to Tanzania on safari, he would always pay a courtesy call on the president of Tanzania, Dr. Julius Nyerere, spend a night at State House, and fly from Dar es Salaam to the large airfield nearest our destination. Smaller twin-engine planes were then chartered to take us to the bush airstrips.

The prince would always bring longtime friends with him on his trips: Coen Geertsema, Hans Teengs Gerritsen, Mo de Meir, and Dr. Stanhope Furber, known as Stan. He sometimes brought his taxidermist to assist my skinners with the preparation of the trophies.

For my first safari with the prince, I chose a picturesque campsite just outside the Katavi Game Reserve in the western province of Tanzania. This area was ideal for a month's safari because it had large numbers of the Big Five: elephant, numerous buffalo, and plenty of lion, as well as leopard and a few rhino. I should mention that the herds of buffalo in the Katavi Reserve were perhaps the largest in the whole of Africa at the time— one herd numbered over three thousand. The prince's second favourite animal in Africa, apart from the elephant, was the mighty *nyati*, Swahili for buffalo, so this was the place to bring him and his entourage. There were many other species of wildlife, including the majestic sable antelope and spectacular greater kudu. Two lakes, Katavi and Chada, provided sanctuary for thousands of ducks and geese as well as hundreds of hippo and crocodile. Huge groves of Borassus palms provided a wonderful setting for our camp, and a crystalline stream full of fish flowed past the front of the tents. The prince and his friends loved to relax in the cool water during the hottest time of the day.

I remained in camp making sure that all was in readiness for the arrival of the VIPs while Bill Moore-Gilbert drove to Mpanda, where there was a dirt airfield capable of taking the Fokker Friendship without any risk of overshooting the strip. The plane arrived on schedule, and the few local inhabitants were excited to see such a large airplane land near their village out in the "sticks." After all the food, drinks, and personal paraphernalia were carefully packed into one Land Rover, Bill and the prince's party set off in another, more-comfortable Land Rover station wagon on the long and tedious journey back to camp. The prince's aircraft and crew flew off to Nairobi to rest and await the conclusion of the safari, when they would return to collect everyone.

On the journey back to camp, Bill went around a sharp corner a little too fast and saw the roof rack fly off to his left. Atop the rack were some crockery and glasses that we had asked Coen to bring from the Netherlands especially for the safari. Not one plate or glass remained usable. The prince had a big laugh as he told me what had happened, but it wasn't such a laugh for me as we did not have enough plates and dishes to go around. We would have to make do with some enamel plates and mugs that we used to issue to our game guards. One of the first things I learned about Prince Bernhard was that he did not care about inconveniences. He in fact enjoyed eating from tin plates and drinking out of tin mugs; new and unusual experiences were enjoyable to him.

Apart from wanting to film elephant and buffalo and possibly find that fifty-inch buffalo (the prince would agree to shoot a buffalo only if its horn span measured fifty inches or more from outside curve to outside curve), this trip's goal was to try to find the elusive spotted zebra

and one or both of the rare albino giraffe that we knew roamed the shores of Lake Rukwa, and perhaps to shoot a world-record puku. The puku is an antelope that belongs to the kob genus and is found only in southern Tanzania and northern Zambia. The swampy puku habitat around Lake Rukwa was about a hundred miles from where we had our main camp.

I had previously made an arrangement with the director of the International Red Locust Control (IRLC), headquartered in Abercorn, Northern Rhodesia (when Northern Rhodesia obtained independence from Great Britain in 1964, the name of Abercorn was altered to Mbala and the country to Zambia). The IRLC used to carry out regular surveillance flights, using both Super Cub planes and helicopters, to keep a close watch on the breeding grounds of the destructive red locust, looking especially for fresh outbreaks of young locusts known as hoppers. The massive swamps in and around Rukwa were the main breeding grounds in eastern and southern Africa for this insect. I had obtained permission for a helicopter pilot to land at our camp and take Prince Bernhard on some flights so we might locate the spotted zebra and the giraffe. I had also arranged for our two Land Rovers to travel to a preselected fly-camp site on the shores of Lake Rukwa with our gear and cooks, for we planned to spend a few days there in search of our quarry.

Everything went according to plan. The morning the helicopter arrived, I instructed the Land Rover drivers to leave, as it would take them at least six hours to travel over country tracks to their destination. The helicopter was able to carry only four people, so two flights had to be made to ferry us all to the shores of the lake. During the first flight I showed the pilot, Ted, where to go. I had seen both the spotted zebra and what looked like a world-record puku a few days before and assumed they would still be in that general area.

Luck was with us, for we soon found the famous spotted zebra. The prince was thrilled and started to take plenty of photos, knowing that this animal was the only one of its kind in the world. I told the pilot to avoid scaring the zebra—it was with about a hundred others, and they were nervous. Noise from the helicopter would frighten them more than anything else.

I found a patch of trees with shade on high ground and asked to be left there while Ted flew back to pick up Bill and the rest of the party. I had a lunch box, and we settled down under a huge mosquito net that I erected between some trees. The net gave us some peace from the millions upon millions of mosquitoes. We could see herds of topi antelope plus smaller groups of puku almost running to try to escape the hordes of "mossies" that attacked them from all directions. Soon we heard the drone of the helicopter returning. I signaled for the new arrivals to join us under the net, which they gladly did as they were already being bombarded by the hungry little devils.

After a good lunch and a snooze, we decided to try to find the albino giraffe. I knew where I had last seen them and was able to direct Ted to that location. Again luck was with us; we soon found one of them in a small herd of about a dozen animals. They were completely out in the open plain and very easy to see. We all took great pictures from the helicopter, helped by the fact that Ted had removed the doors to make more room. It was pleasant to be able to cover so much ground with the helicopter. What took us a few hours would have taken a week or more to do by vehicle.

Our "mosquito camp" was a few miles from where we were to make our fly camp for the night, so I asked Ted to fly the prince, Hans, and myself to the place, drop us off, and return to take Coen, Stan, and Bill to see both the spotted zebra and the albino giraffe before flying them back to our camp. As I pointed out where our fly camp would be, I saw that the Land Rovers had already arrived and that the game guards had started to erect the small tents. These were mosquito-proof, so we could dash into them, zip up the entrance, and sleep in comfort. I made certain that the large net was up and ready for us to enter so that we could at least eat our meals in peace. Actually, the farther one got from the lake's edge, the less one was bothered by the mossies, especially if the wind was blowing.

Just before sunset we heard the helicopter, a pleasing sound. A big fire was already roaring as we prepared for our dinner. The prince, already dressed against the mossies with a long-sleeved shirt and thick, long pants, squatted next to the fire. But as it turned out, the breeze was blowing in our favour, and the heat from the blazing fire kept the irritating creatures at bay. Before long dinner was served, and everyone was amazed at how the cooks could produce such a fine meal over merely some hot coals. We washed it down with beer or wine

Ted, the pilot, had to return to his base early the next day, so he excused himself and retired early. The rest of us chattered well into the night about the sightings and filming of the rare spotted zebra and the albino giraffe.

Very early the next morning we were awakened by the hum of the helicopter engines. Ted got airborne as we made our way to the mess for a quick breakfast. The prince always had a cold beer to start off his day, thanks to our portable kerosene refrigerator. During the meal I discussed with Bill the order of the day. It was agreed that I would take the prince and Coen to hunt for the giant puku while Bill took Stan and Hans after some buffalo and perhaps a zebra.

As our party drove slowly along the lake, we passed hundreds of topi, their newborn calves sleeping or resting on the short green grass that grew along the shore. The prince was happy to snap away with his camera, occasionally asking the driver to stop whilst he took some 16mm movie footage.

We were lucky to see many bushpigs, which had not yet disappeared into the reeds. Suddenly, John, the driver, stopped, and we saw a leopard stalking some of these pigs. We were too far for photos but could follow the leopard as she moved stealthily through the grass, unaware of us. She entered a clump of reeds and waited; I told John to drive very slowly toward the reeds, hoping we could see her kill and get some good photos.

What happened next happened too fast. As the vehicle came close to her hiding place, there was a snarling roar, and the leopard charged out of the reeds and attacked the front tyres of the Land Rover. I had grabbed my rifle and was ready in case she tried to jump on one of us; however, she decided to attack the spare wheel, mounted on the bonnet. She tore lumps of rubber off the tyre, snarling and hissing furiously. I told the prince and Coen to crouch down just in case she decided one of us would be her next target. Luckily for us, she jumped off the bonnet and commenced to attack the front tyres again. I fired a shot into the ground right beside her, which drove her back into the reeds as John pressed down on the accelerator and soon had us out of danger. On glancing back, I saw that she had some tiny

cubs hidden in the reeds, which accounted for her actions.

Phew! What a start to our day! No one had been able to get any pictures, for it all occurred so unexpectedly and quick as lightning.

A few miles farther along the shore I spotted the giant puku. I instructed John to stop as I checked him out. Only the males of the species have horns, and after close scrutiny I could see he was definitely the world record. I planned our stalk and told the prince to climb down the back of the Land Rover. I followed. As John drove slowly off, we sat down and waited. Just as I had hoped, the puku were watching the vehicle and hadn't spotted us.

Shortly afterward we began our stalk on hands and knees. We had to travel 220 yards or so before we got into shooting position, and we used every clump of grass and reeds to cover our movements. Everything worked beautifully. John stopped the vehicle a long way ahead, and all the puku were still looking that way, which made our approach much easier.

When we arrived at the small trees I had selected, I told the prince to relax and rest whilst I surveyed the scene. This was the biggest puku I had ever seen, so I told PB to take his time before shooting. His shot rang out, and the puku just stood there. I said, "Shoot again, Sir, you missed." He had already chambered another round, for he was an expert hunter and marksman; he took aim once more at the bewildered puku, which had turned around to see where the noise had come from. It was standing broadside not more than 150 yards away. PB squeezed the trigger and the shot rang out, echoing for miles, but to his amazement and mine, his second shot also missed. This was most unusual, for PB was an excellent shot.

The puku actually started to walk toward us with its head held high, inquisitive about some movement it must have seen amongst the trees, its curiosity having got the better of it. The animal stopped, stamped its front feet, and snorted, a typical danger signal, but continued to glare straight at us. Prince Bernhard looked at me and shook his head, lowering and unloading his rifle at the same time.

"Eric," he said, "I just cannot bring myself to shoot such a magnificent animal; let him live, to father many young." He raised his binoculars and focused them on the puku, which was still snorting at the strange objects in its domain.

I beckoned for the vehicle to come pick us up. In no time we were taking pictures of what was doubtless the world record for this species. It was great to watch the animal dashing about trying to round up his harem, which had scattered in all the commotion.

I found out during that and later safaris that PB would commonly not shoot unless it was to put a wounded or sick animal out of its misery, to feed the camp staff, or perhaps to bag one or two guinea fowl or francolin for ourselves.

We spent the remainder of the day taking photos and enjoying the wonderful bird life, the big game, and the scenery. Nearing camp, we could hear John telling the cooks and camp staff all about the leopard episode; they were laughing as he waved his arms, showing his white teeth and mimicking the enraged leopard's snarling. Meanwhile Bill and his party had heard the shots and were anxious to know what luck we had had, so they hurried back to hear the stories around the campfire.

They themselves had had an interesting day but had seen nothing worth shooting. After a quick bush-shower (from a bucket filled with hot water suspended from a branch), they joined the party, savouring a nice cold beer whilst watching the huge flocks of colourful flamingos strutting or flying in all directions along the lakeshore. Literally thousands upon thousands of ducks and geese grazed or fed everywhere one cared to look, and mixed in with them were herds of topi, zebra, and puku—a spectacular sight.

PB was itching to make his friends jealous and couldn't wait to tell them about the leopard's attack on the Land Rover.

"Well, what luck did you chaps have today?" he asked.

"Nothing much," Hans replied, "but you must have had some action as we heard shots. What did you bag?"

"Ha-ha, my friends, wait till you hear what happened to us!" PB said and immediately told the whole story in minute detail, ending with the tale of how he had missed the possible world-record puku. Everyone clapped, for the prince was a very good orator. Dinner was served, and, exhausted from the day's outing, we soon retired for a good night's sleep.

An early start was made the next morning, for we had to get back to base camp while it was daylight. The hot, dusty trip was broken up by stops in several local villages, where PB liked to stop and talk to the old folk. We arrived back in camp just in time to watch a large herd of about fifty elephant making their way to the Borassus palms, which were in fruit at that time of the year. The elephant relished this delicious offering, and the prince asked me to arrange for another fly camp right in the middle of the huge palm grove sometime before the end of the safari, to watch the fun

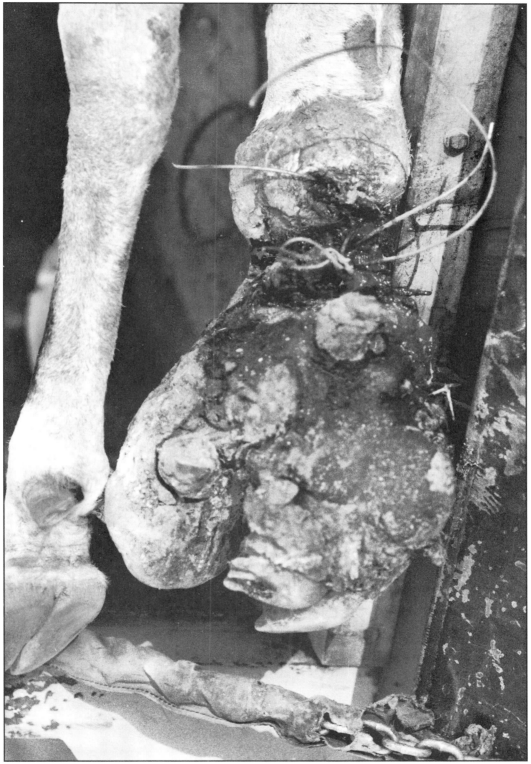

The author had to shoot this gemsbok to put it out of its misery. A poacher's wire snare had cut right down to the bone of his leg, and a hard lump had formed around the hoof. A buffalo that was in a similar situation once charged the author and his party. An animal in this state would have been in great pain and a danger to anyone with whom it came in contact. Namibia, 1990.

and antics of the elephant feeding. This I will tell you about later.

It was on this safari that we were charged by a wounded buffalo, a monster crocodile, and a very angry hippo.

One morning PB said he would like to take a leisurely stroll right around Lake Chada. He inquired who would like to go along with him, but only Hans was enthusiastic. Bill said that we should take along two game guards and porters to carry the lunch box and camera tripods and other paraphernalia, and he would head off toward the hills with the others to seek sable or greater kudu. It was about a fifteen-mile walk around the lake, so we decided to start immediately after breakfast. I shouldered my trusty .470 Rigby double, the prince had his .458 and a camera, and Hans only took his camera and a notepad.

After we had been walking for a couple of hours, I saw some vultures perched on the trees ahead. Maybe they were still roosting, waiting for the thermals to develop before they took flight in search of food, but I had a hunch that a lion kill or some dead animal was nearby. I told PB to load his rifle; I had mine at the ready all the time whenever we walked in the bush, for you never knew what could be waiting just around the corner.

As we approached, the vultures took off, and I expected to see a lion's head pop out of the reeds. Nothing appeared, and we continued our journey. Suddenly, from a clump of reeds behind us, I heard a scuffle and snorts and turned to face a huge bull buffalo in full charge. Luckily for us, it was muddy and the poor old buffalo had an injured front leg, so he was struggling. I had just enough time to raise my rifle and shoot, as he was lowering his head to toss PB. My shot hit his brain, and he

somersaulted just past where the prince was standing, covering him with blood and stinky mud. Hans also received a face full of mud. The game guards and porters, walking some distance behind, came running up to check if we were all right.

The prince and Hans were still in a state of shock, especially poor old Hans. PB's boots were stuck firmly in the mud, and as we pulled him free, he said, "Thanks, my friend; that could have been worse. Was that a fluke shot?" he asked jokingly. "I think that calls for a drink to celebrate that we are still alive."

Whilst we were enjoying a refreshing cold beer, Rashidi, my head game guard, was looking over the dead buffalo. He came over to us and said, *"Bwana, kweli leo ni bahati ya Mungu."* (Master, truly today you all had the good fortune of God.) This Swahili saying is used to describe anything unaccountable or unexpected. He went on to say the *nyati* (buffalo) had a wire snare around a front foot, which was rotting and infested with maggots. No wonder the poor beast was as mad as hell. We went to see the terrible wounds and were all relieved that the big fellow was dead. If I hadn't ended his misery, he could have killed someone for sure.

Rashidi and his helpers gutted the buffalo and covered it with branches to prevent the vultures, already circling above, from ripping the carcass to pieces. I told the other game guard to remain with one porter to keep vultures and other creatures away from the meat. The rest of us made our way back to base to collect a Land Rover to recover the meat for the camp staff. This incident cut short our plans for a walk around the lake but led to some more bizarre excitement when we returned with the vehicle.

As we approached the dead buffalo, the game guard came running toward us waving his arms. He stumbled to my side of the vehicle and said fearfully, "*Bwana, hatari, mamba mkubwa sana ana chunga nyati.*" (Master, there is danger—a big crocodile is guarding the buffalo.) We couldn't believe it. I instructed John to drive slowly up to the dead buffalo, and as we did, a huge monster of a crocodile charged out from behind the covered carcass and commenced to chomp at our bumper. I didn't want to shoot the reptile, for it was not hurting us, and it gave PB and Hans an opportunity to snap a few unique photos.

Then the croc turned its anger on the front tyre; its sharp teeth soon punctured it, and the loud hissing as the air escaped chased the fifteen-foot creature away. We all started to laugh at the sight of the big croc hightailing it at full speed back to the lake. PB remarked, "Can you believe it that we would be charged twice in one day, and that the poor tyre eventually succumbed after being savaged by a leopard and now a croc?"

It took some time to cut up and load the buffalo. The rotten front leg was dumped into the shallow waters of the lake in hopes that it would feed the big crocodile, which must have been very hungry to act as it did. As we pulled away, hundreds of hungry vultures swooped in to gobble up the remaining morsels.

I would like to point out here that the croc's behaviour was most uncharacteristic, especially on dry land, but I think that this was a very unusual reptile, because he attacked our boat a few days later.

Due to the enormous numbers of hippopotamus in Lakes Katavi and Chada, I decided that it was too dangerous to venture onto their waters with an ordinary boat, so I designed a sturdy flat-bottom craft six feet wide by sixteen feet long, built out of 1.5-inch hardwood; it wasn't built for speed but for safety. Of course, it was very heavy, but eight men could lift it off a truck and push it into the water. On it I placed a thirty-horsepower outboard motor fitted with a short shaft to allow navigation in shallow waters. We used this boat to explore the narrow channels and waterways, and its flat-bottom construction made it almost hippo-proof—it would be very difficult for even an enraged hippo to overturn.

A couple of days later, tired of tsetse bites and sore buttocks from riding over rough terrain, we decided that a day on the lake was in order. Bill took Hans and Stan on a cross-country hike, whilst PB, Coen, and I went fishing. It happened to be a beautiful day with a cool breeze blowing in our faces as we launched. I took Rashidi and Salum with us; both were reliable shots in case we ran into trouble. The lunch box was full of goodies plus the usual cold beer and wine. The lakes had several species of tropical fish, but we were after the common tilapia, a fine-eating and sporting member of the bream family; one could catch them with earthworms on a small hook.

As we idled along, looking for a suitable fishing spot amidst lovely scenery and water lilies, we entered a narrow channel and disturbed some hippo sunning on a small sandbank. I throttled down and attempted to turn around, to avoid the big bow waves caused by their massive bodies rushing into the water. The propeller, jammed by weeds and water lily stalks, refused to respond. Soon irritated hippo were popping up and snorting all around us. PB and Coen were snapping away with their cameras, totally unconcerned. I told Rashidi and Salum to load their rifles and made sure mine was close at hand.

I was nervous about one particular female with a very young calf—she didn't move away like the others. In fact, she submerged and came up right under the boat with an almighty thump—she was actually trying to overturn our boat. Luckily it was stable and heavy and she couldn't capsize it. She then surfaced right beside the craft, blowing water all over us. I took hold of an oar and hit her hard on the tip of her nose, but this only made matters worse. She submerged, and the next thing we knew her enormous teeth were biting the front end of the boat. Both PB and Coen, realizing that we were in danger, kept their heads low. I didn't really want to shoot the hippo, but she was persistent in her attacks.

Rashidi shouted, "*Wewe nataka mimi kupiga, Bwana?*" (Do you wish me to shoot, Master?)

"*Hapana!*" (No) I retorted. I had switched the outboard off and grabbed my .470, telling PB that I would have to shoot the hippo or else she might sink our boat if she decided to jump aboard, which she was capable of doing in her rage. Sadly, I placed a bullet into her brain as she surfaced to make another charge. Females of this species can be dangerous, especially if accompanied by a calf.

"Boy, Eric," Prince Bernhard said, "you sure have some frenzied animals around this place. Is that why you brought us here? Hell, we have been charged four times in as many days."

"Well, Sir, at least we are still in one piece, and it could have been worse," I replied as I bent over the stern to clear the weeds from the prop. I started the motor and moved slowly away to more open waters. I was concerned about the baby hippo now that it had no mother. I searched the area with a binocular to see if the baby would

surface, but it never did, so we shifted to another part of the lake where I knew some herons and egrets were nesting. This would ease the tension, allowing PB and Coen to photograph the birds building their nests and squabbling during their courtship displays. Both of my charges were delighted and insisted we spend the remainder of the day right there. Rashidi and Salum managed to catch some tilapia for us and some barbel for themselves.

When we returned to camp, Bill and company were curious about the shooting. PB took them down to the boat and showed them the scars on the bow where the mad hippo had bitten off big chunks. I repaired the two gaping holes before nightfall, for we would leave pretty early the next morning to retrieve the hippo, which would have floated to the surface by then. Usually it takes four to six hours for the gastric juices to produce enough gas in the stomach to make a dead hippo float.

Soon after a remarkable breakfast we were on our way to find the hippo. As we approached, I glassed the area for any signs of the baby. I thought I caught a glimpse of its head, but it submerged before I could be certain. It could have been the head of a big crocodile, so I kept my thoughts to myself. I edged the boat to where the carcass floated belly up, the four short legs pointing skyward. The rest of the herd was about a hundred yards away, grunting, and a couple of large males showed their aggression at our presence by opening their huge mouths and splashing the water with their heads. I drew alongside the floating body so Rashidi and Salum could tie a rope around the hind legs. We would drag her back to camp, where the staff would make biltong (jerky) from the fresh meat, which they and their families relished.

Suddenly, all hell broke loose as a monster of a crocodile plunged at Rashidi, almost grabbing him with its sharp teeth. I hadn't expected this, although I was aware that a big croc was somewhere about. Crocodile are usually afraid of humans unless they are really hungry or guarding their nests or young, although occasionally a villager would be caught while bathing or fetching water.

Rashidi fell backward and nearly knocked PB into the water. I had taken out my .470 by this time. The attacker had submerged, but I knew it would be back for another go at the boat or one of us. Its huge size told me that this had to be the same croc that had hassled us a couple of days ago. Sure enough, a few seconds later it surfaced, opened its jaws, and charged the boat. Coen was in my line of fire and I couldn't shoot. The big fellow snapped its jaws closed, sinking its teeth into the side of the boat a couple of feet from where PB huddled. The timber creaked as it shook its massive head from side to side in an effort to break off what was in its mouth. I stepped aside to get a clear line of fire and shot the reptile right between the eyes. It was stone-dead the moment the bullet entered its brain.

I was worried when I saw that its teeth were still firmly embedded in the thick timbers and knew that the heavy body, which must have weighed at least a ton, could drag our boat under if we didn't unlock his jaws immediately. I reached for a small ax that I always carried in my haversack and began to chop the wood away around its teeth; meanwhile, both of my guards were struggling to force the creature's mouth open with an oar. Amidst all this turmoil, we were getting a good drenching from the twitching of the croc's tail in its death throes. Thank goodness we were able to pry open those

mighty jaws. We just had time to place a rope around its front leg before it sank.

"Eric, let's get the hell out of here. We have had enough excitement to last us for some while," the prince said as he opened a can of beer.

With both carcasses in tow, I steered a direct course across the lake back to camp. Progress was very slow due to the drag on the boat exerted by three tons of dead weight, and the small outboard motor laboured all the way. Most of the camp staff had gathered on the shore, and were singing and clapping their hands as they jumped up and down with joy to greet our safe return. They were thrilled to see the hippo but aghast at the big crocodile. They all shook hands with PB and the rest of us, chanting *"Asante sana, Bwana Kingi"* (Thank you very much, Mr. King) as we made our ways to our tents to change into dry clothes.

A few nights later we were sipping our sundowners and listening to the shrill squeals being made by excited elephant eating the ripened fruits from the Borassus palms that had fallen that day. The fruit from this palm is a little bigger than a softball, with a thick outer skin. Inside is a seed surrounded by a succulent orange-coloured flesh that tastes not unlike the mango. During the drought and famine years in Tanzania, the villagers survived by eating these tasty fruits. Elephant and other animals love them also.

On hearing a trumpet from an enraged elephant (they fight over these morsels), Prince Bernhard asked if we could spend a night or two right in the midst of the palm trees, which covered an extensive area and numbered in the thousands. I was not very happy about this suggestion but agreed to go along with it just to please our guest. Over the years, I'd had some frightening

13

experiences trying to do this very thing. Can you imagine yourself surrounded by hundreds of hungry elephant running all over the place on a dark night, searching for delicious morsels?

The following morning I made preparations for our fly camp whilst Bill, Coen, Hans, and Stan went off in search of a buffalo. PB relaxed, enjoying the sun and reading his book (he was a real bookworm). I made certain to pack our mosquito nets, comfortable bedrolls, and plenty of beer and coffee.

The main forest of palms lay about six miles north of our main camp; together with Rashidi and Salum, I loaded the Land Rover and gave orders that we would leave directly after lunch. This would give us ample time to find a suitable high, flat anthill on which to camp for the night. Before long we entered the biggest bunch of palm trees. It was tricky driving in and around them—so much so that Rashidi and Salum had climbed down and were directing me which way to manoeuvre. At one point we were all walking to scout for that elusive anthill, and eventually I sent the two men ahead in the hope of locating one. Meanwhile, I picked up a freshly fallen ripe fruit and cut off some pieces for PB to savour. He really enjoyed the flavour but not the stringy fibres.

Soon a whistle indicated that the men had found a good spot. I drove whilst PB walked. The anthill was perfect, located on the banks of a small stream with a good vantage point. The stream was dry but damp; green grass grew in it. In no time we had our camp set up and a nice fire going to warm us and help keep the mossies at bay.

It was beginning to get dark as we prepared ourselves for a long night. As we rubbed plenty of insect repellent onto our necks and faces, we heard the first of many trumpets. The coffeepot was on the boil as we sat down to enjoy our evening meal—roasted duck and potatoes plus other goodies.

Before we ate, Rashidi pointed at some elephant that were heading in our direction. Both the guards picked up their rifles, and I made sure mine was close at hand. The lead elephant, usually the matriarch, suddenly skidded to a halt and exhaled a loud, angry trumpet at the same time—she must have picked up our scent. The rest of the herd came to a sudden standstill and raised their trunks, looking for the enemy. After a short while the matriarch gave some signal, and they turned about in unison and moved off a short distance before stretching their trunks groundward in search of fruit. They must have considered us no danger, for they moved all around us, uttering their funny little squeals of delight. It was still light enough to enjoy their antics, and PB was thrilled. So was I. All our fears faded away and a strange peaceful atmosphere set in, a wonderful feeling.

As we dined and enjoyed the night sounds of frogs and crickets mingled with happy elephant, PB raised his beer can and toasted, "To the mighty *tembo*—long may they reign." *Tembo* is the Swahili word for elephant. I said to Prince Bernhard after dinner that we should try and get some sleep before the main onslaught of *tembo* arrived. He said he was happy to be amongst the elephant even if they kept him awake all night—as long as they left us alone.

It was almost pitch-dark when Rashidi crept up to where I sat and whispered that an elephant was coming very close to the vehicle. Suddenly there was a terrifying trumpet from just below us. Rashidi said, "*Leo kivumbi, Bwana*," which, literally translated, means

"Today dust, Master" but has another meaning when used on occasions of danger or trouble.

I could just distinguish the outline of a big elephant, its huge ears outstretched, standing not ten yards from us. I handed Rashidi my strong flashlight and indicated that he should shine it on the elephant. PB had by this time crawled behind me and was looking over my shoulder. He said, "Please don't kill the elephant—just shoot over his head to chase him away." I nodded just as Rashidi switched on the torch. The bright beam in the face of the old elephant caused an immediate mock charge combined with a very loud trumpet. I fired a shot over its head, which immediately

stopped its run. An instant later the hulk swung around and loosed another terrific trumpet as it retreated into the dark.

This sudden turmoil caused all the other elephant in the vicinity to trumpet and squeal as they rushed off in a panic. The noise of some two hundred elephant trumpeting and charging off is something I shall never forget. I never had an experience like that again (until some twenty-five years later in Mozambique—that's another story I will tell you about later).

Soon there was dead silence. PB looked at me, smiled, and said, "Thanks, my friend." He was so pleased that I hadn't had to kill the enraged bull.

This was Prince Bernhard's preferred attire for long walks. Behind him are Joe Newby and the game guards. Selous Game Reserve, Tanzania, 1970.

We sat by the fire, to which Salum had added some more dry wood, for it was getting near midnight and the cold was setting in. I heated some coffee as PB lit his cigar.

"I don't expect that we will be troubled by any more elephant tonight—what do you think?" he said as he stood with his back to the fire.

I replied something to this effect: "This is wildest Africa, so one never really knows what is going to happen next."

He took a big puff on his cigar and laughed. In later years he told me many times that the night amongst the elephant and the story I am about to relate would be etched in his memory forever.

We had just gone to bed and I was very comfortable when there came a strange noise like nothing I had ever heard before or could relate to. I heard Rashidi and Salum loading their rifles and adding more wood to the fire. I crawled out from beneath my net with my gun in one hand and my torch in the other, making my way to the fire. PB was up and standing beside me, also wondering what was happening. Both Rashidi and Salum were scared; I could tell by the look on their faces. I asked them what was making the funny noise.

"*Shetani*," said Salum (which in Swahili means evil spirits or demons). I shook my head as I translated for PB, who nodded and looked just as bewildered as I was. The strange noises seemed to be heading in our direction, as though moving up the riverbed. It was as if floodwaters were coming upstream. But we'd had no rains, and water doesn't flow uphill. Rashidi asked if he should shoot toward the sounds. I shook my head and handed him my torch. PB had his torch as well. The noises grew louder and louder, and I could hear small snorts and grunts—most eerie, to say the least. The sounds were by this time right below us. I told Rashidi and PB to shine their torches into the river bed where, to our astonishment, we saw thousands of "mudfish," or barbel fish, sliding, slithering, or wiggling over one another, heading upstream.

This phenomenon has yet to be explained to me. In other times when rivers were in flood, I have witnessed fishes moving upstream to their spawning grounds, but they were using water to get upstream, not traversing a dry river bed.

Rashidi and Salum soon replaced their rifles with pangas, a type of machete. With these they chopped behind the heads of many unfortunate mudfish until they had collected sufficient to take back to camp and sun dry for their families back home. Rashidi told me, after all the excitement had died down and I had stopped their killing frenzy, that his father had once told him about this type of migration. He said that if this species of fish did this, then heavy rains were imminent. Sure enough, the very next day, as we were returning to camp, there was a thunderstorm that soon had the rivers in flood. It was a most unusual storm for that time of year.

A few days later we drove to the foothills only to find our way blocked by a huge lake that had formed due to the flooding of the rivers. Of course, now this made sense as to why the fish were heading upstream to spawn.

The thunderstorm had brought about a sudden change in conditions; it was much cooler, and the countryside was covered with water holes. Everywhere we went we got bogged down, but it was fun and something different for a change. Hans and Coen had shot nice buffalo, so they were happy, as were the camp staff, as this meant plenty of *nyama* to dry and take home.

Due to the sudden weather change, we all agreed that some brisk walks were to be the order of the day. Only Stan opted out as his legs "were not up to scratch," as he put it. Prince Bernhard generally liked me to accompany him on his walks as I knew most of the trees, grasses, and birds by their common and scientific names. The clients are more interested in their surroundings when they know what's going on around them whilst they are in the bush. PB, Coen, and Hans were all keen amateur ornithologists and were always excited to find a new bird to add to their lists.

Bill was a good bushman but didn't know the flora and birds as well as I did, so he took Coen and Hans in one direction whilst PB and I went off in another. Salum took Stan to see the bird colony and do some fishing as they all raved how delicious the tilapia were. Each party had porters who carried the boxes and water.

It was a lovely cool morning as all parties set off. The prince always insisted on carrying his own rifle. We walked toward an escarpment about ten miles away, passing through the Borassus palm forest where we had spent the night. A few elephant were still about, and PB took some photos, especially of an old bull fast asleep with his head against a palm tree and his large penis touching the ground. We joked as to what he was dreaming about, then left him to his dreams and moved on. The small stream was still flowing, but we were able to ford it to continue our journey. We walked in silence, letting PB go where he wished. Occasionally he would stop to check out a bird and inquire about its habits and name. He would sometimes ask for its scientific name, trying to stump me in a jovial way; luckily, I always knew the answer.

After a few hours we arrived at the base of the escarpment, part of the Great Rift Valley, and decided it was time for lunch and a rest. During lunch, PB did his daily routine of toasting Queen Juliana, his wife, and then set about peeling some garlic cloves, which he proceeded to chop up and mix with bully beef and beans, his favourite snack on safari.

Once we had rested, I suggested that we make tracks back to camp or else we might well bump into some elephant heading toward their favourite fruit. During the daytime, most of the elephant, especially the breeding herds, would leave the palm trees and seek refuge in dense thickets far from any human activity. At this time of the year, honey hunters were allowed to enter the Katavi Game Reserve to harvest their beehives, which they made and hung from big trees high above the ground, out of the reach of honey badgers. During their forays into the reserve, the honey hunters would make straight for the Borassus fruits, which augmented their food supplies. Often they would chase away the elephant.

PB took the lead but set off in the wrong direction. I knew from past knowledge that his bush sense was not very good, but I didn't want to upset him. After we had to make a big detour to get around a large herd of buffalo, I said to him, "Sir, I think it is time that we turned back." He was puffing on his pipe, his rifle over his shoulder, when he turned about and eyeballed me, saying, "Sorry, old fellow, I thought I *was* going back to camp," and just chuckled to himself. It was nearly nightfall when we reached camp and joined the others by the huge fire.

Soon it would be time to send a radio message for PB's crew to fly in, pick them all up, and head back to the Netherlands. Everyone was reluctant to leave, but duty calls. It had been a most pleasant and exciting safari that would remain in memory for a long time, if not forever.

Tragically, Bill Moore-Gilbert was killed in a plane crash less than a month later. Bill's death was a heartfelt blow to all his family and friends, and to his friend the prince.

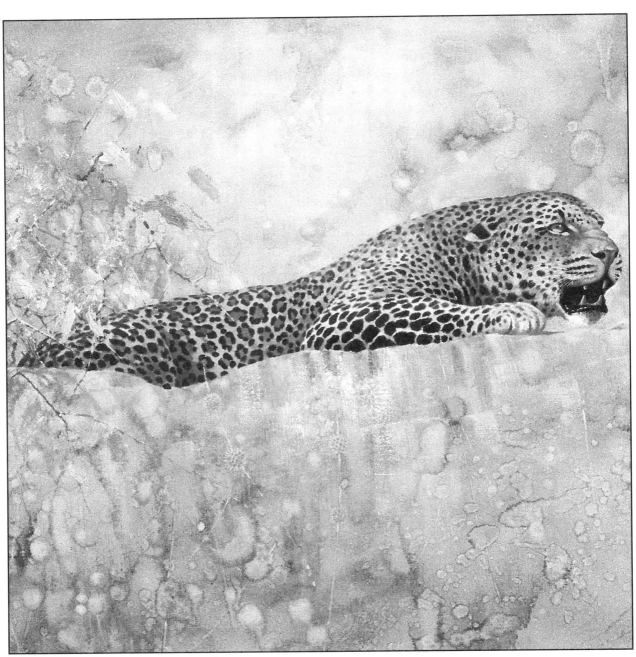

"Growling Chui" *(leopard) by Mike Ghaui.*

CHAPTER TWO
Relatives, Reptiles, and Romance

Soon after Christmas 1969, Viva and I faced up to the inevitable after receiving a letter from the office of the president of Tanzania stating, "Your appointment and your services with this government will terminate on the expiry of your leave." Slowly and sadly we began to pack up the contents of our house in Mbeya, capital of the Southern Highlands province. I say slowly because it's very difficult to pack into some forty wooden crates and suitcases the accumulation of three-quarters of a century of living in this intensely beautiful part of eastern Africa.

I have nostalgic recollections of this place that go all the way back to 1899. In that year, two Victorians who were to become my grandparents on my mother's side, the Bennett family, bought an ox wagon in Pretoria, South Africa. They loaded into it a couple of barrels of salt, flour, dried game meat called biltong, some milk cans filled with fresh drinking water, a couple of rifles and a shotgun plus an ample supply of ammunition, some camping tarpaulins, pots and pans, and other equipment. Then they harnessed a team of unhealthy horses and headed northward toward the equator into the great unknown in search of their Shangrila.

A few years later, in 1906, Viva's grandparents on her father's side, led by William Klapprott, who hailed from Germany, were also searching for new pastures. They traveled by ox wagons from Mombasa to the Kenya Highlands before finally settling on a farm in the Uasin Gishu district at a place called Kipkabus. Sadly, all the photographs of my grandparents' heroic journey were destroyed in a fire, but Viva's grandparents had theirs safely stored, and they now reside with her cousin, Nickolas Klapprott, who has kindly allowed me to publish them in this book. These old pictures open a window on how the pioneers/settlers traveled and the hardships they had to endure before finding their promised land.

Viva and I knew little of our future destination when we prepared to leave our beloved East Africa in 1969. But our grandparents had known even less about theirs. As Viva and I looked into the void, we were fairly certain that we were as unsuited to the outside world as a lion is to Alaska; our grandparents at least had set off with high hopes of finding their Utopia. They believed that there would be a place for them somewhere north, far beyond South Africa, beyond the vast thornbush country of Matabeleland, perhaps even in the high, rainy mountains of eastern Rhodesia, now known as Zimbabwe. They were Victorians and had been brought up to believe in dreams and the God-given rights of the pioneer or settler Englishman. They had plenty of examples to follow. Cecil John Rhodes, just a few years before, had told Queen Victoria that he intended to make Africa British from Cape to Cairo. And he had already fulfilled a good part of that promise. All of Rhodesia had been made safe for the Queen by the efforts of just two hundred settlers endowed with the sense of the blind, hoping to make their fortunes from prospecting gold. These were people of unquestioning spirit, the same kind that had motivated my grandparents.

Where my grandparents were concerned, though, there were only two of them to show the way, to read the Bible at night, to sit on the wooden driving seat of their covered wagon at dawn and head into the unmapped and virtually unknown country, accompanied by their three sons and two young daughters. Only one of the three sons remained by journey's end. My mother missed the journey; she would be born after they had found Shangrila and settled. It was a very long, tedious, and hazardous journey. In Rhodesia they found that the dream of Cecil Rhodes had gone badly wrong. The Matabele, a renegade regiment of Chaka's ferocious Zulu, were the rulers there, and, although cowed initially by the many Martini Henry rifles and the magic beam of a steam-driven searchlight, they were preparing to go to war against the new settlers. They were almost starving anyway. Rhodesia had been settled by fortune seekers who came in search of gold. The early hunters/explorers had headed north with reports that Rhodesia had so much gold that it was bursting out of the ground. But when they arrived, they found that

to be untrue. Unlike the mighty seams of gold of the Rand in South Africa, the gold here was mainly alluvial, only on the surface, though it carried into the sand rivers, where it had to be panned, a tedious task that was unrewarding more often than not.

So my grandparents moved on. They purchased some more mules and donkeys (the only animals immune to the dreaded tsetse fly, which carried sleeping sickness; even dogs fell victim to this pest) and spare parts for their wagon (especially wheels) from destitute miners who by then had turned to farming. These ragged men and women were attempting to farm bush land without proper tools or knowledge, battling the ravages of insects and parasites. In later years they found that with the right knowhow and machinery, the climate would grow crops like tobacco in great abundance, but for men and women who were little more than common gardeners, the land was useless for wheat and potatoes and the other crops they needed to survive day to day.

My grandparents moved on into Northern Rhodesia, now known as Zambia. The country was fairly flat and very dry, though evergreen forests of *Brachystegia* (*miombo*) coloured the land. Few settlers had even bothered to farm here, mainly due to the dreaded tsetse fly and the high costs of clearing the woodlands. The country in the north was of interest largely for its embryonic mines, driven into abundant seams of copper and coal. My grandparents knew this was not their kettle of fish; they were looking for fertile farmland, and so they headed farther northward, crossing another border into German East Africa, later known as Tanganyika and now Tanzania. There their trek collapsed.

The cheap mules and horses had done well to get them this far, but in the arid hinterland, the poor beasts either succumbed to disease or were too weak to carry on, and all perished. Six people sat for two months around their battered old wooden cart, living off the land. Hunting kept them alive; the plains were a teeming mass of wildlife.

Some fifty years later, as I recall, it was possible to drive all day past never-ending herds of wildebeest, zebra, and gazelle moving in their annual migration from the Masai Mara, through the Serengeti, Maswa, then back via Lake Ndutu, the famous Olduvai Gorge (renowned for the discovery of early man), and finally through the Loliondo District back across the border into Kenya's Masai Mara Park. Admittedly, at the turn of the 1900s, there were many predators, in direct ratio to the size of the herds. There were enough male lion still for every young Masai to become a man by killing one in personal combat, armed only with a spear and a sturdy shield made from buffalo hide. During the British rule in Tanganyika, this tradition was forbidden as too many male lion were being killed, almost to the point of endangering the species—much to the annoyance of the Masai warriors.

My granddad used to tell us stories about how he and my uncles would have to chase away the many lion, hyena, and jackal that came around their wagon in search of food, despite the plains being full of game. But in a strange way, my grandfather would relate, the lion were their friends and their company, "as hardly anyone else came to call."

The trek finally resumed, with the wagons being pulled, erratically and dangerously, by ragtag teams of mules and donkeys, semi-wild beasts bought or bartered off the roving Masai herdsmen. It took weeks to train these animals to adjust to their new task of pulling a heavy wagon, but at least they were immune to the tsetse fly. Eventually this extraordinary caravan wobbled into Kenya and headed for Nairobi, the main town. The people had wandered almost the entire length of the Great Rift Valley (which stretches through most of eastern Africa) in a semibemused state of hunger and disillusionment—was all of Africa sun-baked earth and thorntree country? But finally, as if in a mirage, the Ngong hills loomed before them, and they could see the snowcapped peaks of Mount Kenya far to the north. They knew that they had arrived at their Shangrila, or as close as one could have imagined it.

Here the lush plains (now called the Athi Plains) teemed with wild animals, mostly wildebeest (gnu), gazelle, and zebra, with some giraffe and ostrich. Along the rivers the fever acacias (*Acacia xanthophloea*) were in full bloom with their fragrant, golden yellow, powder-puff flowers. Most important of all, there were people here, people carrying on the kind of life my grandparents had dreamt about for years. They made their first encampment about fifteen miles outside the then-small town of Nairobi—which is today, a century later, a huge city and the capital of Kenya—on a site that I have since established to be the main runway for jumbo jets at Jomo Kenyatta Airport. For almost a year they lived there, building two small "mud and daub" huts and establishing a vegetable garden, which they had to protect with a huge thorn-branch fence to keep the wild animals at bay. They were content to do odd jobs for better-established settlers; their contentment, I think, was based at least partly on their having gotten there alive.

The arduous trek had cost them almost everything but their lives, and they very nearly lost those in their first week in Kenya. The small patch of land where they chose to settle was part of the grazing grounds of the nomadic Masai, without a doubt East Africa's proudest and most intransigent tribe. At the time of Viva's and my departure from eastern Africa, no outside influence had ever been allowed to change the Masai's way of life; they had survived the blandishments of the British and the Germans and even the appeals of other black African political groups such as the Mau Mau.

During the Kenya emergency in the 1950s, many farmers hired these Masai warriors, with their long spears and *semies* (long, sharp knives used to cut up almost anything) and buffalo-hide shields, to guard their farms and plantations from marauding Mau Mau bands. Usually a few of these warriors patrolling the farmhouses, workshops, and labourer lines night and day was enough to deter any intruders or would-be killers. Even today, although the Masai's dress mode has changed to the brightly coloured *shuka* (a piece of calico about two yards long, worn as a loincloth and usually tied and knotted over one shoulder), their tribal habits have changed very little, and they still remain aloof. Their stance has become a grave concern to many African governments and anthropologists worldwide, because their aloofness will ultimately lead to their race becoming an "endangered species."

A Masai friend of ours, Solomon ole Saibul, who worked with me on the Ngorongoro Conservation Authority[1] and later became head of the Tanzanian National Parks, made many compassionate, if stern, attempts to bring clans of his tribe into the modern world. He once told me that his efforts had been largely a dismal failure; the Masai just want to be left alone and remain themselves. In his words, "The Masai cannot stand still, and any group that cannot progress in this chaotic world in which we find ourselves, will become extinct."

The Masai came upon my grandparents' encampment on the first night. I shall always remember my grandpa telling us this story. Upward of fifty Masai warriors surrounded their camp. They danced, screamed, and waved their spears in the light of the fires; they played cruel games with the mules and donkeys. In the morning they were still there, a silent ring of tall men, their hair and loincloths coloured a red ochre, each brandishing his spear, standing behind their buffalo-hide shields on which the owner's specific design was painted with red ochre and gray wood ash. They wanted to speak with my granddad.

Their leader told my grandparents, via an interpreter, that this was their land and that the intruders should leave immediately or they would all be killed. Fearing that the Masai would carry out their threats, the Bennett family once again harnessed the donkeys and the mules to the creaky old wagons and moved out across the dew-encrusted grass into the slum outskirts of Nairobi. There they stayed for five years. The many months of hardship and this terrifying night had exhausted their spirit.

---

1. The Ngorongoro Conservation Authority was established to urge the Masai, who moved about the world-famous Ngorongoro Crater, to live in harmony with the thousands of tourists who visited the area to see them and the marvelous array of wildlife. I knew from first-hand experience what a difficult task this would turn out to be. It never really worked. But in 1900 the Masai were far from extinct. Their tribal structure and traditions were more highly developed than those of the embryonic Kenya colony. Most of the land that these new *Wazungu* (Europeans) were using to park or drive their ridiculous vehicles and to build their houses was land the Masai needed for their herds of cattle and sheep. A Masai has no need of transport; he can jog thirty miles or more a day comfortably.

But during the following five years, their spirits were revived. My grandfather opened the first blacksmith shop in the fast-growing town of Nairobi and earned enough to expand into the more-profitable business of gunsmithing. During the first decade of the new century, the flow of settlers increased, and the Bennetts, with friends' help, a solid business, and a vastly increased knowledge of the country, decided to "trek" once more to set up a farm.

On the Athi River about twenty-five miles east of Nairobi, they decided to build an enclosure of mud huts and tents surrounded by a thick, dense thornbush stockade. Sadly, the Masai again came down on the encampment, and the terrifying experience of five years previous was repeated throughout a long night. But in those five years the odds had changed, materially and psychologically. This time their camp was built like a fortress, and their right to stay conformed to the rights of their friends and neighbours—settler's rights. This was confirmed by the British administrators, who at the turn of the century had never been questioned by any of the tribes, including the Masai. The following night,

Viva Balson's father, Rudolf, and her two uncles used to hunt on horseback and wait for the beaters to chase the stock-killing lion or leopard to them. Kipkabus, 1919.

Grandfather Bennett and my three uncles decided to carry the war to the Masai camp.

I have little doubt, after a lifetime of contact with Masai, that my ancestors made a terrible mistake this night. I can even postulate that the Masai's tactics—the screaming and shouting antics around large fires—were nothing more than a test of the Bennetts' nerve, for the Masai have great reverence for nerve, and their antics could have amounted to nothing more than a bizarre initiation ceremony for this new tribe that had come to live as their neighbours. Certainly, if the Masai had determined to kill the Bennetts, they would not have announced their presence and numbers so obviously. They kill quietly, stealthily, and preferably at close range, where their sharp *semies* can be brought into play.

The four Bennetts rode down on the Masai *manyatta* (a stockade built to protect themselves and their livestock from enemies and wildlife) carrying firebrands, which they tossed onto the mud-and-cattle-dung lean-tos, hoping to chase the occupants out into the open. But their plan failed, and two of my uncles were killed by the Masai warriors, paying the price for underestimating their enemy. Within minutes the two survivors were in full flight with the warriors in hot pursuit, but the Bennetts' horses were faster than the Masai, and the riders were soon out of danger. They headed for the nearest neighbours, the Destros, who were looking after the rest of the Bennett family whilst the men went to attack the Masai. It wasn't allowed to end there— pioneer settlers believed in "an eye for an eye" as a prime law of survival, and that particular Masai clan was eventually driven back into the hinterland by a posse of white farmers and other settlers led by the remaining men of the Bennett family.

Grandpa Bennett told me that the family tried to hold its land, but always the Masai came back. Lone warriors would cry out in the darkness; small groups would light fires and wave their spears in defiance. The Bennetts were marked men, and finally they had to acknowledge defeat and move once again, to join forces with an already established farmer in another part of the country not too many miles away. The farm was that of the pioneering Tarlton brothers, Henry and Leslie, who at that time had some 100,000 acres under their tenuous ownership and could use all the help they could get. By 1920 the partnership had grown into an extremely lucrative business, essentially cattle ranching but with an unusual "cash-crop" sideline: ostrich farming. It was the age of hats, and the best ladies' hats required elegant ostrich plumes.

My father, Walter James Balson, arrived in Kenya from England at about this time, and his job reflected the changing times in the East African colony. As the newly appointed representative of the Goodyear Tyre Company, he met the Bennett family when he went to the ranch to sell them rubber car tyres. This was when Model T and Model A Fords were leaving curling trails of dust across the open plains and the Rift Valley. During his extensive sales tours, Walter developed a lasting interest in the African bush and was one of the first to take a professional interest in photography. He developed a close friendship with Alan Tarlton, the son of Henry Tarlton, and also a very keen interest in Rose Bennett, who was to become my mother. They married in 1928. Sadly, my father does not feature very significantly in my memories. He was killed in WWII when I was just ten years old, and my recollections of him are little more than faint echoes of what had already become an exotic childhood.

In real terms the Tarltons were my family, and my home was on their great ranch at Ruaraka. The Tarlton brothers were first-generation white Africans who were later to apply their special knowledge to the establishment of one of the first hunting and safari businesses in East Africa. Their abilities as bushmen, animal experts, and hunters had all been hard-earned, and those lessons brushed off onto Henry's son Alan. Coincidentally, three Australians, a Mr. Newland and the Tarlton brothers, established what I believe was the first safari-outfitting company in East Africa, called Newland and Tarlton Safaris.

Viva's grandparents, the family Klapprott, likewise had their trials and tribulations. By 1907, Wilhelm (William) Klapprott, who had a wife and seven children to support, lost his entire herd of cattle to the dreaded cattle disease, East Coast Fever, and they were desperate. But Wilhelm was offered a job by the veterinary department because of his considerable knowledge of cattle. He worked as a livestock officer and supervised the moving of some 10,000 Masai people plus their livestock—some 200,000 head of cattle and over one million sheep—a task that took about four years to complete. The movement of the Masai from the Laikipia district was done to enable the white settlers to farm this very fertile area, which the Masai could not possibly have done as they were pasturalists, not farmers. Naturally the Masai were reluctant to uproot, but they were forced to move to the Southern Province in Kenya.

Wilhelm Klapprott obtained a farm in what was later known as the White Highlands on the Kinankop, and moved from there to another farm, the last family farm, on the Uasin Gishu at a place called Kipkabus. Photos show

their first houses, the ox wagons, and Viva's uncles carrying a leopard that had been killing their livestock. Another photo shows a group of Nandi tribesmen who were employed as beaters to flush out leopard or lion that threatened the family's precious livestock. Those early days in eastern Africa were hard times for the new settlers, but they persevered.

The Bennetts and their children also survived the struggle, with Grandfather Bennett growing older and, unfortunately, bitter. In his later years, he became, I am sad to say, a drunken, irascible depressive with a terrifying capacity for violence. It was hard to believe some of "carryings on" that my mother told me about. I especially recall one story, which always made me stay clear of him when he had one of his drunken spasms. It went something like this:

In about 1917–18, as WWI was about to end, the British and Germans were fighting at a place called Longido, one hundred or so miles south of Nairobi. One night during this campaign, my Uncle Alec returned from the front line, almost falling from his horse in a malarial fever. In his delirium he told Grandfather Bennett that the Germans were coming, which caused the old man to rush for his 12-bore shotgun. He lined my mother and her three sisters up against the wall and announced that he would rather shoot them than have them taken prisoners and raped by the "Bosch."

Luckily for them, my grandmother talked him out of it, but in the years that followed they lost control of him, and by the time of his death in 1934, almost all his share in the ranch had been sold and the money squandered. My mother told us other stories about how he used to make them run home from Nairobi as he drove behind in his Model T Ford, and if they failed to reach home, some ten miles, he would tie them to the ox-wagon wheel by their long hair and give them ten lashes with his rawhide whip. He would take his temper out on whoever happened to be near. His temper was no doubt another reason for his ludicrous attack on the Masai, which caused the death of two of his sons.

During WWII, Alan Tarlton arrived one day with a scheme that at first seemed so exotic as to be beyond belief. He proposed that my mum and he join forces to farm snakes! After my father's death, Alan formed a lasting relationship with my mother and took on the role of my stepfather. With Alan I properly entered the African bush, much of it totally unexplored. If I have any real understanding for the wide horizons of Africa, in particular the wild animals that populate it, it was kindled in me and brought to maturity by Blinkie, our nickname for Alan, who believed in direct contact with and exposure to the land, no matter how young and inexperienced we were.

I shall always remember Blinkie by the following. He would NEVER go anywhere in the bush without wearing a .45 on his right hip. I can recall him telling us that over fifty percent of hunters that were killed by wounded or enraged animals would be alive to tell the tale had they worn a heavy pistol on their belts to shoot at very close quarters, especially when

Claude Klapprott and a leopard. Kipkabus, 1919.

their attacker, be it a lion or leopard, was on top of them. He was an excellent shot with his .45. I remember watching him and his pal, Bud Cottar, shooting empty food cans off each other's head at twenty paces; neither of them ever missed. (Lucky for them!)

Blinkie always wore a cowboy type of hat and was never without a red scarf around his neck. He told us it was his trademark, which he inherited from his father. He loved classical music, and his favorite singer was the well-known opera singer Beniamino Gigli.

When I was out hunting with Blinkie, he gave me a feeling of utter confidence, despite his small stature. He had a curious way with all animals. He was a superb bushman in every sense. He seemed able to read the mind of an animal. "Spend your life with these animals, and in time one gets to know their habits and judge their next movement," he told me.

In his early years he was a crack jockey, due to his small stature, but gave it up for life in the bush. He was always seeking new hunting grounds, places where other hunters hadn't been. The rivalry between professional hunters was fierce; they kept secret their territories, equipment, and their good gunbearers and trackers. All his crew were warned never to disclose his "new hunting grounds."

It all may sound idyllic, but in fact those formative years were very hard for all the families. In 1934 Henry Tarlton was fishing one afternoon on a small dam on the ranch when he was stabbed and probably drowned by an African cattle thief. Ironically, Alan was passing on horseback when he heard his father yelling. Alan gave chase and caught the killer, not knowing that his father was dying from severe stab wounds. From that day on, Alan would not go near that dam, and his father's death haunted him until he passed away in 1958.

As the new head of the family, Alan saw the great ranch collapse during the slump years, the early 1930s. The ostrich industry went almost overnight, and most farmers in Kenya were reduced to subsistence levels of poverty and, like the Tarltons and Bennetts, were forced to sell off huge chunks of their land to meet loan debts and mortgages.

Grandmother Bennett turned her few remaining acres into a poultry and rabbit-farming venture, and we children were almost as wild and undisciplined as the livestock— literally free-range youngsters who spent most of our daylight hours in a competition to see who could find the most eggs so cunningly hidden in the bushes by the almost-wild chickens and turkeys. We also used to go hunting for snakes, and for each snake that was useful to their business, my mum or Blinkie would reward us with a small tin of condensed milk, which we loved. We snake hunters did very well, and the area's small shop, run by a family from Goa in India, had to order cases of Milkmaid condensed milk to keep up with our demand. Mr. de Souza, who owned the shop, thought we were a crazy family. He didn't like snakes, and here were young kids catching poisonous snakes. He used to shake his head and tell us, "Please be careful. Don't let those snakes kill you, otherwise I won't be able to sell you any more condensed milk, and I will get poor."

Snakes are not popular with many people throughout this world except to a herpetologist (the name given to a person who studies reptiles and amphibians). One of the most famous of these scientists was the late Charles Darwin.

No animals are more misunderstood than snakes. Their eyelids are fixed, giving them a scary, staring look. They are said to be deaf, as they have no eardrums. These fascinating creatures actually have a very sensitive smelling system. A snake catches smells on its tongue, which is a Y-shaped organ. It then pushes the tips of its tongue into a small hollow inside the mouth. This hollow has nerve endings that transmit a message to the brain. Strange but true. If one comes across a snake that appears to "push" its tongue out very fast, this is a sign of an angry or nervous snake, so be careful. A slow-moving tongue usually means a friendly or peaceful snake.

Another remarkable thing about a snake is its jaws. These dislocate at the joints, allowing it to swallow a large meal. I have witnessed a python swallowing a hog deer in the Chitwan National Park, Nepal. Now a hog deer is about the size of a full-grown sheep or goat, just to give one an idea of the size. It took three hours for the python to swallow its meal—most interesting and educational, to say the least.

Alan's scheme remained, well, deadly, but it had considerable commercial prospects. By now very well known as a hunter and bush expert, he had been approached by the British

Hermann Klapprott, Viva's uncle, shot this 10-foot, 4-inch lion. Kipkabus, 1919.

Army with an offer of finance if he could establish a source of high-quality snake venom. It had been found to be an invaluable blood coagulant in the treatment of shell or bullet wounds, particularly in the lungs, where the casualties could literally drown in their own blood without treatment.

I immediately offered to be Snake-Catcher-in-Chief and, to my considerable astonishment, my offer was accepted. It emerged later, however, that the money the army allocated for our service was just enough to build a few wire enclosures, so no doubt I would have been roped in anyway. But it did mean that we now had to go deep into the bush on regular safaris. These delightful sojourns thus became delightful business trips and still resulted in many tins of condensed milk. We went looking for the deadliest snakes the bush had to offer, the main requirement being that you brought them back alive.

I was forced in a few short months to become a tracker and learn the tricks and skills of the conservationist as opposed to the hunter. Admittedly, hunting for the pot remained important for our safaris. We literally lived off the game, and in those days, which are not that far in the past, the plains of East Africa were at times, especially during the migration, a shifting mass of animals, their outlines distorted by the heat mirages or "waves." Today, when I see a horizon that doesn't have these etchings, I am aware that something has happened, something is wrong—where have all those animals gone, especially on the Athi Plains of Kenya?

But in those days, poaching and human settlement had not yet taken their toll on the animals. I was just eleven and being paid to hunt and capture the deadly gaboon viper and puff adders, plus any cobras we happened to find. My new status also brought certain changes. I was allowed my first rifle—a Mauser .22 given to me for my birthday that year. Blinkie taught me how to shoot and take care of that lovely little rifle. The week after my eleventh birthday, I scored my first kill, a male Thompson gazelle.

This book is about hunting as well as the conservation of animals, birds, and trees. There are perhaps three categories into which hunters can be placed. There is the genuine hunter, who seeks to shoot nothing but the biggest or the best, most of whom will pay thousands of dollars for the privilege. Then comes the person who kills for subsistence—just to survive. Lastly and no doubt the worst are those who hunt for commercial purposes, for money or for greed, irrespective of how much damage it does to the animals or the environment. These bad types are the ones that I wanted to catch, for I could see the damage they were causing, and so could people like my friend, Prince Bernhard.

Don't get me wrong, I feel very strongly that there should be recognition of the excitement of the hunt. I can still remember vividly the thrill of my first real kill. In Africa, hunting and conservation have always constituted a curious marriage, and I am aware that my reputation is based as much on my shooting abilities as on the work I did for the Tanzanian Game Department. My friendship with Prince Bernhard reflects the strange marriage. The prince has done more than any man I know for African conservation and has assisted me in almost all of my conservation projects over the past forty years. But I first met him when my game warden friend Bill Moore-Gilbert was looking for an expert with the big-game rifle and knowledge of the bush.

I have thought about the vicarious excitements of hunting a great deal and suspect

Claude and Hermann Klapprott, Viva's uncles, with a leopard. Kipkabus, 1920.

that they are a basic paradox—a human failing like infidelity, if you like—against which it is possible to preach eternally but which in the end remains viable, perhaps because it stems from our most basic instincts.

But let us return to the snake-hunting Balsons, for I am better at recounting events than I am at homilies, and I'd be lying if I were to suggest that I did not enjoy my hunting as a boy. And the stories of those bush-days experiences are a source of never-ending delight to me.

At boarding school, my brother David and I couldn't wait for the last day of term to arrive. When our mother drove up the driveway to collect us for our July–August holidays, we jumped into the back seat, happy to know we had six weeks to go on "safari" once again. It was the norm at this time of year to go down to the coast, so we waited with baited breath to hear our mother or Blinkie say, "I

think it is time for us all to visit our friends the Nightingales at Watamu."

As far back as I can remember, even when my dad was alive, we used to go to either Malindi or Watamu for our holidays, but we preferred Watamu because it seemed always to produce plenty of snakes, especially huge puff adders around Gedi Ruins, an old Portuguese fortress. And Watamu had magnificent, almost-pure-white sandy beaches, which in those days we had all to ourselves— just the Nightingales and us, plus a few local fishermen and their families. The trip there took two to three days of traveling over rough and dusty roads, so en route we would stop off at our friends' coffee estate just outside Arusha. We as kids enjoyed the company of our school pal, John Stewart-Smith, plus we all loved to hear the hunting stories told by John's grandfather, a well-known professional hunter.

When he and Alan Tarlton got going on their stories around the huge bonfire, we used to sit in silence and listen with awe. I still remember the stories about the almost-world-record buffalo and the largest lion ever recorded shot by a hunter at that time.[2]

Alan Tarlton—I shall refer to him as "Blinkie" from now on—was a superb raconteur, and when his stories paled, the bush itself stepped in to provide my brother David and me with stories of our own. Amongst the most vivid was the night he and I were asleep in the back of the safari car; our sister Eileen was in a nearby tent with our mother, whilst Blinkie slept under the stars next to a huge campfire. We could hear lion roaring not too far away, but Blinkie assured us that they wouldn't harm us, which gave us some confidence when we climbed into our sleeping bags, protected only by canvas curtains and a hard deck roof. That afternoon Blinkie had killed a hartebeest for our camp rations and hung the carcass in a big tree alongside the truck.

Some time in the night, David and I awoke when the truck bucked and shook under a heavy weight. We opened our eyes to see a pair of hairy thighs rising like tree trunks just alongside our heads—the bulging, muscled legs of a full-grown lion. The animal was after the hartebeest carcass and had decided to use the mudguard and side toolboxes of our "house" as steps to jump on the roof.

We survived the experience only because both of us were literally struck dumb! My little brother disappeared stealthily back into his sleeping bag, pulling it right over his head, but I could neither move nor take my eyes off the scene as the huge lion pulled the carcass free with much grunting and rocking of the springs. It jumped down to pick the load up in its big mouth, and then looked me straight in the eyes from a distance of no more than a few feet. I have always had a vast respect for the intelligence and, certainly, the instincts of lion. This one reasoned that it had literally a mouthful and there was no room for the bug-eyed kid

2. Viva and I happened to hear that John Stewart-Smith was living in Canada somewhere, so when we arrived in Canada in 1994, we made inquiries. One day as I did farm chores on our son's Bobcat, a vehicle drove up and a young man got out and came over to where I sat on the machine. I switched it off.

"Good day," he said, extending his hand for me to shake. "I see you are driving a Bobcat. How do you like it?" I told him it was a super little machine. He looked at me sideways, then said, "What type of accent is that?" I told him that we are from East Africa. He smiled and told me that his father, Brandon Dansie, was from East Africa—Kenya—and asked if I knew him. I laughed and told him that his dad went to school with me and that I knew him very well. I then asked him what he did. "I work for Bobcat in Calgary," was his reply. "That is why, when I saw you driving one, I was interested to see if you were happy or needed any parts."

I asked where his father lived, and he told me that he was retired in High River, doing some carpentry as a hobby. I then asked if he knew John Stewart-Smith. His eyes lit up as he replied, "Do you mean Boozie Smith?" and when I nodded, he said, "Hell, man, the Stewart-Smiths are my parents' greatest friends; we have spent perhaps the past sixteen Christmases together. We and their three children are good *rafikis* (friends)." I was excited to know that I had found John and his wife Avgi again after some forty-five years.

I phoned John, whose nickname at school was indeed Boozie, Swahili for goats. John used to have a small herd of goats at his parents' farm, thus the nickname. He was very happy to hear from me and invited us to visit immediately. Viva and I arranged it for the following weekend, and when we met up, I asked him what had happened to two old pictures that his parents had hanging on their lounge wall. "Just hang on for a few seconds," he said with a smile, and disappeared down some stairs, only to return hiding something behind his back. With a glint in his eyes he handed me those very same photos that I remembered from some sixty years before.

cowering in the darkness. It gave a muffled growl, turned its back on me with slow contempt, and ambled off into the night, dragging its bounty between its front legs. I didn't dare start screaming for help for at least ten minutes.

The snake farm prospered. At one time we had about 580 puff adders, several gaboon vipers, and many cobras—but no dreaded black mambas, which moved too fast, were very aggressive, and didn't produce enough venom to make us risk our lives. Judging by my experiences in Africa, stories of how quickly a snake can kill a human are vastly exaggerated. I know of only one African snake, the beautifully marked gaboon viper, whose venom (until recently) had no antidote. There is a serum that can counteract the poison of all other venomous snakes. How dangerous a snakebite is depends on a number of factors, especially its location in relation to the main arteries or nerve clusters, and the amount of poison in the snake's sacs, which normally depends on how recently it has used its poison to kill prey. Most humans are bitten when they step on or trip over a snake in dark or thick grass. Snakes don't usually attack unless they are provoked or disturbed.

Let me tell you a story that happened to me in 1962. Early one morning I was looking for a sitatunga, sometimes known as the marsh antelope because it inhabits dense reed beds or papyrus swamps. Sitatunga are strong swimmers and have peculiarly long and narrow hooves, an adaptation for walking over marshy terrain. I had heard reports that sitatunga had been seen in an area where they were never recorded before, and so I was reconnoitering to see if the reports were true.

I was leading the way, using a forked stick to push the tall, wet grass aside as we made our way toward a swamp. I very nearly stepped on an enormous gaboon viper; its fantastic colouring struck my eyes just as I was about to put my foot down. I stopped in midair, but one of my game scouts suddenly bumped into me, and I had to do an acrobatic jump so as not to land on top of this deadly snake. I always carried an antivenin kit, and it must have saved at least ten lives during my days in the bush of Africa. But there was no cure for the gaboon viper's bite; it meant certain death for the victim. That thought dashed through my mind as I leaped over the snake, shouting *"Nyoka!"* (snake) to those following. You might be surprised at the reactions one gets when this word is uttered. Ninety-nine percent of all Africans are scared stiff of snakes, mainly due to the fact that many of them don't have access to the serum and die each year from being bitten; most deaths occur miles from any hospital or clinic.

As I hit the ground, I rolled over, but I was soon on my feet again looking for the snake. My three game guards were nowhere to be seen, but the snake was still there, coiled in an S bend, ready to strike. Eventually I managed to get the guards to bring me a gunnysack from my vehicle. I wanted to catch this beautiful specimen to take home and show Viva and our sons before taking it to a friend of mine who adored snakes. My head game guard approached sheepishly and said, *"Bwana mkubwa, huyu nyoka mbaya sana, usi cheza na yeye, ua tu."* (Big man, that snake is very bad. Don't play with it; just kill it.) But I was determined to capture this fine specimen and hoped that I had not forgotten the skills learned many years before during our snake-farming enterprise. I used a forked stick to hold its neck down so I could take a firm grip on the neck. I had not anticipated its strength and weight. As I gripped it, I instructed my guard to hold open the gunnysack so that I could drop the snake in headfirst, but he just stood there dumbfounded and shook his head. I got really anxious and shouted for him to hold the sack open immediately, which he did. That was the end of the sitatunga recce for that day.

When I arrived home and shook the snake from the sack, I noticed it had a swollen neck—I must have injured its neck whilst holding it so tight. I know from previous experiences on our snake farm that a reptile injured like this has an almost 100 percent chance of dying, so I put it out of its suffering and took the specimen to my friend. He was delighted and said it had to be the biggest and the best specimen he had ever come across.

At our farm we had several hundred deadly snakes in captivity. Most were capable of delivering three to four lethal bites because we deliberately allowed the poison to accumulate. The sleepy, fat puff adders plus several gaboon vipers were particularly sluggish, so an observer was inclined to become complacent, but Blinkie and my mother always warned us to be on our guard because any bite from the gaboon viper meant certain death. Ranging from three to five feet long, they had wide, flat bodies and spent most of their time curled up asleep. Both vipers and adders could convulse into a lightning strike if their slumber was disrupted.

Of the some 2,300 known species of snakes worldwide (I stand to be corrected on this number), only about 765 are known to be venomous. Of these a mere seven percent are capable of causing death to humans. The salivary glands of venomous species are modified to hold poison, and in most cases a pair of primitive teeth are transformed into fangs. The vipers and adders (Viperidae) have very large fangs in the upper jaw and no other teeth behind them except replacement fangs, which move into place as soon as the working fangs are broken or fall out. These snakes drive their venom into the victim the same way a hypodermic syringe operates, so they don't seize their victims and hold on after the bite.

The family Viperidae, which includes the rattlesnakes and moccasins of America, are all ovoviviparous, meaning that the eggs are incubated in the genital tract of the female and the babies are born alive. Some female puff adders gave birth to forty (and sometimes fifty) babies, so a keeper had to be extremely careful when walking in the snake pens because a bite even from one of these newborns could mean almost certain death unless an antidote was administered immediately.

We also kept thirty to forty cobras—active, aggressive snakes that have a habit of spitting poison at their enemy's eyes—and they were difficult to "milk." We milked all the other snakes by using a catching stick to trap the neck. Then we held the snake behind the head and allowed it to strike into a piece of flexible rubber stretched over a wine glass or, better still, a beaker marked with measurement graduations; this made it possible to measure the amounts as well as the toxicity of the venom but also enabled the laboratories to develop suitable antivenins.

Cobras were another matter altogether. Eventually I became quite fond of the vipers and adders, especially the gaboon viper because of its extraordinary beauty, but I never learned to like the vicious, spitting cobra, although I admired its courage.

The venom-collecting technique we used for the cobras involved a sheet of plate glass

Walter James Balson and Rose Bennett Balson, the author's father and mother, on their wedding day, 29 February 1928.

about three feet square. You held the sheet by the fingertips—and there was always that lingering danger of a bite on the fingers—and gingerly walked directly at the cobra. At a distance that varied from three feet to six inches, the cobra would strike and spit, covering the glass with a fine spray of venom, usually aimed directly at your eyes. It would do this three or four times, and after the first two sprays you could no longer see the snake, which made the whole exercise that much more frightening. Once it had exhausted its venom, you backed away, being very careful that another snake hadn't slithered across your line of retreat in the meantime. Then the venom was allowed to dry and scraped off for storage.

I was bitten seriously only once. A smallish puff adder hit my shinbone when I didn't see it and stepped on its back. Luckily, only a small amount of poison entered my body, for its fangs hit the bone. Blinkie administered the antidote, and after a few months the wounds healed. For some reason the bite from these adders takes a considerable time to heal; sometimes victims lose an arm or leg.

I had been taught to be wary rather than frightened of wild animals and in the bush would treat a big snake with the same amount of respect I would accord big game such as elephant and buffalo. The fact that we had so many dangerous snakes in our compound tended to reduce our natural wariness. Ironically, my mother and we three children all came through the snake-farming period virtually unscathed. Poor Blinkie was not so lucky.

We were on a snake-collecting safari near Lake Jipe on the Kenya-Tanzania border when a local *jumbe* (chief) made contact with us, saying he knew of a cave famous for its big cobras. He took us there. The cave was deep,

dark, and full of bats; one could smell their droppings and urine from some distance away. Blinkie insisted on going in alone, and after switching on the powerful torch attached to his hat, he disappeared inside.

Only a few seconds later we heard an anguished shout and some thrashing about, and then he staggered from the entrance, his face drained of colour. He told us he had been bitten in the chest—an extremely dangerous point because of the position of the heart—by a huge cobra, and that he'd fallen into what amounted to a nest of cobras! To this day the thought of being in that black hole with those deadly snakes sends cold shivers down my spine.

My mother injected him immediately with the antivenin, and we started a mad dash to the nearest point of habitation, a small town called Taveta, but by the time we reached the place, Blinkie had collapsed and was already semicomatose. Fortunately, a doctor was on duty at the Moshi hospital some fifty miles away, where Blinkie was treated in the trauma unit. Whilst all this was going on, my mother called Wilson airport just outside Nairobi and managed to arrange for a small plane to fly in and airlift Blinkie to a private hospital. He was in a coma for three days, and the doctors said there was little chance of saving his life. The doctors showed my mother the cobra bites—they had found *nine!* But my mother insisted that he be flown immediately to Johannesburg in South Africa, where there were facilities for massive blood transfusions.

They changed Blinkie's blood three times over the next few days, and he lived to tell the tale, though it took a considerable toll on his constitution. A few months later they decided enough was enough and released all our farm snakes back into the wild, and we returned to a normal life once again. My mother did her turkey farming, and Blinkie took out safari clients once he was fully recovered.

Against a domestic background as exotic as this, school was little more than an obligation. I got a good basic education from the local primary and high schools and took my Oxford—Cambridge Overseas School Certificate. What I was learning in the bush was at least as important in that my ambition, for as long as I could remember having one, was to go into the game department or similar work when my schooling was completed. Almost everything I did on the farm was good training for that. Our early safari cars were Model A and T Fords, and you had to know how to repair one before you dared take it into the wild. During the war my mother bought two ex-army motorcycles, a B.S.A. and a Harley Davidson, and we soon learned to ride them. I managed to get to know my huge Harley intimately whilst David had the smaller B.S.A.

My closest friends were the Taylor brothers, whose father owned Taylors Brewery at Ruaraka and also Taylors Farm on the Athi River. We managed to wrangle petrol for our motorcycles from the man who drove the brewery lorry. At night we would go out on our bikes in pursuit of springhares, commonly known as night hares, for which we used to get paid 10 shillings (approximately U.S.$1.50 in those days) by a local game catcher; the animals were in demand at that time by zoos around the world. It was an extremely dangerous sport requiring night vision, the ability to ride a motorbike, and ignorance about what hazards lay ahead, as one couldn't see where one was going. It also required quick reflexes as you got near the fleeing quarry. You had to jump off your bike (which would have

done credit to a stuntman) and chase after the springhare, which would jump all over the place on its two long hind legs, not unlike a kangaroo. Hazards hid around each corner, especially huge holes dug by antbears. We fell down a few of these holes, and I almost broke my leg a couple of times. But it was great fun, and we had many good laughs.

The Taylors allowed me to shoot my first big-game rifle, an old army .303 that knocked me on my back and bruised a shoulder the first time I pulled the trigger. Blinkie, who had very strong views about the use of guns and saw little need for me to own anything bigger than my .22 Mauser, was very surprised when he discovered that I was already a crack shot with a heavy rifle by the time he judged me old and big enough to handle one. I shot my first elephant when I was just fourteen (highly illegal, of course) with his .375 Magnum.

The whole concept of game conservation in parks and nature reserves was created during the time I was a boy, but very few of them were in existence when I finally left school. However, an awful lot of eager young boys like myself ached to go and work there. One needed the right contacts, and since my father was dead and I was too proud to ask Blinkie, a job was not forthcoming. Instead I went to work as a surveyor, assigned to assist a civil engineer named Max Lawrence-Brown (an elder brother to the two well-known Lawrence-Browns, professional hunters working out of Kenya) in surveying a new railway line from Kaliwa to Mpanda. This job took me many miles into the wilds of western Tanzania, where I got the real sense of being "in the bush." Plenty of wildlife roamed the area, whetting my ambition to become involved with the fauna and flora of eastern Africa.

Alan Tarlton—Uncle Blinkie—holding a young python. This picture was given to me by my mother in memory of a great man and naturalist.

Once the survey had been completed and the plans handed over to the authorities, we went to work for an incredible man, Colonel Grogan, whom I had met during our snake-hunting safaris. He lived in a castle, Girigan Castle, on top of a hill overlooking Lake Jipe. The colonel owned some 500,000 acres of land that was split up into three sisal estates, Jipe, Zawani, and Taveta. How he obtained these would take up another whole chapter.

Legends abound worldwide about Colonel Grogan. One of his most outstanding feats was to walk from Cape Town to Cairo. This came about, so the story goes, when he was a young man and fell in love with a lady named Gertrude Watt (a descendant of the famous Watt who invented the first steam engine) whilst convalescing in New Zealand from wounds he had received in 1896 during the Matabele Rising in southern Africa. When he asked her stepfather for permission to marry her, the man replied, "Young man, what have you done to prove you are worthy of my stepdaughter?" Colonel Grogan personally told me that he was stunned and at a loss for words and suddenly replied, "Nothing, Sir, but I will prove my worth and show the whole world that I am a man. I will walk from Cape Town to Cairo—the length of Africa." So it was agreed that if he achieved this feat, he could marry his sweetheart Gertrude. Believe it or not, Colonel Grogan achieved the almost impossible. He commenced his epic journey in 1898, and it took him two and a half years to complete. Emerging from obscurity, he suddenly found himself a hero. He survived to tell the tale—braving cannibals, hunger, and illnesses—and to marry Gertrude.

Max and I were employed to survey and construct some irrigation schemes on the colonel's vast estates. He had great vision and always looked ahead twenty to thirty years. He told me his trademark was "Be one step ahead of everyone else." All my friends told me I was mad to go to work for the eccentric colonel, but we became very good friends despite our age gap.

He was eccentric, to say the least. Soon after my arrival at the construction camp on the outskirts of Taveta, I went down with a bad bout of malaria. In a state of high fever and semiconscious, I was taken by the colonel to his castle. I can remember waking there and being convinced I had died and was in some reception room to heaven!

Colonel Grogan's castle had been built by Italian prisoners of war right in the heart of the Jipe Sisal Estate, surrounded by hundreds of square miles of African bush. And here I was, a sick and nervous young man, occupying a four-poster bed in a huge, tapestry-hung room. When I had recovered enough to get back on my feet, I went down to the dining room, which had the largest table I had ever seen, surrounded by twenty-four beautifully carved chairs. At dinner that night, Mrs. Towers, the colonel's housekeeper and friend, told me to seat myself opposite her, which I did just as the colonel entered the room. He stared at me and said, "My young friend, you must be seated at the far end of the table until we are certain that you have not contacted some awful contagious disease," and he smiled as he sat down.

The job was all right. I was out in the open and involved with water, a vital commodity in Africa. I worked with a skilled civil engineer and picked his brains to gain practical knowledge of the problems and technology. This knowledge was to stand me in good stead many years later, when I would be asked to join the game department to survey roads and dams in game reserves and conservation areas in which the most important construction element was water conservation and supply.

And even better, I found Viva. That is perhaps an odd name for a girl born in a tent in the heart of the African bush, but it suits her very well. Her mother, Edith, had a school friend with the same name, and wanted that name for her daughter. Viva is small, blonde, and determined, and has always looked half her age.

I saw her for the first time at a club dance in Morogoro, a small town some 120 miles inland from Dar es Salaam, the capital of Tanganyika (since renamed Tanzania). In case you don't understand what the word "gauche" really means, imagine a young man with my background, on a night off from an engineering camp, seeing for the very first time an object that invoked in him all the feelings that a man is supposed to have for a woman! And to say that there were more men than girls at the monthly Morogoro dances is the understatement of the past century!

Fortunately, a good bushman has to have a high degree of animal cunning. I knew the compère (master of ceremonies) and asked him to call a "Paul Jones," in which couples were obliged to drop their present partners, and the ladies would all join hands and dance around in a circle counterclockwise whilst the men danced in an outer circle clockwise. When the music stopped, you danced with the lady right in front of you. I gave the compère strict instructions to try to stop the music when Viva would be right in front of me. Given the pace of the dance, I had about one chance in ten of being in the lucky position. But, with me throwing the MC threatening glances, he managed to stop the music at the right moment, and I finally managed my first meeting with Viva. She was then just sixteen and still in high school.

Viva's family background is even more exotic than my growing up on a snake farm. The most important part of it, for us at least, is that we were both born in the bush, and our love for it is "organic." Her parents were of German and English backgrounds, and her grandparents on her father's side, as mentioned earlier, trekked by ox wagon in the early 1900s to the highlands of Kenya, where they settled and farmed. Viva's father decided to try his hand at mining.

I managed to dance just enough with Viva to extract some rather vague information as to where she was living. She mentioned a place with an unpronounceable name (which I found out later to be Kigimarkala). She told me that her family lived in a type of long house built out of timber and thatched with grass and that her parents were mining mica and that she had three sisters and two younger brothers. Viva was the second eldest. I had already decided that she was the woman I wanted to spend the rest of my life with.

A week later I mounted my own safari to try to find this place Kigimarkala. Nobody I asked had ever heard of it, and now I wasn't at all sure that the place even existed. Perhaps she had tried to put me off the scent by some girlish joke.

Still, I was determined to find her again, so I drove off in the general direction she had described to me. I found a small track leading off into thick bush at approximately the place she told me to look. There were no signboards or any sign of habitation anywhere, so I drove on. There were many signs of elephant in the area—huge trees were pushed over, and droppings and tracks were all over the place. I had a couple of elephant licenses and told myself I could perhaps at least shoot a big tusker!

On coming around a corner, I suddenly spied a rocky outcrop, just what I needed to survey the woodlands for any signs of humans or elephant. I parked my pickup off the track and made a beeline for those rocks. I soon was squatting up there and making a 360-degree sweep with my heavy 10X40 binocs, steadied by my elbows on my knees. Out in the middle of nowhere I spotted a large grass shack with some smaller outbuildings also made of grass. That must be the Klapprott encampment, I thought to myself, and focused my lenses more sharply. Suddenly, three young girls started to chase one another around the compound. It was like something out of a Greek legend, so incongruous as to be close to fantasy.

I came down from my rocky outcrop like a wild thing, clutching an elephant rifle and an excuse that I just happened to be in the area hunting elephant and saw their encampment from the top of the hill. This was indeed the home of the family Klapprott, as Hans Christian Anderson a group as I had ever come across in life or in fiction—cheerful, warmly hospitable, and full of enthusiasm and everlasting stories about searching for pots of gold or mica or copper at the end of rainbows. I was swept in by the whole family and ordered to stay the night, even though it was quite obvious that my intentions were anything but honourable and my excuses hollow.

For a few happy months I was able to enjoy that extraordinary household, and the joy of seeing Viva again blossomed into a mature emotion that has lasted me all my lifetime to date; we have been happily married for forty-five years. Sadly, Viva had to complete her schooling and was sent to Nairobi to learn to become a nursing sister; her mother had been a trained nurse at St. Bartholomew's in London and wanted Viva to follow in her footsteps. It was only by

coincidence that she went to Gertrude's Garden Children's Hospital, which had been built by Colonel Grogan in memory of his wife. It was there that I introduced Viva to the colonel, whom she enjoyed meeting. He remembered me, although we hadn't seen each other for a few years. Whilst Viva was learning her trade, she wrote and told me that the colonel had passed away at the ripe old age of ninety-two.

We were suddenly 800 miles apart, and it was completely unbearable. At least once a month for the next two years, I drove up to see her over roads that were dry, corrugated, and dusty, and in the rainy season were reduced to a slippery quagmire. Then I would drive back on Sunday night, a 1,600-mile round trip.

We were married on 10 December 1955 and have three sons. I think that if one of them ever came and told me that he was in love with a girl and wanted to marry her, I'd tell him he should do a bit of long-distance driving for a year or two before making up his mind. There can't be any better test!

Over all this time, the job in the Water Development Department had grown less and less fulfilling. Some of my friends from school were making a name for themselves in the game department or national parks in Kenya, and one, Brian Nicholson, had joined the game department in Tanganyika. All were doing important and brilliant work. Several others had become good professional hunters, and here I was, slogging away at building dams and irrigation schemes. This was no life for me, important though dams were and despite the fact that I'd become something of an expert at my work and had in fact just built the first-ever irrigation scheme in Tanganyika. But for a young man with my background, dams could never equate with animals.

I'd become an honorary game warden and was known as something of a shot, but the hoped-for move from the water department to the game department seemed a pipe dream. In fact, I was later to discover that my first two applications for a transfer had been "spiked" by my own boss, on the grounds that I was the only good irrigation engineer he had.

Then that strange marriage of hunting and conservation, which I have mentioned before, came to my rescue. In 1954 there was a famine in Sukumaland in the Western Province, and I was asked to supplement the game department staff on the edge of what is now the Serengeti National Park in a culling operation to provide food for the starving villagers. On this trip I met face-to-face the head of the game department, Gerry Swynerton, and over a campfire told him of my ambitions. He was enthusiastic and listened to my plea for a chance to join his staff, which gave me some hope for the future. Even so, I had to wait three more years.

But in that time, the embryonic game-conservation projects had grown into game reserves and also national parks. Their tourist potential was expanding and had been recognized as a top money earner for foreign exchange. My boss, trying to keep me under his wing, seconded me to the Ngorongoro Conservation Unit and the famous Ngorongoro Crater, hoping that I would be happier there working on dams for the animals and the Masai cattle. I was instrumental in helping build one of the main accesses down into the crater. And then my third application for a vacancy in the game department was finally accepted. I was a game warden, at long last!

If this story had been set anywhere but in Africa, it could very well end here. The next twelve years were a time of total fulfillment. Viva and I spent most of it outdoors on safari. Born to the bush, we were completely contented with the kind of home one could keep in a safari Land Rover followed by a 4x4 Bedford loaded with all our camp gear, supplies, and food. Our company was a few of my faithful game guards. We camped many times in picturesque places on riverbanks, and in the shadows of Africa's great mountains, Kilimanjaro and Meru. We rode a mounting international wave of interest in the protection of Africa's wild animals, driven by the concern of countries like the United States, where conservation awareness had come almost too late to save some of their indigenous wildlife. The world was concerned, or so it seemed, to see that the same tragedy did not happen in Africa, and the money to support this ideal began to flow in to East Africa in particular.

I became so immersed in this narrow field of domestic politics that the other changes going on in East Africa—the movement of colonies to independent nationhood, for example—were somehow outside my scope. I was not a politician, except in working for the territorial interests of the wild animals under my charge. And even this effort was naïve. There is no protection in remoteness; the winds of change will reach even Shangrila eventually. Nevertheless, when they did finally blow down my neck, I was shattered—and totally unprepared.

The irony of it was that we bushmen of the game department were not directly caught up in the various "Africanization" programmes that followed Tanzanian independence. But a ridiculously petty squabble developed between the governments of Great Britain and Tanzania that landed us directly in the eye of the storm. It involved who should be responsible for paying our meager pensions! Tanzania argued, in my view quite correctly, that it should be responsible only for the pensions of civil servants working on contracts after independence. Britain disagreed, insisting that Tanzania, in spite of its obvious economic problems, take on all pension liabilities. When Tanzania refused, Britain cut off diplomatic relations and all aid to the fledgling state. Tanzania responded by giving notice to all "expatriate" civil servants on contracts predating independence.

Thus, on Christmas Eve 1968, as I mentioned at the start of this chapter, my office messenger arrived at our house with a reply to an application I had made for annual leave. The letter was an acceptance of my application, but it contained notice that I was being fired as of "the expiry of your leave." What a terrible Christmas present.

During this most devastating period of my life, Viva and I groped desperately for some good alternative, for we still had our three sons to educate. I became obsessed with my lack of qualifications. For the first time in my life I began to realize that the job I had desired more than anything else and for which I had given the best part of my working life was extraordinarily limiting. Only East Africa, with its vast game parks protected by their huge tourist potential, required senior game wardens!

Viva suggested that I travel to Kenya, where I had many school friends in the safari and tourist industry, and seek some opportunity in that fast-expanding business. This I pursued vigorously. I'd developed an interest and some skill in taxidermy, and for a time it seemed we might set up a business in that area.

But all the time there was the nagging doubt that stuffed animals were not for us, especially Viva. It didn't matter how often I told myself that I had a family to support and that taxidermy

was a better prospect than a job in some English safari park, sharing a compromise with some sad lion. What's more, Kenya at that time was like an unexploded volcano. The Luo leader, Oginga Odinga, had quit as Jomo Kenyatta's vice president, publicly confirming the simmering differences between Kenya's two main tribes, the Luo and the Kikuyu. Odinga created his own Luo opposition party and for his efforts was promptly arrested and locked up by Kenyatta's ruling Kenya African National Union. The last remaining hope for tribal peace in those troubled times, the gentle, intelligent, and enlightened Luo politician Tom Mboya, who had remained in Kenyatta's party through all these machinations, was shot and killed outside a chemist's shop in Nairobi.

Viva and I, trying hard to be business people, were staying in Nairobi's Ambassador Hotel the day it happened. We were only a few blocks away and heard the commotion. We looked at each other, our eyes expressing not so much fear as a kind of total confusion as to what was happening to this wonderful Africa of ours. With very little discussion, we packed our bags, paid our bill, and pointed the car back in the direction of the Tanzanian border. As we drove through Nairobi trying to avoid the many police vans and ambulances that seemed to be driving aimlessly around, some Luos who had heard that Mboya had been killed started to stone cars. We managed to escape unscathed.

Some months previously, I had made arrangements to attend the second Big Game Conference being staged that year in San Antonio, Texas, by an organization called Game Conservation International. It seemed a good opportunity to meet people who might be able to help me find a suitable job. In preparation for that conference, I made a quick safari through the game areas and conservation parks in northern Tanzania. My own personal problems had tended to push into the background the startling facts I unearthed on that tour, but now I began to prepare notes and to discuss the situation with various officials and informed experts in Tanzania. I talked freely and frankly—there was nothing very much for me to lose!

I had a long session with a man whom I hold to be one of the greatest protectors of game I know, Myles Turner, deputy chief warden of the famed Serengeti National Park. Myles had chosen to stay in the Serengeti come what may, as was reflected by his voluntary "step down" to deputy status. I had always presumed that this decision was based simply on the fact that he had worked in and fought for this paradise for many years, and he and his wife Kay loved the place. In fact, Myles had unfinished business of a more direct nature.

As we sat on the veranda of his concrete-block house at Seronera headquarters in the middle of Serengeti Park, Myles told me, "Eric, my old friend, it's not like it used to be. The past problem of poaching for meat you can forget. Things have changed dramatically. We are now faced with the commercial poacher armed with those dreaded AK47s—we have a war on our doorstep."

I knew Myles very well. I also knew how he personally disliked even the mildest form of poaching. I'd seen him come back from long, dusty anti-poaching safaris to the far end of his territory with his Land Rover cluttered with wire snares, muzzleloaders, and piles of poisoned arrows. He had a very efficient field force, a paramilitary group largely composed of reformed poachers—and some not that reformed. They would have been a highly suspect bunch of

villains had they been commanded by anyone but Myles. But on those occasions, he would come home confident that he had an edge on the men who came in to kill a few wildebeest and sell the smoked meat to villagers.

But now he felt differently. "It's like sitting under an avalanche," he told me grimly. "We haven't got a chance. They're even using automatic weapons, and they shoot to kill, be it my Rangers or animals."

I tried to console him with a few homilies: Times were changing. Law and order weren't what they used to be. But it would get better. Things had to sort themselves out, especially now that the Tanzanians were in charge of their own destiny—just give it some time.

"That's all very well, my friend," Myles said slowly, "but you must know that we may not have the time. I estimate that we lost 30,000 head of game over a nine-month period."

I couldn't keep secret a figure as appalling as that. And I couldn't sleep at night, thinking of how a few of us dedicated people had looked after the wildlife and its habitat for so many years, and now it was being decimated right before our very eyes. I had to do something quickly.

I mentioned it to various top officials in the government, and to John Owen, then-director of National Parks, Tanzania, and to my surprise there were no real denials, nothing to reflect the sense of shock I had felt when Myles told me. What's more, I began to hear reports of terrible poaching in other areas.

But there was little I could do. I had been given notice, and Viva and I had already commenced to pack our things. I told her that I was going to call Prince Bernhard and tell him what was happening, as he was a close friend of the president, Dr. Julius Nyerere. I had to go to the Big Game Conference, and I would see what could be arranged there.

My flight was due to depart from Mbeya to Dar es Salaam at 1:30 P.M. on 20 May 1969. That morning the phone rang. The operator said he had an urgent call from the office of the president of Tanzania. An official asked me whether it was true that I was planning to leave the country that night. With some trepidation I confirmed the information. At that time in Tanzania, the Instant Deportation Order had been applied extremely freely, and it flashed through my mind that perhaps I should have kept my big mouth shut. The prospect of having to leave everything, taking nothing more than Viva and the boys, was truly frightening.

The voice at the other end of the line did nothing to quiet my fears. I was told that an urgent letter was to be delivered to me and that I must read it before taking my flight. The letter would be handed to me personally by a messenger from the president's office.

I put down the phone and went back into the sitting room, where Viva was putting the finishing touches to some notes I had prepared for the conference. I debated in my mind whether to tell her of my fears and then reasoned that there was little point. If it were to be a deportation order, I would cancel my departure and go back to Mbeya to get things organized. If it was something else—well, there was no need to add to her worries.

In a situation like this, it is difficult to behave normally. On my arrival at Dar es Salaam airport, I was met by a young civil servant who was extremely courteous, which by itself increased my suspicion. I told myself, as I fingered the envelope he handed to me, that his demeanor was designed to prevent my complaining about the way I was treated.

"Do you want me to open it now?" I inquired.

"Yes, Mr. Balson. I think that some reply is expected."

The letter read: "I am pleased to offer you reemployment on contract, immediately following your retirement on pension, and on completion of your retirement leave, as a senior game warden."

"What is this?" I asked stupidly, taken completely by surprise.

The young officer looked me straight in the eyes and said, "I believe it asks if you will accept and then a contract will be prepared. I am empowered to accept your initial decision. What will it be?"

"But what's it all about?" I inquired.

"I'm afraid I can't tell you that, but as you can see, the letter is from the office of the president himself. I do know that it is very confidential."

In my quandary I hadn't looked at the letterhead.

After reading the letter again, I asked the young officer, "Could I possibly speak to the president?" He winked at me and smiled.

He then phoned the State House and handed me the phone, and I heard President Nyerere say, "Hello, Mr. Eric. I have met you before during those visits when His Royal Highness Prince Bernhard came to stay with me. I would like to know if you would be prepared to come and work again to try and stamp out this outrageous poaching epidemic that is currently sweeping my country."

I told him that I would be honoured and that I would think it over and give him a reply once I had discussed it with Prince Bernhard. He replied, "Please do, and give my warmest *salaams* to the prince. Thank you, Mr. Eric, and enjoy your leave."

I immediately phoned Viva, who was waiting anxiously to hear my news. She was relieved to hear about this special assignment but expressed her concern about the dangers that would undoubtedly come with the job. I told her not to worry and that I would probably change my flights and travel to see Prince Bernhard to get his advice. Viva was happy that at least I had a job to come back to.

I boarded the plane in a complete daze. I was desperately in need of some guidance and decided I would break my flight in London, then take a shuttle to consult with Prince Bernhard, whose wide experience in game policies could help me in my dilemma.

But there was not enough information, and the prince advised me kindly to examine how much I really wanted to stay in Tanzania. If that was a dominant notion, my decision was perhaps not that difficult. He also told me that President Julius Nyerere had phoned him about the terrible devastation of his country's wildlife and asked for advice on how to combat the problem. The prince had advised Nyerere to employ someone like me. I thanked him graciously for his advice and for helping me find a job.

Even so, when I landed in San Antonio sleepless and jet-lagged, I still was not sure what to do. When I reached the hotel where most of the East African representatives were staying, I found another note waiting for me at the reception desk. It was from the chief game warden of Tanzania, a Mr. Mahinda. There was a room number, and I found that Mahinda was in his room. He asked if I could please come and see him immediately.

He welcomed me with an embrace and came directly to the point.

"We know now that the poaching in the northern areas of Tanzania has reached appalling proportions, Eric. I don't need to tell you that. I want it brought under control, and so does the president . I have asked him if he would allow me to send you to the Arusha area for that purpose." I told Mahinda that I had to consult with my wife before I could give my final reply.

So started another interesting, dangerous, but rewarding saga in my life.

"Browsing Bull" *by Mike Ghaui (portrait of a greater kudu).*

CHAPTER THREE
Four Princely Safaris

Katavi Revisited: 1963

The prince had enjoyed his first safari so much that he requested an encore for 1963—to the same area. Bill Moore-Gilbert was no longer with us, so I inherited the role of chief professional hunter and guide for the prince, a rewarding but challenging task that I was honoured to take on, for I admire PB very much as a man and friend. I made the arrangements, and before long we were on safari once more.

On this trip, only Coen and Hans accompanied the prince. I set up our camp not too distant from where we had headquartered for the previous safari. Instead of overlooking a lake, we had our setup on the bank of a river with a big, deep pool full of hippo and croc.

Coen had told me that PB wished to collect a big buffalo with horns spreading more than fifty inches for a museum. I knew that this was a possibility, for I had seen a couple of big bulls in a large herd that congregated on the flood plains of Lake Katavi during this time of the year, August–October. This herd was estimated to number over three thousand head. I had also come across a few lone bulls with exceptionally massive horns that would fit the

prince's criterion, so I knew our chances of finding the right one were good.

One morning, as we neared a lookout point from which we could glass a large *mbuga* (low-lying grassy plain), we could see the big herd assembled there, most of the animals lying down and chewing their cud. PB, Coen, and Hans just gazed in amazement, unable to believe their eyes. I switched off the Land Rover, and we all climbed down and took up our binoculars. We were about two miles from the buffalo, so they couldn't see us, but we could see them clearly through our 10X glasses.

"*Phew!* What a fantastic spectacle," remarked PB as we sat down to check the herd.

Coen said, "I think I can see a beauty" and proceeded to direct our eyes to the spot. The bull looked good, but it was difficult to say if it was over the fifty-inch mark. As we enjoyed coffee and sandwiches, I worked out how we might attempt our approach and prayed that the wind would keep in our favour.

Before long we arrived at the point from which we would commence our stalk. I planned to drive the vehicle a certain distance and then proceed on foot. The wind was still right, so I slowly drove forward, using clumps of thick shrubs and bushes to conceal our approach to a big tree some two hundred yards ahead, where I planned to park the vehicle.

As we approached the tree, we had our eyes fixed on the herd, which was still unaware of our presence. I took up my binocular and scanned for the big bull. Prince Bernhard was sitting up front with me while Coen, Hans, and Rashidi sat on a high seat in the back. The Land Rover's hood and canopy had been removed, giving everyone an excellent view all around. The prince preferred it like this.

I was evaluating the size of a big buffalo grazing on the far side of the herd, some three hundred yards in front of us, when I felt a touch on my shoulder. Rashidi did not speak but pointed into the tree above us. Crouched down on a thick branch just above Prince Bernhard's head was an enormous black-maned lion, his tail twitching from side to side, a typical gesture of feline annoyance. PB looked up, and his eyebrows lifted as if in shock. I was afraid the lion was preparing to spring on top of one of us. I heard the click of a camera; it was Hans. I had my .470 in hand, but PB looked at me and shook his head. My camera was hanging from my neck, so I quietly put my rifle down and risked taking a photo. That

This is just a part of a big herd of buffalo that used to congregate on the Katavi flood plains during the months of August to October. Balson estimates that there were at least 2500–3000 head in the herd. He comments, "The herd was too large to fit into one picture, so I had to take two pictures and join them."

picture is perhaps the best I have ever taken of a lion. I am rather proud of it.

Nervously, I started the engine, engaged reverse gear, and inched away. Once we were out of danger, I stopped, and at that moment the big lion slid down the tree and made off in the opposite direction. Immediately, the nearest buffalo stood up and started to run en masse toward the fleeing lion.

"*Hmmm*," said PB, "I see that our luck is still with us. That was a scary situation."

We all agreed and forgot completely about the buffalo. Hans said, "I bet my photo is better than yours. I was only ten feet from his head and shall never forget the look of his yellow eyes staring right into my lens." I drove back to the same big tree, which provided super shade, and we decided it was time for a drink to soothe our nerves, and some lunch.

During the break PB asked, "What was that big fellow doing up in this tree?" I explained that lion are not prone to climbing trees and do so only when herds of buffalo are about or they are troubled by the biting *Stomoxy* fly. Buffalo hate lion and will give chase, especially if the buff have young calves.

I had seen this behaviour before, in both Tanzania's Manyara Park and the famous

Ngorongoro Crater. I have come across several lion and their cubs trampled by herds of buffalo. The lions' carcasses were flattened.

After our meal and drinks, a siesta was called for; it was too hot, anyway, to travel around hoping to find animals, most of which would be resting. We all helped to tie the large mosquito net between some bushes, and soon we were all snoozing.

After an hour's rest we were up and away. I drove toward the edge of the plain where the buffalo had been, and the air was still full of dust mingled with the stench of dung. It smelled like a farmyard. In the far distance we could see that the buff had stopped running and were grazing peacefully once more. It would be impossible to get near them that day, however, for there was no cover for a stalk and the cattle egrets and tick birds would see us from miles off and warn their hosts. These two species of birds live harmoniously with most wild animals here and act as their eyes and ears in case of danger.

The cooks had asked me to bring back some *kanga* (common guinea fowl) as the makings for a special dinner for the *Bwana Mkubwa* (big master). Coen was given the task of shooting some on the way home, and he did so with only one shot each.

It was almost dark when I steered the Land Rover into camp. The hippo were already grunting and groaning, anxious for the night to fall so they could wander in search of tender grasses. These huge grazers consume many pounds of grass each night to fill their big stomachs. They feed at night because they have tender skin; although it is over one inch thick, it gets badly cracked and sunburned during the day. Thus they spend their days in water. During the evening meal we decided to

return to Lake Katavi the following day to try for the fifty-incher.

After an early breakfast, John brought up the Land Rover for the day's outing. PB said he wished to sit in the back for a change, so Hans and I joined him there, Coen sat in front, and Rashidi stood in the back as we set off. The tsetse flies were bad, indicating that there was plenty of game somewhere close by.

We hadn't gone a mile when our nostrils picked up that familiar farm smell. Rashidi pointed ahead to some large black objects moving through the trees. "*Nyati*" (buffalo), he whispered. John slowed to a crawl just as the grass got much taller; it was difficult to see much, let alone try to select a fifty-incher running through the stuff. We entered an open area and suddenly found the herd looking at us. John stopped as we lifted our binoculars. I could see mainly females with calves and one or two young bulls, so I told John to go around them. We passed a small herd of sable—again only females with young—and so we continued to the lake. At this time of the year you could count on seeing a big herd of buff out on the *mbuga*, and sure enough, as we climbed our lookout hill, there they were, a mass of black amidst the green swamp grass.

We spent at least an hour admiring and checking over the herd but couldn't locate the big bull, so we decided to follow yesterday's routine. John simply followed yesterday's tyre marks. As we passed behind a clump, an old lioness jumped down right in front of us. She'd been using the bush as a lookout and a safe haven. The buffalo were grazing and lazing much nearer to the tree line and had not noticed the lioness or the vehicle.

I told John to stop the vehicle—an easy stalk could be made from right there. I told everyone

This large crocodile attacked the tyres on the author's hunting vehicle. Lake Chada, Tanzania, 1963.

This photo demonstrates how wide a hippo's mouth is. This was taken in the Katavi Game Reserve, Lake Chada, where the author was charged by a hippo. Tanzania, 1963.

The famous spotted zebra of Lake Rukwa Valley. Eric Balson found this freak black zebra in the Lake Rukwa Valley of Tanzania and protected her for seven years. He later heard that she had been killed by poachers. Tanzania, 1966.

Male puku, a picture taken at sunset. This may well have been a world record puku, but we will never know for sure; Prince Bernhard allowed him to walk away because of his dignity and magnificence. Tanzania, 1966.

Vultures on a kill. Poachers had killed a zebra for the skin and left the carcass. This picture was taken on the day on which Balson floated his Land Rover across a flooded river. The culprits were apprehended that very day. Lake Rukwa, Tanzania, 1967.

An old buffalo bull and his sentinals, cattle egrets, watch the author's movements as he approaches to take photos.

Some female hippos with their young getting out of the way as the author and Prince Bernhard approach in a boat. This is when one has to be cautious, as some females protecting their offspring can charge and overturn a boat. Banks of the Rungwa River, Tanzania, 1967. (Photo by Viva Balson)

A wonderful photograph of some old bull buffalo and one old cow, with Mount Kilimanjaro in the background. Amboseli, border of Kenya and Tanzania, late 1960s. (Photo by Paddy Curtis)

This young bull elephant charged the author and his party and chased them for about a mile. Luckily it was open country, and the hunting vehicle was able to make its escape, with the author shooting pictures the whole time. In the second picture, the bull is making a turn to have another go at it. Lake Rukwa, Tanzania, 1963.

to walk behind me in "crocodile" formation and to keep their eyes open for hippo.

"Why hippo?" PB asked.

"It's funny," I replied, "but around this lake I have found that some of the old hippo bulls prefer to lie up in the shade under these thick bushes."

As we walked along in a crouch, there was a loud crash to our left as one of those old hippo darted out and, snorting, wobbled off toward the water. The buffalo looked up, but they must have recognized this as a daily occurrence and carried on with their business, whilst we were able to carry on with ours. When we arrived at the edge of the trees, we all raised our binocs to observe the mass of black, not one hundred yards away. Egrets were perched on their backs, just waiting to gobble a locust, grasshopper, or some other unfortunate insect. The tick birds, with their bright yellow beaks, were hopping from one buffalo to another, checking in their ears and under their stomachs for their favourite food, ticks.

We must have spent a couple of hours there, but suddenly the wind changed, and so did the scenery. Instead of lazy buffalo sleeping or feeding, three thousand of them were in full flight, bellowing as their mighty hoofs churned up clouds of dust. In a few seconds all you could see was dust and all you could hear was the thundering of stampeding buffalo. It was quite an experience; I was glad they hadn't come in our direction.

A majestic and beautiful fish eagle. Katavi, Tanzania, August 1963.

We sauntered slowly back to the vehicle and climbed aboard, and John drove us along the shore between the lake and the trees, looking for other interesting subjects to photograph. Soon we saw a suitable cool place to rest up and have our midday refreshments. The cooks had prepared some cold buffalo tongue served with chopped onions and tomatoes, plus some cloves of garlic for the prince. After toasting Queen Juliana, we all tucked into the food and had a long rest before it was time to return to camp.

A nice hot shower soon took away all the aches and pains. We dressed suitably to ward off the mossies, then sipped our drinks beside the hot fire, waiting for dinner to be served. Both cooks really outdid themselves that evening, serving roasted guinea fowl with potatoes and assorted veggies, plus PB's favourite sweet, a superb hot chocolate mousse.

This most enjoyable safari was drawing to a close; it didn't seem possible we had been in the bush for just over three weeks. The prince bade his farewells to all the staff and, as always, gave each of them a good *zawadi* (gift or keepsake). At the airfield, where PB's plane and crew were waiting, we shook hands and embraced one another, and the prince said to me, "My friend, thanks for a wonderful safari with so many memories to tell my family and friends. And for our next safari, would you please take us to your Ruaha Game Reserve? From the stories I have heard, it is a fantastic paradise."

"Sure thing, Sir. I will arrange everything."

PB smiled and patted me on the shoulder and climbed into the cockpit.

The Ruaha and the Rungwa: 1967

When Dr. John Owen, director of the Tanzania National Parks and a close friend of ours, heard that Prince Bernhard was coming to visit the newly established Ruaha National Park, he asked me if PB would officially open the park. PB's safari was to be in August 1967, and after making the request, I awaited the go-ahead from State House, Dar es Salaam, and the Netherlands embassy. I would make all the arrangements. The prince agreed and would, of course, spend one night with the president out of courtesy before retreating to the bush and its wild animals. But he asked that the pomp and ceremony be kept to a minimum, for he had to deal with it the whole year round.

I motored with all the required camp equipment to the Ruaha, where I reported to the newly appointed park warden, John Savidge, and told him that I had come to set up the camp for Prince Bernhard's safari. From there I went to an area that I knew had some big *Acacia albida* trees, which would supply shade and overlooked a section of the Ruaha River that was a drinking spot for elephant and many other animals.

As the game guards were setting up the tents, I took my camp chair and sat overlooking the big pool, where I must have counted fifty hippo sleeping on top of one another and saw many croc sunbathing on the far bank. It made me feel good.

I had directed that the big mess tent be erected on the river's edge where a sheer thirty-foot drop to the pool below permitted a 180-degree lookout. As we were placing the tent, a breeding herd of elephant wandered down to drink and cool themselves in the river. What a perfect setting.

I arrived back in the town of Iringa the day prior to the arrival of PB's party to make final purchases of fresh eggs and vegetables from the local market. I booked into one of the town's two hotels, did my shopping, and returned for lunch. As I picked up my room key from the reception desk, the attendant handed me an official envelope with *HARAKA* (haste/urgent) written in red ink at the top. Inside was a message from the regional commissioner. Written in Swahili, it said, "Report to my office immediately you receive this."

I didn't think much of the message, so I took my time over lunch before going to the regional headquarters. I introduced myself to the secretary, who stood up and uttered softly, "*Bwana Mkubwa ana hasira kabisa.*" (The big boss is very angry.) She ushered me into his office.

The regional commissioner, whom I had met before at meetings, sat at an enormous desk littered with hundreds of documents and didn't even look up as I entered. He just pointed to a chair and gestured for me to sit, and to my annoyance shouted at me, "Stand up when you speak to the regional commissioner!" slapping his hand on the papers in front of him. I despised all politicians, for they seemed to know only politics and nothing else. Just after independence, they took over all the senior administrative positions throughout Tanzania, and most of them considered themselves little gods.

He continued, still not looking at me, "Don't you know that I am in charge of this region, and who gave you permission to take the prince of the Netherlands to the Ruaha Park, which is under my jurisdiction?"

I was seething mad but dared not show it; I just kept my cool and answered, "I was only carrying out my orders, which I received personally from Mwalimu [the president of Tanzania]." He nearly choked when he heard that my orders came directly from State House.

"Why don't you ask the president himself?" I added "He is the one who asked me to take Prince Bernhard to open the Ruaha National Park."

This must have scared him—he immediately sprang up from his chair, darted around his big desk, grabbed my hand, and said, "*Tafathali samehe mimi, na kosa tu.*" (Please forgive me, I made a mistake.) He then went on to say he thought my actions were presumptuous, and therefore he had sent his two senior security men to search and inspect the camp and that they were to remain with the safari until we passed out of his region. I told him straight that this certainly would not be well received by the prince and advised him to send instructions recalling his men. He assured me that this would be done and virtually begged me to allow him the honour of meeting Prince Bernhard. Knowing that PB wanted peace and quiet, I told him that as long as he came alone and without the local press, he would be welcome.

The following morning I drove PB's private Land Rover station wagon to the Iringa airfield, about seven miles from the town. The regional commissioner was already there. He smiled and was very cordial—quite a different person from the previous day in his office. Soon we heard the sound of an aircraft approaching, and the plane made a perfect landing—thanks to the pilot, the prince himself—then taxied to a halt where we were. Once greetings were concluded and the safari supplies were packed securely for the rough six-hour drive to the park, PB said *kwaheri* (good-bye) to his crew and the regional commissioner, climbed into the driver's seat, and said, "Show me the way, Eric."

As PB pulled onto the main road, I noticed he was driving on the wrong side of the road.

In Africa one drives on the left-hand side, just the opposite of Europe's system. The prince had forgotten he was in Africa and kept to the right. We rounded a sharp corner and saw a seven-ton petrol tanker heading straight for us, the driver flashing his headlights. I expected PB to pull over, but he kept on going in the same lane. Luckily for us, the tanker driver moved over and passed us on the wrong side of the road, shaking his fist as he went by. The prince calmly said, "What the hell was that all about?" I explained that in fact he was at fault as he was now driving in Africa and not the Netherlands! PB apologized and moved over to the left, saying, "Gosh, I am sorry for putting you all in danger."

The remainder of the journey was uneventful, and we soon arrived at the ferry crossing the Ruaha. The craft was on the other side, and I could see John Savidge standing on the deck as it moved slowly our way, pulled by four ferrymen straining on a thick wire cable. John jumped off as it reached our bank and saluted the prince, and I introduced PB to everyone. He told us that two security men were waiting to escort Prince Bernhard for the duration of the safari, had been through everything in the camp, including the refrigerator, and had helped themselves to cold drinks. When PB heard this, he was as mad as I was and told John that he would sort it out once we reached the other side.

As the ferry pulled up, PB jumped off and talked to the two men very politely, telling them they must immediately drive their vehicle onto the ferry and return to Iringa. They were reluctant to go but eventually consented. All hands were pleased to see them go; having such "overseers" on safari is a nuisance.

It was agreed that we would stay in the park for three days and then move to a new campsite about sixty miles away in the adjoining Rungwa Game Reserve. We had a fantastic three days around the Ruaha, spending many hours walking along the picturesque river with its numerous species of birds and always seeing new animals around each bend and literally hundreds of hippo and crocodile. The

A large breeding herd of elephant drinking. Ruaha National Park, Tanzania, 1997.

Enjoying lunch in the bush under an enormous fig tree (no doubt over 100 years old) are Coen, P.B., and Hans.

melodious call of fish eagles was enjoyed by all. These beautiful birds are found in pairs wherever fish occur. A lucky observer might see two flying eagles suddenly lock their talons and spin around in circles, playing.

On our last day in the Ruaha, the prince invited John and Yvonne Savidge and another senior warden, John Stephenson from the Mikumi National Park, to have drinks and a farewell supper at our camp. As our guests arrived just before sunset, a big breeding herd of elephant came down the opposite bank for a drink, and as we watched their antics, refreshments and "toasties" were served. Then

the hippo commenced their evening chorus as they left the water and climbed up the bank. This camp had proved to be a real paradise for wildlife. Several greater kudu, both male and female, came to quench their thirst, and every night "the king of the jungle," *simba* himself, roared all around the camp and on both sides of the river.

As the evening shadows faded to blackness, the lamps were lit while everyone sat around the glowing embers of the campfire. Suddenly, PB excused himself, got up, and walked toward the mess tent in a hurry. I thought he was merely going to fetch something. Then I heard the head waiter shout, "*Loo, loo, loo—kuja upesi Bwana Kingi ameangukia ndani maji!*" (*loo* is used in this context to express horror; the rest means Come quickly—the king has fallen down into the water!)

I rushed to where the cooks and camp staff were gathered on the high bank, staring into the darkness, but we couldn't see much. Suddenly we heard moans and groans coming from just beneath us, then some chuckles, followed by laughing. We all were relieved to hear PB's voice: "Hey, fellows, give me a hand?" By this time Rashidi had brought my strong flashlight, and its beam revealed PB hanging from some roots protruding from the bank about twenty feet down. I lowered myself with some ropes and was able to tie another rope around PB's waist. The others hauled him up. I followed a few minutes later.

The prince explained that as he walked to relieve himself in the shadows of the tents, he looked back toward us to see if he was out of sight and suddenly fell over the edge. The roots broke his fall, and he was able to grab one, which luckily held his weight and prevented him from falling into the croc-infested waters some thirty feet below. Who knows what his fate might have otherwise. We joked about the episode later, whilst enjoying a scrumptious dinner and washing the food down with plenty of beer and wine, but I always shudder when I recall it. Can you imagine the headlines in the world press if PB had been injured or killed?

We had some hard going ahead of us in the morning. I was up very early, as was the prince.

"That was a long night," he said as he made his way over to check the scene of his fall.

"How do you feel, Sir?" I asked.

He rubbed his shoulder and replied, "Now I see it in daylight, it could have been much worse." He lifted his shirt and showed me his bruises; he was black and blue all over, but he assured me that he was fit and ready to travel.

I made sure we had sufficient food and equipment for a fly camp because I knew we would be at least a couple of days en route, and PB really enjoyed our fly camps. The game guards, cooks, and camp staff would pack up camp, load it all onto the 4x4 Bedford truck, and follow our tyre tracks.

I drove one Land Rover and John Jonas the other. There were no roads from that point on, but I knew in what general direction to go. Using my bushcraft, I navigated across country, following the Ruaha River downstream for about thirty miles, then heading southwest. It was rough and tough going, but fun, except for the tsetse fly.

Around one o'clock PB asked to stop for a rest, some snacks, and a toast to his wife, then to his and our families. I found a big, shady wild fig tree that suited our needs, and we set the lunch box down in the shade. In no time the drinks were served and the tins of bully beef and baked beans opened. PB offered his garlic cloves all round. It was extremely hot and humid, so we expected a thunderstorm before nightfall. I only hoped we would be able to cross the big sand river before the rain made it flood.

We packed up and left just as the dark clouds gathered. The banks along the sand river were too sheer, so we motored up and down searching for an elephant crossing, but we had no luck until late in the afternoon, when, to our relief, we came across a suitable place. Even here, we had to dig the banks away on our side, and were spurred on by lightning and the first clap of thunder.

Before long I drove the first vehicle down the steep slope. The others thought I might turn over. I told them that they would have to walk across the wide river because once I started to go, I'd have to give it full throttle or the wheels would likely dig down and get stuck in the soft sand. All went well, and I was soon leaving deep ruts in the riverbed as I made it across and up the other bank. John followed on my heels but didn't give his engine enough power, and his heavily loaded vehicle became firmly stuck. I looked skyward to check on the cloud formation. There was still lightning and thunder, but farther away, which pleased me.

We unloaded John's vehicle, and I let most of the air out of his tyres to give them more traction. After an hour's digging, I climbed in and asked everyone except PB to start shoving as soon as I revved up. This they did, and the Land Rover managed to get out and up the other bank. Soon we were on our way once more.

But I was worried about the truck that was to follow us. If it rained hard upstream, floodwaters would make it very difficult for the heavy truck to get across. But thank goodness, as we were setting up our fly camp, Rashidi said he could hear the sound of the truck approaching.

Just as we finished erecting the small tents, a sudden but not unexpected cloudburst sent everyone scurrying for cover. The drivers covered the truck with a large tarpaulin, which they held down whilst sitting under the truck. In a few minutes the heavy rain ceased, giving the cooks a chance to start their fires for the evening meal.

We still had about twenty-five miles to go to reach the preselected campsite, which I had seen from the air a couple of months previously. That night lion roared, so we would have to be on the lookout for them when we continued our journey the next morning.

Just as dawn was breaking, a staffer knocked on my tent with the usual greeting, "*Hodi, hodi, Chai Bwana?*" (May I come in, Tea Master?) The morning air was fresh and brisk, and the birds were already singing in the trees along the river.

As we ate breakfast, the staff folded the tents and the cooks packed our lunch boxes with a cold snack and placed Thermoses of hot water and coffee in our Land Rover. I told the guests to keep their eyes open for vultures because the lion had certainly killed during the night and would likely come to water or lay up in the shade by the river.

The elephant find water under the sand and dig holes with their front feet. Once they hit water, they wait for it to filter through the sand and then suck it up with their trunks and pour it down their throats. It is fun to watch them digging and fighting over water, especially at the height of the dry season. They invariably cover up the holes again, but the clever baboon and warthog find these places and dig them out for themselves, and they don't cover the holes, thus enabling other animals to drink. It is interesting to note that the water in these sand rivers is nearly always crystal clear and fit for human consumption. In fact, most of the water used on safaris is obtained from sandy riverbeds.

We had been traveling for some time when I caught a movement in thick bushes to our left and the huge gray body of an elephant walked straight into our path. He had an enormous pair of tusks. Goose pimples formed on my body at the sheer sight of such a remarkable animal.

I said to PB, "Now, there is a big tusker for you."

He nodded and replied, "How heavy do you estimate his tusks to be?"

"I don't really know, Sir, but each is well over the 150-pound mark. I have never seen such thick tusks before. Do you wish to shoot him?"

He gave me a scowling look and said, "No, thank you. I will take some cine and photos instead." As I stopped the vehicle, the big beast turned toward us and spread out his ears. The whir of the movie camera caused him to take a couple of steps toward us, and I told PB to climb back inside. I prayed silently that the elephant wouldn't charge, but I had my .470 ready just in case.

I started the car and turned it so that PB could have a better angle to photograph. Just then, a second elephant parted the bushes and stood behind the big fellow, putting his trunk into the air to smell. They both turned and headed for the river, disappearing just as quickly as they had appeared. I drove as close to the river as I could, and we watched them walk round a bend out of sight.

There is a sequel to our confrontation with this enormous tusker in the Rungwa Game Reserve. Allow me to digress from the flow of my narrative to relate it to you.

Some time after this safari, I was sitting in my game department office in Mbeya when an informer who worked for me stopped by. He said he had heard that a certain policeman in Iringa had bought a pair of very large tusks from a poacher. My ears perked up, and I was angry.

I drove home right away and told Viva I was off to Iringa. I took the informer with me, dropping him off a few miles outside of town so no one would see us together and telling him where to meet me the next day. We had to be discreet, especially in matters involving the police.

My informer gave me all the information that I needed to confront the suspect about where

and when he had shot the elephant. In past experiences involving this type of deal, I found it was productive to ask the so-called hunter, who likely had never set a foot outside of town, where he shot his elephant and to demand that he take me to the place and show me the carcass. Invariably, the reply would be something like this: "Oh, *Bwana Nyama*" (Mr. Game, or Mr. Meat), "it is a long way out in the bush—*kule-e-e-e-e.*" Prolonging the final vowel and saying the word in a high pitch meant that the distance involved was *verrry* far.

The suspect hoped that the distance would discourage me from going to look. But I was dead sure that our policeman—who had an elephant license and had filled in the date and place of the kill—was lying; the place he had written down did not exist in that region. I pressured him some more, and eventually he admitted that "*Ndugu yangu*" (my brother) had actually shot the elephant. He begged forgiveness and said he would lose his job. I told him that it was his job to help prevent crime, not condone it, so he must pay the penalty and go to court. I confiscated the pair of huge tusks.

My investigations turned up the poacher, and I had long discussions with him. He was an old man who used to hunt legally with a muzzleloader, taking out his license yearly and hunting for the pot. But just after Tanzania attained its independence from Great Britain, unprecedented poaching of elephant began, and that is how the old man now made his living, selling the tusks illegally for a few pennies whilst the buyer sold the same for many British pounds.

The long and short of the story is that this large pair of tusks almost certainly came from the very same elephant that Prince Bernhard turned down during our Rungwa safari.

The poacher showed me where he had shot the elephant, just outside the Ruaha National Park, close to where we had seen the bull. The tusks became government trophies and were exhibited at the 1971 World Hunting Exhibition in Budapest, Hungary, where they won the overall prize for "most outstanding trophy" in the entire exhibition, plus a gold medal for being the second largest pair of tusks ever recorded since Rowland Ward began measuring game heads before the turn of the century. Those ivory tusks weighed 206 and 202 pounds (I stand to be corrected on the exact weights) and can be seen in Dar es Salaam.

The No. 1 world-record tusks came from an elephant—also killed by a poacher—on the slopes of Mount Kilimanjaro near the turn of the century. They weighed 226 and 222 pounds and can be seen in London's Museum of Natural History.

Back to my narrative: As I reversed away from the river, PB pointed upward, and there, circling above, were many vultures. As we watched, they suddenly folded their wings and

Prince Bernhard was injured in a horseback-riding accident early in life. Part of his daily routine was to stretch his neck each day using a special neck harness. He was also a great believer in exercise, often involving his hunting partners in his daily calisthenics. Rungwa Game Reserve, 1967.

stooped toward the ground. *Ha-ha*, I thought, *that's where the lion will be*, and pointed the nose of the vehicle in that direction and drove slowly along. The vultures were sitting on the treetops, an indication that something lethal remained on the kill. *Could it be poachers?* went through my mind. *No, they would have heard the noise of the vehicle and been long gone. It must be lion or leopard, likely the former.*

I eased the Rover forward, trying to avoid the bushes, which scrape along the sides of the vehicle and scare the animals away. We soon were rewarded for our efforts, as there, right in front of us, was a fine tawny-maned lion in his prime. He and another, younger lion had killed an old bull buffalo. You could see that quite a battle had taken place as all the bushes were flattened.

PB and Coen were keen photographers whilst Hans and Stan just loved to look. Hans always said, "I like to observe what's going on with both my eyes, not have one fixed to a small peephole trying to find what to photograph." We spent a long time watching the bigger lion fill his stomach before he would allow his pal to partake. As I drove away, hordes of vultures descended on the remains and both lion walked with swollen bellies toward the river.

This exciting start to our day was tempered by the thousands of tsetse flies that continuously attacked us from all angles. Stan swelled up in big welts from the bites, which even penetrated our clothing. I gave him some antihistamine lotion to rub on his bites. Insect repellent had no effect whatsoever.

At midday I chose a suitably shady lunch spot beneath the canopies of fig trees, where several species of fruit-eating birds sang to their hearts' content. Coen, a keen ornithologist, wandered about with a binocular, checking for new birds to add to his list. PB,

Stan, and Hans had their books handy for a few minutes' reading. After a good hour's rest, I said it was time to move on as we had still some distance to go yet. PB, though still very stiff and sore, never grumbled one iota, and climbed up into his seat.

As it was cooling down that afternoon, I saw a welcome sight ahead: some twenty very large wild fig trees with lush green foliage, the ground beneath them covered with a fine star grass similar to that used on golf-course greens, where the tents were to be pitched. A crystalline stream flowed several yards away, and as we came to a halt, a large herd of graceful impala leapt high into the air before darting off in all directions. Then, to our delight, a troop of baboon climbed down from the trees, barking at us as they ran across the stream. PB remarked, "What a delightful campsite."

As the staff unloaded, I suggested we all go for a dip in the cold stream. The water wasn't very deep, so I dug a hole in the sand to make a deeper place and beckoned the prince to have a soak. The others soon caught on and dug their own "wallows," sighing as they sank into the cold water. After cooling off, we dressed and walked upstream a short way, finding fresh lion, leopard, buffalo, and big elephant tracks in the sand. Back in camp, the fire was blazing away and the tents were up, so we each entered ours to change and dress for the evening.

As our safari drew to a close, Prince Bernhard asked me about the famous Selous Game Reserve. He had read a lot about it and heard only good reports from many sources. "How about the Selous for our next safari?"

I replied, "A wonderful idea. I will contact my friend Brian Nicholson and get him to book the best block for us." Nicholson had worked out the quotas for the reserve and split it up into many hunting blocks; he knew the Selous intimately. None of us had ever been to that part of southern Tanzania.

The remaining days of this safari seemed to fly past much too quickly, and it came time to pack up and head to a town called Dodoma, 175 miles away. I had radioed the Netherlands Embassy to make sure that PB's plane was there to meet us.

The Selous: 1969

There is some interesting history attached to the Selous. The Germans colonized Tanganyika (then known as German East Africa) and were the first to establish a game reserve, in 1905. I believe that Kaiser Wilhelm created several game reserves there and bequeathed them to his wife as a birthday present. Some very old Africans told me that this is where the name "*Shamba ya bibi*" (wife's garden) came from. *Shamba ya bibi* was a term used during my years in the game department to denote a game reserve or national park, and I believe it is still in use to this day.

In 1922 the British delineated an enormous piece of land (over 22,000 square miles or 14,080,000 acres—larger than the state of Maryland in the United States or Wales in the United Kingdom) in southeastern Tanganyika and named it Selous Game Reserve, after the great naturalist, elephant hunter, and explorer Frederick Courteney Selous. Selous was buried there after he was shot in the head on 1 April 1917 by one of General Count von Lettow-Vorbeck's crack guerrilla snipers. The British thus honoured Selous for his efforts leading up to the sinking of the German cruiser *Koningsberg* in the delta of the Rufiji River, and for his courage in fighting a long rear-guard action against the equally courageous German count, all during World War I.

I should also mention that General Count von Lettow-Vorbeck, nicknamed the White Ghost, was never captured or beaten in battle. The British honoured his courage by allowing him safe passage across the Ruvuma River into Mozambique at the end of the war in 1918. This astonishing man repelled the British forces, said to number 300,000 men, with an incredibly small force that never exceeded 14,000 troops (3,000 Germans and 11,000 askaris, or native Africans). On his return to Germany in 1919, von Lettow-Vorbeck was welcomed as a hero. Though a member of the right wing, he was never a Nazi and, in fact, attempted unsuccessfully to organize an opposition to Adolf Hitler. In the 1960s he returned to Tanganyika and paid his old soldiers. Quite a man.

The Selous Game Reserve was and probably still is the largest wildlife sanctuary on the African continent, almost four times the size of the world-famous Serengeti National Park, also in Tanzania. And it is perhaps one of the remotest reserves to reach. Few roads lead to that part of Tanzania. There are, however, numerous bush airfields, most built under the stern supervision of Brian Nicholson, who opened up the area to controlled hunting under the auspices of the British and Tanzanian governments.

I had a long conversation with Brian Nicholson, whom we used to refer to as Little King of the Selous because he always acted as if he owned the place. But I had known him very well since our school days and was able to get along with him despite his grumpy attitude. He assured me that everything was arranged for "your Prince Bernhard," emphasizing *your*—his way of being sarcastic—and urged me to come to Dar es Salaam so we could get together and tie up any loose ends. I had to travel to Dar anyway on other business related to my work as head of the anti-poaching unit for northern and western Tanzania.

Melva, Brian's wife, invited Viva and me to stay with them, which we did. This made a big difference, enabling us to discuss matters and plans over sundowners, which eased the tension. Brian suggested booking the Beho-Beho block, which had plenty of wildlife, picturesque lakes full of fish, and interesting bird life with the added attraction of the mighty Rufiji River close at hand if we needed a change of scenery. So the scene was set.

Prince Bernhard flew into Dar es Salaam. For the first time on his many trips to Tanzania, President Julius Nyerere was there on the tarmac to greet him. They embraced, then PB immediately excused himself to dash over to shake our hands and say how pleased he was to be back, adding that he would be slightly late in the morning as he wished to spend a little more time with the president. This suited us perfectly—our vehicles would have to travel overnight to reach our Behobeho camp before we flew in on a chartered plane.

Mike Carr-Hartley, youngest of four brothers, whose father was the number one game trapper in all of Africa, was my assistant hunter for this safari. Mike traveled with the two vehicles, and as the prince and I flew low over our camp, I saw that they had arrived safely.

As the twin-engine Cessna made its final approach, I could see dust being churned up by the vehicles coming to pick us up. We wanted to reach camp before it got dark, for Mike had passed many elephant near our tents as he drove out. As I drove into the trees surrounding our camp on three sides, I could see the backsides of some elephant feeding on the bushes next to the road. There were some small calves, so I knew this was a breeding herd. The .470 next to my knee gave me a comfortable feeling as I engaged low gear and crept along gingerly.

All of a sudden one old female, probably the matriarch, wheeled about to face us, letting out a loud trumpet. She was joined by two others, who started to pick up dust in their trunks and blow it toward us. There was no room to turn about, and the bush was too dense to drive through. So I did what I had learned from Mike and his brother Roy whilst out with them catching elephant: I pushed the accelerator to the floor and charged straight at the elephant at full speed with the horn blaring. PB let out a soft groan as I nearly bumped into the nearest female, which spun around and sprayed us with dung as she ran off into the bushes. Her companions followed.

Mike shouted from the rear seat, "Hey, Eric, that's a Carr-Hartley trick!"

I replied, "Thanks to you and Roy, I knew what to do, and thanks to our lucky stars, it worked like magic."

In camp, all the staff lined up to greet the *wageni* (guests). I walked PB to his tent, set up a few yards back from a steep bank along the sand river's edge. I reminded him not to wander in the dark unless he wished to repeat his Ruaha "trick." He slapped me on the shoulder and gave me a dirty look, remarking as I walked away, "Thanks, Eric. This looks a nice spot. Just give me a few minutes and I will see you all at the fire."

As we sat by the fire, elephant were trumpeting in one direction whilst some lion roared across the sand river. The prince raised his beer glass and said, "*Gezondheid.*" We all raised ours and drank to the success of our safari.

During the meal we discussed plans for the following day. PB, Hans, and I would hunt for a good wildebeest. Mike would take Coen and Ron to hunt buffalo. An early turn-in was welcome as all were exhausted from a long day.

Prince Bernhard with trophies taken in the Selous: (top) Lichtenstein hartebeest, and (bottom) a fine eland bull. Pictured with Prince Bernhard in the bottom photograph are Eric Balson (left) and game scout John Jonas (center). Tanzania, 1969.

Because we were strangers to this area, the first day was spent getting to know it and its game. Spoor and droppings were abundant along the riverbeds, but the dense shrub habitat made it difficult to see the animals. Soon we came across a nice herd of wildebeest, which differ from the brindled wildebeest or white-bearded gnu, found in the Serengeti and Masailand, in that they lack the white beard but have a striking white chevron between eyes and nose. We found no bulls worth shooting, so instead we took photos.

Traveling on a narrow track, we saw a pack of wild dogs. These are fascinating and inquisitive animals, so I stopped the engine and let the vehicle roll to a standstill so as not to arouse or scare them. It worked, and they started to come toward us, sniffing for scent with their tails in the air. They came very close, and again we were able to take some good photographs. Ahead I could see some Borassus palms, indicating water close by, so I headed in that direction.

I had fixed my Toyota Land Cruiser with a specially designed roof seat, where PB and I sat whilst John did the driving. We didn't have seat belts, so we had to be alert in case we hit an antbear hole whilst traveling cross-country. I would allow people to sit on this high seat only if we were traveling slowly; otherwise it was too dangerous. It served as a good lookout and photography post. As midday approached, we came to a lovely lake, so I looked for a nice place to stop for lunch. At a shady spot where green grass flattened by grazing hippo looked like a freshly mown lawn, I told John to "*Simamisha papa hapa.*" (Stop just here.)

A couple of fish eagles soared overhead whilst a few others perched in the tops of palm trees, rulers of their empire. Many thousands of ducks and geese floated on the quiet water as some white egrets and herons waded in the shallows, snapping up fish disturbed by their feet.

After snacks and a two-hour rest, it was cool enough to move. We passed some southern impala males, which are smaller than those in northern Tanzania but nonetheless very impressive looking. They can jump as high as ten feet, and proved it as we drove past them.

As John steered around a blind corner, there stood a lonely Nyasa wildebeest with a spread of horns one might have found on a buffalo. I could tell instantly that this was a record. I signaled to John to reverse as PB's rifle was inside the vehicle and we had to dismount anyway to stalk the bull. We could hear him snorting and kicking up dust—this was his territory, and he was letting us know it. As PB loaded his rifle, I took my .470 just in case. I always did so in the bush, even with no VIPs around.

Plenty of small trees and bushes made it easy to creep up to within 150 yards. The bull was looking toward us, but I don't think he actually saw us. PB lifted his rifle, took aim, and fired, and I heard the distinctive thump as his bullet found its mark. The wildebeest spun around and sped off at full gallop. I knew it was a perfect shot by his reactions.

We watched him disappear in a cloud of dust, then walked to pick up the generous blood trail. I told PB, "That was a heart shot, Sir. We should find him stone dead just ahead."

"I hope you are right," he replied. "I hate wounding an animal or bird."

He had no sooner stopped speaking than I saw a blackish object through the shrubs. It was the wildebeest. When we arrived, I marveled at the terrific horns and bent down to touch the animal's eye. There was no blink—he was dead. I shook PB's hand and told him that he had just shot a wonderful specimen that would place well up in the record book. We took pictures, then gutted and loaded the animal and headed back to base.

Coen and the others came to look at our spoils. Mike saw right away that it was a record-book trophy and shook PB's hand, as did Coen, who was clutching his measuring tape. Coen was a Rowland Ward official measurer, and so was I, so we measured the horns. They were the second largest ever recorded. Everyone was delighted, and we celebrated with drinks around the roaring fire. It had been a great first day in the Selous.

After a good night's rest, everyone was up early, discussing what we should do that day. I suggested that we all explore the mighty, dirty Rufiji.

Before the commencement of this safari, I had sent word via a game scout to ask the local chief to find a *fundi* (expert) who could make two canoes out of big trees. When I arrived to scout for a good campsite, I was surprised to find that the *fundi* was almost finished making the canoes. It is amazing how these native craftsmen can make such fine things using only a primitive axe or adze.

I was so pleased with his workmanship that I paid him double the agreed-upon price—which was a pittance anyway, but he was thrilled. The canoes would be powered by a couple of outboard motors mounted on the sides.

At the river, we found the boats tied up and waiting. The old *fundi*, Abdullah, was there with a happy smile on his pleasant crinkled face. I introduced him to PB and the others, and as we walked to the moorings, Abdullah pointed to the boats and said, "*Kazi yangu, mzuri sana.*" (My work is very good.) This was true. He had cut down two trees near the river and carved out the two canoes, each over thirty

feet long. Chairs were placed inside, together with our lunch boxes, and we set off upstream. Huge crocodile sunbathed on the sandbanks here and there. As we meandered our way toward a steep gorge that lay ahead, some would slide into the murky waters as we glided past. Hippo kept popping up all over the place. Water birds were everywhere, and the noisy blacksmith plovers would dive-bomb us if we ventured near their nests.

Suddenly I saw an object come tumbling over the 300-foot-high cliff ahead, followed by two others. Rashidi, up front, also saw this apparition and shouted, "*Allah!*" an expression often used to express wonder or disgust. Here he was wondering aloud if what he was seeing could be true.

I had my binocular on the objects and could see that the big one was an eland whilst the others were wild dogs. We concluded that the big eland bull was being chased by a pack of these dogs and suddenly found himself in midair, flying over the edge. Two of the wild dogs followed suit, but the remainder of the pack was apparently far enough behind to slam on their brakes just in time. As we approached, I could see that the eland was dead, his neck probably broken the moment he struck the water. One of the wild dogs swam ashore, but the other was struggling, so I had Rashidi put it out of its misery.

Mike and I looked at one another and shook our heads in disbelief at what had just transpired. We made headway to retrieve the eland, which was floating fast downstream with the current. Rashidi soon had hold of one leg, and we towed the big bull to a nearby sandbar. The others drew alongside, and we climbed out to help pull the two-thousand-pound animal as close to shore as possible.

What a task! I was standing waist-deep with Ewalarn next to me, shoving the animal forward. Without warning, Ewalarn jumped clean out of the water, grabbing his thigh and screaming, *"Mamba, mamba!"* (crocodile, crocodile) I tried to run, but the water was too deep. Then I felt a bite on my bottom–and shot out of that water like a rocket! Rashidi and Coen had their rifles in hand as Mike ran over to check on Ewalarn. PB had his revolver out and Hans his camera.

I could now determine what had happened. The wild dogs had started to rip the belly out of the eland (their way of bringing down a big animal, which carries the poor victim to a painful death). Blood escaping from the wounds attracted the *vundu*. The water was literally boiling around the floating eland as hundreds of fish fed on the offal and blood.

The *vundu* is scientifically known as *Heterobranchus longifilis*, a genus of very large to enormous catfish, which differ from the normal catfish, family Claridae, mainly by possessing a large and well-developed adipose dorsal fin. The flesh of this fish is very nutritious and very palatable, but due to local taboos, many tribes refuse to eat it, saying that the flesh causes leprosy and in some instances, sterility.

With the scare over, everyone was in fits of laughter. Rashidi, Salum, and Ewalarn fell over and rolled in the sand laughing at how Ewalarn had jumped out of the water to escape the big *"mambas."* For the rest of that safari, they teased poor old Ewalarn about being scared of fish. We were so weak from laughing that we simply could not pull the eland out of the water to enable Rashidi and Ewalarn to butcher it for our kitchen. Eland is one of the best-tasting meats of all wild game, with a flavour not unlike that of beef. But finally we managed it, and whilst the butchers were at work, I had the lunch boxes carried to a shady spot.

Meanwhile, I was wracking my brains on how to catch some of those enormous catfish. Foolishly, I had forgotten to take along my fishing kit that day. Then I remembered that I had placed a few three-inch nails in one of the lunch boxes. I found them, fetched a pair of pliers, and bent the nails. Salum untwisted some of the anchor rope, and I had line. I tied small pieces of meat to my "hook," and soon as you can say bingo, one large, fat catfish was wriggling on the sand. Everyone clapped, especially the game guards, who relish these fish. Salum asked me to make some more hooks for them, which I did, and before long twenty huge catfish were on the beach. Coen took my line and landed a couple of fish, which made his day. Well, I had to call a halt to the "slaughter" as the day was nearly over and we had to make it back before nightfall.

Back at camp the staff told us they had been chased by a herd of angry elephant, but no one was hurt. Their eyes lit up when they saw the fresh meat and fish. That night we could hear outbursts of laughter from the staff quarters some seventy yards from the camp kitchen. Apparently, the *mamba* story was making the rounds.

I awoke to the sounds of birds singing away and hot water being poured into a basin for my morning shave and wash.

"Chai na maji tayari, Bwana. Jambo, habari ya leo?" (Tea and water are ready, Master. Hello, how are you today?)

"Mzuri kabisa, asante sana" (absolutely fine, thank you) was my response.

With my ablutions over, I unzipped the tent to collect my rifle and jacket, for it seemed much cooler than normal, and walked over to the mess.

"What excitement have you in store for us today?" PB asked me.

"Nothing exceptional as yet, Sir, but as you know only too well, anything can happen. We will split into two groups and head off in different directions to see what awaits us 'around the corner.' "

Mike drove off with Mo, Coen, and Karl, heading for the lakes in the hopes of finding a shootable buffalo or whatever came across their path. PB, Hans, and I went north. It turned out to be one of those ordinary days when you see little game and end up photographing birds. That is how it goes in the bush: One day you see plenty, the next day hardly anything. But just being out there breathing fresh African air instead of exhaust fumes made it worthwhile. Of course, we had to factor in the nuisance of the thousands of sweat or mopane bees buzzing endlessly around us, seeking the moisture in our eyes or the wax in our ears. Their persistence can drive a man insane. To ward off these little devils and the tsetse, PB always carried his "fly swat," made from a wildebeest's tail.

The others had a much more eventful day. Mo managed to bag a fine buffalo, while Ron shot a very big female elephant that was lame and could hardly move. We heard both stories back in camp that evening.

(left to right standing) Karl (aide-de-camp to Prince Bernhard), Col. Coen Geertsema, Mo De Mer, H.R.H. Prince Bernhard, Mike Carr-Hartley, Hans Gerritsen, (kneeling) Eric Balson, and Fritz, the taxidermist. Selous, 1969.

The days rushed by. I built a tree stand, or machan, in a big fig tree overlooking a place where herds of elephant dug for water in the sand. I think they did this so they would not have to go to the river, where crocodile might have killed their calves. To reach the stand, you had to walk through thick brush. The prince used to sit up there for hours on end, watching and taking photos of the huge creatures digging whilst their youngsters frolicked in the sand.

One day Hans wanted to sit up there, so Mike went with him—luckily for Hans. As they were walking there, a young bull elephant suddenly charged. As the bull was about to knock Hans over, Mike knocked it over instead, killing it instantaneously with a bullet to the brain from his .500 double rifle. It was sad, but venturing into the bush has its risks.

Another day on the Rufiji, everyone wanted to go and see where the main river hurtles through a narrow gap known as Stiegler's Gorge. This mighty stream and its massive tributaries, the Great Ruaha, Kilombero, and Luwegu, make up the largest river basin in eastern Africa. Downstream from the gorge it meanders across the plains, pouring millions of tons of silt each year into the Indian Ocean, creating a delta some forty miles across, where millions of mangrove trees thrive. During WWI a Commander Villiers wrote: "If in this world there is a worse place than the Rufiji delta, I hope I may never find it. The whole delta is gloomy, morose, and depressing beyond endurance." Luckily, upstream it is more hospitable.

As we proceeded slowly toward the gorge, Coen inquired, "What are those large, tall, white trees called?" I told him they were from the family Sterculiaceae, and that their common name was Star Chestnut trees. I went on to say that I believed that there were two species growing in the area,

Sterculia africana and *Sterculia quinqueloba*. I continued to tell him that they grow sometimes to one hundred feet and are useless for anything, even canoes, for the wood is too soft. Prince Bernhard just chuckled and said something to this effect: "Hey, Coen, I bet you can't remember one of those names Eric has just rattled off." Coen just shook his head and smiled.

We cruised past hundreds of hippo floating like logs in the murky waters; they would honk and grunt as we disturbed their slumber. Soon we were gazing at waters boiling through a narrow gap and plunging some four hundred feet, quite a sight but nothing spectacular. In fact, we all remarked on how disappointing the place was, especially after having heard so much about it.

On the way home, someone spotted a very big croc lying on a sandbank and wanted me to glide the boat closer for some pictures. The old fellow was most obliging and just stayed put as if he knew we were not going to harm him. He must have been over seventeen feet long. A croc will grab a victim with its sharp teeth, or sweep it off its feet with a blow from its powerful tail, before dragging it below the surface and lodging it in a hole or amongst some roots until it putrefies and becomes easy to rip apart and swallow.

The next day, Mike agreed to demonstrate how to catch fish with a throw net. Some small streams there had an abundance of tilapia, a species of bream known for its fine texture and taste, so we challenged Mike to catch some for our table.

Mike sorted out his tangled net, explaining how to place most of the net over the shoulder and hold some in the opposite hand. He selected a pool that held many tilapia. Stalking sideways, half bent over, he approached the pool from behind some bushes, stepped out backward, and then flung his left arm toward the place where he wanted the net to land. As he did this, the bunch of net on his shoulder unwound and formed a complete circle as it flew through the air. When it hit the water, it sank quickly, thanks to the many small lead weights attached all around the outer circle. A small rope in Mike's hand was tied to the middle of the net, which he immediately began to pull.

The net started to surface, and inside we could see several large tilapia darting around in panic, trying to escape. Mike's face lit up in a broad smile, and he said, "How is that, chaps? Enough for a couple of meals?" We were most impressed, and PB had captured it all on movie film.

Thus did I learn yet another "Carr-Hartley trick," and over the many years since that day I have used it dozens of times to supply meals for our table.

The water enticed us in for a swim. Later we climbed out to relax and dried our goose-pimpled bodies. It was another of those fun days, which ended on a pleasing note for Karl, who shot a wonderful male kudu on the way back to camp.

That night the cooks managed to produce some outstanding fish and chips wrapped up in newspaper—a good old English tradition! We toasted Mike for his efforts and Karl for his kudu. The roaring of lion could be heard in the distance as we warmed ourselves by the fire prior to retiring for the night.

That night a strong wind made me get out of bed to check the guy ropes on all the tents.

This was a very large, old female elephant who was ready to die of old age. She had no teeth left and was alone. Her tusks were very good for a female elephant, weighing approximately fifty pounds each. (left to right) H.R.H. Prince Bernhard, Rashidi Ramazahi (game scout), Elias Nampungu (skinner), Balson, and Mo de Mer, who shot the elephant. Selous, 1969.

Mike and Rashidi were there doing the same. It drizzled near dawn, which made the air smell fresh and helped chase the stifling humidity that had blown across from the Indian Ocean during the previous couple of days.

As we drove off together the next morning, a smoky haze blurred our view. A big grass fire was raging not too far away, more than likely started by either lightning or poachers. I suggested we take a look. One thing was for sure: lots of insects, reptiles, and young birds and animals would die a horrible death before the fire was extinguished or had exhausted itself. I also knew that hundreds of birds of prey would be hovering above and about the advancing fire, ready to swoop down on some fleeing rat, mouse, snake, or insect. It would be a good opportunity for photography.

We tried to extinguish the fire with branches, but finally, with smoke-filled lungs and watery eyes, we called it a day and headed to some shade to recover and have lunch near a clear stream. Each of us jumped into the clear water to cool off and wash the smell of smoke from our bodies. As we made our way home, the columns of smoke had died down, and most of the haze was gone.

It had come time to radio for the twin-engine planes to fly into Behobeho airfield and pick us up. Mike would remain to supervise the demolition of the camp and then would travel in convoy to meet me in Dar es Salaam before proceeding back to Arusha and then home.

Another memorable safari had been enjoyed by one and all.

Loliondo: 1972

Colonel Coen Geertsema was to alert me to the time and place of Prince Bernhard's next safari. For most of PB's visits I was able to arrange with the director of Wildlife for a special president's license, granted only to VIPs, that allowed them to hunt whatever species they liked and go wherever they pleased.

In 1971 Coen sent me a request for a safari to the Loliondo Controlled Area, just outside the famous Serengeti National Park. I had told the prince that this area held some enormous buffalo as well as plenty of lion and other game, making it the perfect place for wildlife photography. PB always told me that he would love to record the "laughing hyena" sounds, and this was perhaps the best possible area to fulfill his request.

My good friend Myles Turner would come along as my assistant on this safari. Myles was a former professional hunter of great standing and knew the bush like the back of his hand. Dr. John Owen, then-director of Tanzanian National Parks, was reluctant to release Myles from his duties, but I eventually twisted his arm into agreeing to let Myles accompany me.

Myles, a good pilot, told me that the airfield at Seronera within Serengeti Park could handle the Fokker Friendship. This was good news, for it would save many hours and hundreds of miles of travel in motor vehicles. Landing the Friendship at Seronera meant we had to travel only about sixty miles to our safari camp, set up about six miles outside the park. Myles was too busy to leave his post until the very day Prince Bernhard arrived, so I had the task of setting up the camp under some large fever acacia trees surrounding a pure natural spring, a perfect camp setting.

The Serengeti Park is world-famous for its wildebeest migration, which takes place usually in the months of December through March. The main body of animals, estimated then to number well over two million, had crossed the border of Tanzania back into neighbouring Kenya and were concentrated along the Mara River in the Mara Game Reserve, but many thousands still remained behind in the Loliondo Controlled Area. The concentration of so many prey animals in one place brought about an explosion of predators, mainly lion, hyena, and leopard—a perfect situation for filming and recording.

I met Prince Bernhard in Arusha, and we flew out to Seronera, where Myles was waiting to help load the many cases of beer, mainly Heineken and Amstel, plus bottles of wine. Myles was amazed at the amount of alcohol and food supplies that accompanied such a safari. After a quick cup of tea and cookies, which Kay Turner had prepared, the two Land Rovers set out for our camp.

During the journey we must have passed thousands of animals, mainly wildebeest, zebra, and Thompson gazelle. We also saw some spectacular impala rams grazing close to the roads. PB was impressed, as were Hans and Coen. On hearing the approach of our vehicles, the staff lined up to greet PB and his friends.

The prince recognized Rashidi and said, holding out his hand, "*Jambo, Rashidi, habari gani?*" (Hello, Rashidi, how are you?)

"*Jambo, Bwana Kingi, leo mzuri sana*" (Hello, Mr. King, today is very good), said Rashidi with a broad grin, taking the outstretched hand and shaking it vigorously. I should explain here that the word *Kingi* is a nickname the natives gave to the prince because they knew he was married to Queen

Our safari camp. Loliondo, Tanzania, 1972.

71

Off-loading the "hard-tack," wine, and beer at Seronera as Myles Turner watches in amazement. The author, Eric Balson, is on the left. Tanzania, 1972.

Juliana. The usual Swahili word for king is *mfalme* or *sultani*.

PB and the other guests proceeded along the line and shook hands with all the staff, a fine gesture.

When I had showed everybody their respective "homes" for the next three weeks, I went to oversee the unloading of supplies. Rashidi told me the lion had been roaring all night long just downstream from the camp. Most of the camp staff were petrified and came to his tent, for he had a gun. I strode over to tell Myles the news and suggested that we take

a drive in that direction in hopes of finding their kill. He liked the idea.

Whilst we were chatting, PB came over, and when I told him the news about the lion, he yelled, "Hey, Coen and Hans, let's go." All were ready to get cracking. We climbed into the Land Rover, driven by Myles. I stood in the back to look around. Circling in the sky were a few vultures, and as we drove I noticed many more perched atop trees. Myles steered in that direction, and as we drew closer, I saw a huge black-maned lion crouching behind a dead animal, which turned out to be an old bull buffalo. Then a movement in the bushes just to that one's rear revealed a second big male. They looked like littermates.

Myles stopped so we could have a closer view through our binoculars. What a great sight! Their stomachs swollen full of meat, the regal creatures were staying close by, protecting their kill from the vultures and hungry hyena that were lurking around.

I said to Myles that we should drag what remained of the buffalo back to camp and tie it to a tree just outside PB's tent. The prince just nodded and, in his sarcastic way, remarked, "Do you really think that it will work?" As we drove toward the "brothers," they snarled and ran off into the thicket. Rashidi hastily fixed a rope around the buff's thick neck, then signaled to Myles to drive off back to camp. The two lion had eaten most of the back legs during the night. I showed Myles where I wanted to place the remains of the buff. Rashidi, assisted by Salum, cut it loose and tied it securely to a tree. So the scene was set for an interesting night.

After nice hot showers, everyone gathered as usual around the campfire. The cooks had scrumptious goodies for us to munch on prior to dinner.

As we sat down to supper, we heard the first stupid cackle of excitement from a hyena not far away. It was following the buffalo drag. I told Rashidi to take Salum and sit near the carcass to keep the *fisi* away until we had finished dinner. I gave him my flashlight and said that if the lion came, they must come and tell us. With dinner over, PB said he wanted to go and set up his tape recorder to have it ready for the action.

It was a dark night, the half moon hidden by clouds, but I could see the silhouettes of the game guards standing near the bait and every now and then shining my torch around to check for

lion. It was time to take up our positions. Coen, Hans, and Myles retired to their tents whilst I took both my .470 and a 12-bore shotgun loaded with S.S.G. slugs, just for safety, and made my way to PB's tent. I told the guards to go, and we settled down to wait.

Not ten minutes later, a jackal howled very close by, then yelped as it was likely being chased by hyena, which then started making their funny noises. PB looked at me and nodded. I shook my head and indicated with my hand to wait. The next moment the hyena were right beside the carcass—at least twenty animals, judging by the sounds that erupted. I nodded for PB to commence recording. Their weird sounds—shrieks, squawks, and squeaks combined with their famous cackle laughter—sent cold shivers down my spine. PB was giving me the "thumbs-up" signal.

The hyena were fighting amongst themselves when all of a sudden there was complete silence. I looked at the prince and shrugged, but I guessed that at least one lion had arrived. Whilst I was straining to see, there was a deafening roar from right beside PB's tent. I grabbed my shotgun, which is a better weapon to use at close range, especially if one might have to shoot from the hip. PB jumped in the air and fell off his bed just as the lion let out another mighty roar. I could hardly hear as my heart pounded and adrenaline rushed through my body. PB just sat on the floor and gave me another "thumbs-up" signal to indicate he was all right, followed by a big smile, and then he clasped the sides of his face with both hands. I could hear the big-maned creature panting right next to me, with only the thickness of the canvas separating us. It was a hair-raising feeling, I can assure you. I was almost frozen stiff with fright.

A large male lion attempts to drag a bull buffalo into a thicket (above) and guards it against encroaching silver-backed jackals (below). It is amazing what strength these animals have: The bull must have weighed 1,500 to 2,000 pounds. Tanzania, 1972.

I peeped through the flimsy mosquito-screen window and felt a sense of hopelessness as the lion's eyes stared right into mine from three feet away. Fear gripped me as I thumbed off the safety catch, and I could hear the angry twitching of his tail. I expected him to jump on one of us at any moment. Suddenly, he gave a grunt and charged off toward the buffalo. Apparently he had seen a hyena coming to the bait, for he was obviously annoyed and agitated.

The half moon had come out from behind the clouds, and I was able to make out shadows moving all around us. A pack of hyena had formed a gang to chase away the lion. I had seen them do this before. They started their bloodthirsty laughing once more, and the poor old lion decided it was time to escape. Both the prince and I started to talk aloud with relief.

We could hear laughter coming from the other tents, and then Myles appeared with his .470 in one hand and a torch in the other. "Are you chaps OK?" he shouted.

PB replied, laughing, "Hey, I bet you fellows thought we were lion food." He added, "I think I have some unique recordings—come on over." The entire camp was awake by this time.

We listened to some of the recordings, which turned out superbly, before deciding it was time for some shut-eye. I told Rashidi to take my Toyota and tow the carcass a mile or so from camp so we could have a peaceful night. That evening's entertainment, I can assure you, will never be forgotten. For years later, we always laughed over that event, especially when we listened to the taped recordings at Soestdijk palace.

This safari was not only enormously rewarding but also one of the more relaxing that I have had the privilege to conduct. Everything went so smoothly that I thanked our dear Lord every night in my prayers. Myles, too, told me during the safari that he couldn't ever recall having such good-hearted VIPs who enjoyed every minute of every day and never voiced any complaints.

"What a pleasure it has been for me," Myles said. "I feel really honoured to meet and be with such an outstanding man as Prince Bernhard."

During that safari I wore a greenish shirt that Viva had given me for my birthday a couple of weeks before. PB said to me one day, "Eric, you and that shirt chase away all the animals. Please remember to give it to me at the end of the trip so I can modify it for our next safari." I took him at his word and handed him my shirt the day before he flew home. Sure enough, on our next safari he gave me back the shirt, which he had hand-painted with trees and his favourite creature, an elephant. I still have the shirt some thirty years later and will treasure it always.

On the first day I wore the green shirt on our 1972 Loliondo safari, PB shot a record-book impala ram. Myles was really impressed with my shirt and also the impala, which he said was one of the finest he had ever seen in over forty years in the bush. It was just luck that we came upon this fine specimen. Earlier we had seen a lame lioness with some small cubs. It was obvious that she was having a hard time feeding them, so we decided to shoot some food for the little family. We had just seen a herd of impala, so we backtracked, and right there in front of us stood the outstanding animal. I told PB to drop off on his side at the next clump of bushes. I had his rifle and followed him. John was driving and knew the routine, so he kept on going. The ram's eyes followed the vehicle as the prince and I crept into position. PB shot, and the beast dropped stone dead.

We took some photos for the record and then I skinned out the head and cape. Rashidi and

John loaded the ram into the back of the "Landy," and we went to look for the lioness. She had joined some other, younger lionesses, which was a pity as they would soon help to finish off the food. As John drove fairly close by, Rashidi and I threw the carcass overboard. But as the lioness pounced on the free meal, a big male lion ran out of the thicket and carried off the body.

So we repeated the procedure, this time with a wildebeest. I told PB that we would drag the food past the lame female and her cubs and take it about half a mile away. The plan worked fine; she followed, as did her cubs, and when we left them, they were enjoying the fresh meat.

Myles was out with Coen and Hans that day and returned to camp at the same time as we did. PB trimmed his beard and then sat in the sun reading and relaxing, watching the marabou storks wandering about the camp, which they had decided was now their territory.

The prince asked if we could visit the newly finished Lobo Lodge Hotel, located amongst and integrated with some gigantic granite boulders. PB had heard that it featured a lovely swimming pool overlooking the hills and valleys surrounding the lodge. The next morning I drove PB and Hans to the lodge. Coen decided to try for a big buffalo with Myles.

It was approaching midday by the time we climbed the hill to the lodge, which was cleverly concealed amongst the boulders. As we drove up, two klipspringer jumped across our path and stood on the crest of a rock looking at us. PB and Hans donned their swimming togs and were enjoying the heat emanating from hot rocks by the side of the pool. I walked to the edge and saw a few old buffalo bulls lying in mud wallows just below us.

A super day was had by all. Coen had shot a nice old bull buff for camp food, and as we sat around the fire, he told us all about the long stalk he and Myles had made. The distant roaring of lion was a soothing sound to snuggle into bed with on a cool night.

The days were always too short for the things we wanted to do and passed much too quickly for everyone's liking. We tried to make plans for each day, but more often than not, events threw all plans aside. For example, one day we planned to try to find that fifty-inch buffalo that had eluded PB for so many safaris, so an early start was ordered. The prince was always ready and itching to go long before the others, so we were never late in getting away from camp.

I had seen an old bull that was well over fifty inches, but that was three weeks earlier. These old fellows usually stay in an area they like, especially if they are not molested, so I thought we should give it a try. As we drove along, checking any buffalo we happened to see, PB held up his hand for a stop. I braked to a standstill.

PB raised his binocular and said, "Hmmm, I thought so. Yes, it's a big, beautiful leopard up that tree over there." He pointed, and sure enough, there he was, lying on a branch, checking us out.

"Well done, Sir," I said as I started the car. "That was fine spotting."

"I still have good eyes," he said, smiling, as he got his cameras ready.

I drove very slowly toward the tree so as not to alarm the leopard. He didn't seem a bit nervous, so I edged forward some more, expecting to see him dart down from the tree and disappear. But no, he just stared us right in our eyes, his tail not twitching at all. PB took some good photos as the cat just lay there—his behaviour most uncharacteristic for a leopard in the wild. Usually they are shy and wary, very hard to see during daylight, so this was a bonus.

We spent a good hour watching him before driving off to look for the buff.

The sun was well into the sky as we drove to a hill from which we had a panoramic view and from where I had last seen the big buff. Glassing the valley revealed several old bulls but not the big one. We watched a couple of cheetah chasing a Thompson gazelle. One of them knocked over the fleeing gazelle with a swipe of a front paw, and before the poor beast could recover, the cheetah had it by the throat. We drove closer to get some pictures and watched the predator enjoy his well-earned meal. Strangely, the second cheetah appeared to be frightened of the big male and kept its distance. As we watched the way nature continued its cycle of life and death, I thought to myself, with satisfaction, that another memorable safari was coming to a close.

"Deep Shade" *by Mike Ghaui.*

CHAPTER FOUR
Marshal Tito's Safari

In the 1970s I was stationed in Arusha, the tourist capital of Tanzania, running a special anti-poaching unit. Late one evening the telephone rang. I did not really want to answer it, but after second thoughts I picked it up and was amazed to hear that the vice president of Tanzania wanted to speak to me.

"Good evening, Mr. Balson. I am very sorry to trouble you at this ridiculous hour, but it is important that I speak to you so I can give your answer to President Julius Nyerere in the morning. The president would like to know if you could please take Marshal Tito and his wife on safari next week."

The vice president, Rashidi Kawaha, was very polite and apologetic for the short notice they had given me. Such a request, however, was more like an order. I told him that I would be honored to take Marshal Tito and his wife, Madam Broz, on a hunting safari, and that I would commence preparations immediately. Tito, born Josip Broz, was the leader of Yugoslavia from 1943 to 1980.

I asked for details, such as size of the group, how long they wanted to stay in the bush, and what animals the marshal and his party wished to shoot.

"I will be there myself," the vice president replied, "and I would like you to arrange if possible for my brother, Saidi Kawaha, who is one of your senior game scouts, to be your assistant. I will have the commander of the Field Force Unit send his best men to be on hand in the camp for security reasons. I will call you again to confirm how big the party will be and which trophies they would like to hunt. Thank you, and *lala salaama* (sleep well)."

The next couple of days were hectic. We would have to headquarter somewhere off the beaten track because Marshal Tito was a famous WWII hero and politician who would draw tourists and others, and the last thing I wanted was to have inquisitive and intrusive people around our camp. The location we selected would have to be kept as secret as possible so our guests could relax and enjoy their stay.

I remembered that an old hunter friend of mine, George Dove, had the perfect setup for this safari. His Ndutu camp was situated at Lake Lagaja just outside the Serengeti National Park, and at this time of the year the annual migration of thousands of wildebeest plus other game would be in full swing there. George also was an excellent host and a *cordon bleu* cook. I rushed off to his office in Arusha and spoke to his wife, who contacted George by radio and asked him to return to Arusha so that we could make proper arrangements for this VIP safari.

George arrived that very evening. I asked him what his airstrip was like, because the VIPs were planning to fly in aboard the Tanzanian Air Force's large Hercules plane and the pilot wanted to know the length and condition of the strip. I phoned the details through to Dar es Salaam.

I told George to expect me at his Ndutu camp in three days. In the meantime he would arrange for the fresh food, fine wines, and other supplies to support our VIPs. George had prepared many safaris in the past, and he assured me that it was in his interest to provide a successful safari for our guests.

Dar es Salaam called to confirm that the safari was definitely going ahead and that the Field Force commander would contact me. Saidi Kawaha arrived, and together with my trusty game scout, Rashidi Ramazani, we loaded our tents and all the other gear and headed for Ndutu. We were a day ahead of schedule, which would give us three full days to scout out the area to see where the lion were feeding and how far the migrations had

This is a picture of "Big Boy," taken by Steven Balson, age ten, with a Brownie box camera. This particular lion was much sought during the Marshal Tito safari in 1970. July 1970.

progressed. George had told me that thousands upon thousands of wildebeest were heading in his direction, and we saw plenty of these stupid animals en route to our destination.

We made our staff camp some distance away from the main camp so we could "do our own thing," especially once the Field Force arrived the next day. I hated the thought of this so-called security business, which to me meant too many people carrying loaded rifles.

George showed me where he had set up special new tents for the visitors, with attached facilities, including hot and cold running water. What a luxury in the bush! It was a hot day and everyone was tired, so we had a rest after a superb cold lunch. I told my head game scout, Rashidi, that we would go on patrol at four o'clock, using two Land Rovers specially fitted with trap doors cut into the roof. This gave guests a good viewing area for shooting or photography. I sent one Land Rover off in one direction with strict instructions to look for—not to shoot—a big, black-maned lion, as I had been told that the marshal was anxious to hunt the "king of beasts."

The Serengeti lion are fantastic. Some have huge black manes; others are just as grand with tawny manes. Either would make a wonderful trophy for any hunter.

I headed off to a big rocky outcrop I knew of that would make a very good lookout point. I passed herds of wildebeest, zebra, and Thompson gazelle. *This is a game paradise,* I thought to myself, *and there must be numerous good lion about.*

No sooner had the rocky outcrop come into view than Rashidi knocked on the roof to indicate that he had seen something of interest. Not far ahead lay a big male lion, staring straight at us. I stopped and fumbled for my binocular

to check him out. What a sight! He was with two younger lion, good trophies in their own right, but Big Boy, as I christened him right there and then, was one of the best-looking lion I had ever come across, and I have seen plenty. We left them still lying down and drove away to see if we could shoot a wildebeest to drag back and use as a bait. If I could keep Big Boy fed for the next couple of days, he would not wander far and would be a wonderful trophy for Marshal Tito to take home.

I found some permanent water not too far away; lion have to drink regularly and do not wander far from that precious commodity. Soon I spotted an old wildebeest bull that was limping badly and no doubt would have fallen prey to lion or hyena, perhaps that very night, so we put him out of his suffering. Rashidi was a "deadeye" with a rifle and dropped the old devil with one well-placed shot.

It was getting dark, and I wanted to make sure that we dragged the carcass back past the lion and toward the water, which was about one mile from where the lion were first sighted. As we approached, the beasts were already standing and stretching, preparing for their night's hunting. We drove by about 250 yards upwind of them so they could catch the scent of blood and guts. When they lifted their heads and began to follow, I drove off quickly. We had to get ahead of them because one of us had to jump off the Land Rover to cut the carcass loose, and darkness was fast closing in.

It was pitch dark when we arrived back at George's camp. Saidi and his scouting crew had already arrived and came to meet us. They, too, had found lion—two prides feeding on kills. One male had a big tawny mane, but after my scouts told Saidi what we had seen, he reckoned ours had to be the best.

A lovely hot shower and tales told next to a roaring log fire with the stars sparkling made a wonderful ending to a long but fruitful day. During dinner we suddenly heard lion roar quite close by. The hyena's laughing and chattering told us that the lion had killed something and that the hyena were probably trying to steal the lion's meal. As I made my way back to my tent, I listened to the sounds wafting through the trees—what a chorus of grunts, squeals, and snorts mingled with the occasional roar from lion both near and far. The comical cackling sounds of laughing hyena, the crickets and frogs, plus the odd hoot of a little scops owl added to the bush symphony as I literally fell into bed and tucked the mosquito net well under my mattress. Despite the cacophony, I fell straight off to sleep.

I awoke very early, washed, and shaved, feeling fresh and rested, and sat down for a quick breakfast. George joined me as I watched a herd of wildebeest with newborn calves canter by the log fire, still smoldering from the night before.

Rashidi and Saidi were waiting by the Land Rovers, and—still in our presafari scouting mode—we were soon on our way to find Big Boy and his mates. Hordes of wildlife ran here and there as we progressed. I stood in the observation hatch, enjoying the sights as we drove along. We saw a small pride of lion feeding on their kill, jackals awaiting their turn. It was strange to witness hundreds of wildebeest walking right up to and around the feeding lion. They seemed to know there was safety in their huge numbers; wildebeest were everywhere, and many more seemed to have moved in during the night. The morning air was brisk, making the smells of the bush even more invigorating; we felt glad and lucky to be alive in this paradise.

Soon we were approaching our wildebeest bait, but I could see nothing. I told John, the driver, to proceed slowly. The lion and the bait were gone. Signs showed that the lion had dragged their meal to a thick clump of bush, presumably to hide it from vultures and other scavengers. We followed the drag marks and soon found the animals, but Big Boy was not with the two others, which still had blood all over their faces and looked bloated. Big Boy must have fed first and then wandered away to look for female company, or to be alone—something old males like to do. I sent Saidi to search in the opposite direction from where I was going—which was back to the rocky outcrop, one of my favorite lookout points.

Rashidi, Elias (the head skinner), John, and I climbed over the hot rocks and found a shady overhang where we could scan the countryside for miles around. Thousands of little black spots dotted the vast Serengeti landscape. The great migration was in full swing. An estimated one and a half million wildebeest join this annual spectacle, which, once witnessed, is never to be forgotten. Their incessant grunts and snorts fill the air all day and all night long.

Some vultures circled, using thermals to soar ever higher in their endless search for food. Suddenly, one bird folded its wings and swooped to the ground a couple of miles from where we sat. Others soon followed, and so did we—it meant a kill or a dead animal was in the vicinity. The place was easy to find—all we had to do was follow the vultures. Most of them were perched atop thorn trees (flat-topped acacia), a sure sign that lion, leopard, cheetah, hyena, or wild dogs were in attendance; we drove up very slowly.

I was standing in the hatch but could not see which animal had made the kill. Then a movement caught my eye. I told John to stop.

My binocular revealed a cheetah lying flat on its belly, trying to hide. We sat watching for a long time, and finally the cheetah grew accustomed to our presence, stood up, and gave a high-pitched whistle, a signal for her cubs to join her. There were four of them, perhaps out on their first hunt. I took a few pictures and went to search for Big Boy.

Midday was upon us, so I signaled to John to drive to a big acacia tree, where we stopped for a snack and coffee. My radio came to life; it was Saidi and his crew, calling to tell me that they had just found a very big male lion feeding on an old bull buffalo it had killed. Saidi said it had a tawny mane with some black in it and was *"mzuri sana."* (very good)

He gave his location, and I told him to keep track of the lion and we would be with him in about one hour. Driving across those open acacia woodlands can be dangerous; antbears dig huge holes there, and if your vehicle falls into one, it usually means a broken spring, so we proceeded with caution, all eyes ahead.

As we made our meandering way through the zigzagging wildlife, I could see the small hill that Saidi said he was near and pointed it out to John. The radio crackled again, and this time it was George back at base camp, letting me know that the Field Force had just arrived and were busy setting up their headquarters. I told him that we were on our way to check out a big male *simba*.

There was still no sign of Big Boy, but I wasn't worried—there would be many more chances. We had a day in hand before the VIPs arrived. We drove up to where Saidi was. He signaled that the lion was sleeping under a small bush. The huge-bodied lion had what looked to be a fantastic mane. I could also smell the buffalo kill.

I crept down and climbed into Saidi's vehicle. We spoke and waited for the lion to make the first move, for we didn't wish to upset him. He obliged us by standing up and stretching, giving me enough time to see he had a perfect mane and would make a good substitute for a black-maned lion. I told Saidi, "Well done—he is *kubwa sana, tena sana."* (very big indeed)

We called it a day and returned to camp. Lots of meat remained on the dead buffalo, which usually meant that the lion would feed on it for a couple more days—unless we were unlucky and the hyena chased him off.

The Field Force commander greeted us as we drove into camp. He had set up his camp, and his troops had settled in. I invited him to join us for supper and drinks by the fire. We discussed plans for the hunt. I told him that I did not want to have a convoy following us when we went out with the marshal. He replied, "We will await our orders from the *bwana mkubwas."* (big men)

After dinner and some hot chocolate, we departed for a good night's rest, knowing that once the guests arrived, we would have to be on our toes twenty-four hours a day to make sure nothing happened to the VIPs.

Come morning, I sent Saidi and Rashidi to keep an eye on the big lion. I went with the commander and George to check the landing strip for holes dug by the aardvark (antbear) or by feeding warthogs. We drove up and down the strip to chase off the hundreds of gazelle. These small animals like to rest and feed in these cleared areas, which allow them to see their enemies approaching. All was clear.

We returned to camp to check things over one last time. We hadn't been there long when we picked up the drone of an aircraft. We boarded our vehicles and headed for the airfield once again. The Hercules made a low flyover to check the strip and then circled for final approach. The undercarriage was lowered, and the pilot made a perfect landing. The engines roared as he put them into reverse thrust to slow down. The strip was plenty long, so there was no worry about an overshoot. The pilot taxied toward us; the Hercules is a noisy plane, so there was dead silence once the engines were switched off.

The gangplank was lowered, and Vice President Kawaha was the first to disembark. He waited to assist Madame Broz and Marshal Tito and then walked to where we were waiting.

After introductions, we left for the camp. The aides and other helpers saw that the guns and luggage were off-loaded and brought to camp. We showed our guests their quarters and left them to ready themselves for a quick lunch, for they were excited to go after the big lion as soon as possible.

During lunch I told the vice president that his brother had found a big lion and was out keeping an eye on its movements. He told the marshal, "You see, I told you that my brother, Saidi, was a good hunter; he has found a super big lion for you." Everyone smiled. I, too, was happy because it transpired that Madame Broz could speak good English and that Marshal Tito himself could speak some English, though haltingly.

I had spoken to the vice president about not having too many cars following us on the hunt. He told the commander that only two vehicles—carrying the aides-de-camp, a doctor and nurse, plus a few photographers from Yugoslavia and Dar es Salaam—were to follow the main car. We worked out a system of signals and set out.

In our vehicle were the vice president and his guests, plus their respective aides; Marshal Tito stood in the back, and Madame Broz sat up front with me.

It had cooled down, and the guests had their cameras at the ready as we drove to see where Saidi was. He told me over the radio that the lion had wandered down to a small riverbed to drink and was still there.

We drove slowly to where Saidi was parked. I signaled the other vehicles to join us, for Marshal Tito wanted to have his official photographer catch him shooting his first African lion.

I worked out a strategy for how we would conduct the hunt. I must admit that I was not very hopeful the lion was still in the riverbed. Still, I instructed Saidi and his scouts to go around to the far side and to walk slowly while talking, hoping to drive the old lion in our direction.

Marshal Tito had his gun ready, as did I in case of a charge. The photographer was ready, so I gave the go-ahead to begin the drive. Everyone was excited and silent, especially as Saidi and his men neared the place where he said the lion was sleeping. They disappeared into the riverbed, and I told Marshal Tito to be prepared for a shot at a running lion. Nothing happened, and soon Saidi came into view. No lion. We drove down to the river—I wanted to check the tracks to determine what direction the cunning old blighter had taken.

Everyone had recovered from the disappointment of not seeing the quarry. We discovered that the lion had drunk his fill, lain down for a short while, and then made his getaway by creeping upstream and vanishing. We tried to locate him again, but no luck.

Arriving back at camp just as the sun was setting, the VIPs disappeared into their tents for a hot bath/shower before we all gathered around a huge log fire that sent sparks into the sky like fireworks. Everyone seemed relaxed and happy.

The aides tended to their duties, and drinks and toasties were served as people began to chat with one another. The mood was good as we enjoyed dinner. Marshal Tito really liked George's waxed mustache. It was indeed the biggest and best mustache that I had ever seen, and George was proud of it.

"How is your mustache today?" Marshal Tito would ask every morning.

Marshal Tito sat on one side of Vice President Rashidi Kawaha and Madam Broz on the other. Saidi Kawaha sat opposite, as did the Field Force commander. I was placed next to Tito, and some of the top aides also sat at our table.

During dinner Marshal Tito asked me if it was possible for his wife to shoot a nice zebra. I told him that we had to shoot some bait to attract Big Boy and that a zebra would fill the bill nicely. He smiled and added, "My wife isn't a good shot, but let her try."

The general conversation was about hunting and the migration. Everyone was astonished at the amount of wildlife they had seen so far. The chief photographer was in his element, snapping pictures one after the other. The food was top of the line, and the marshal asked to be introduced to the cook. George was actually the chief chef, but he sent Ali, his assistant, to meet the VIPs. Ali came in all smiles, his white hat making him look every inch a chef.

We were served a fine five-course meal, with good wines to wash it down. Everyone cleaned their plates. After dinner we again settled around the fire. The night choruses were heating up, spiced with an occasional roar from a lion,

and we were lucky to hear a leopard grunting as he prowled nearby. Hyena were "*oooowing*" in all directions, and the wildebeest calves were calling for their mothers.

Soon people began to yawn. I told everyone that we should leave very early, as there might be a chance to come upon some lion before they headed for the shade to rest. A light breakfast would be ready by 5:30, and we would leave by 6 A.M.

I was awakened by a gunshot. I said to myself, "What the hell is going on?" I leapt out of bed, grabbed my .470, and rushed outside. The commander was up and giving his men hell. Apparently, one of them had fired accidentally whilst unloading his rifle. Luckily, Marshal Tito and his party were sound asleep and didn't hear a thing. No further mention was made of this episode.

In the morning we hurriedly drank and ate, and then climbed aboard the vehicles. I told Saidi to head for where he last saw his lion and to keep us informed if he spotted a shootable trophy. I drove off in the hopes of finding Big Boy and perhaps en route finding a nice zebra for Madame Broz.

The sunrise was a spectacular sight. Animals danced and pranced all around as we headed for the open plains. We hadn't gone far when I spotted a fine zebra stallion. Madame Broz handled her rifle like an expert (which I found out later she was). The group of zebra moved away as we approached, the females and young in front with the stallion at the rear. Estimating that he was about 250 yards out, I told her to aim just behind the shoulder and about a third of the way up its body. The stallion had stopped and was standing broadside. She took aim and fired. I saw a puff of dust on the other side of the zebra.

Marshal Tito laughed and said, "You missed; shoot again," as the beast tore off across the plain.

I said, "You have hit just right; you watch, he will fall over any minute now."

The words had hardly left my lips when there was a cloud of dust and the zebra was on the ground kicking in his last death throes. Everyone clapped, and Marshal Tito said jokingly, "You must have had a fluke shot." Madame Broz just turned and smiled.

When we reached the zebra, it was stone dead, its perfect black-and-white skin free of blemishes or bite marks from fighting. Pictures were taken. The second Land Rover arrived, and after the animal was skinned and its stomach opened, I told Rashidi to drag it around and pull it slowly to a big clump of thorn trees not far from where we had last seen Big Boy. Whilst the skinner, Elias, was doing his work, an aide produced some schnapps, and we all toasted Madam's fine shooting. It was here that another of the aides told me that Madame Broz had been a top-ranking resistance fighter; that's how she came to meet the marshal.

Saidi had told me earlier that his brother, *Ndugu Yangu*, the vice president, wanted to take some good meat back to his family and friends in Dar es Salaam, and also to President Nyerere. It happened that whilst we were cruising around,

Marshal Tito with his Patterson's eland. Left to right: Saidi Kawaha, brother of the vice president; Vice President Rashidi Kawaha of Tanzania; Madame Broz, Marshal Tito's wife; chief skinner Elias Nampunju; Tito; Game Scout Vincent; and Eric Balson. Tanzania, 1970.

I spotted a fat bull eland, which carries what some would say is the best-tasting meat of all wild game. I told the marshal that we would go and stalk the eland on foot.

Another look at the bull showed that it was a particularly good trophy, so we could kill two birds with one stone. I wanted only the marshal to come with me, not his entire entourage. He agreed, told everyone to stay behind, and said, "I want to prove that I can still stalk. Come on, Eric, let's go."

The wind was in our favour, and we used some large acacia trees and clumps of bush for our approach. We moved only when the eland was feeding or had moved behind some bushes. He was alone, which helped, and he hadn't any idea we were after him. We crawled on hands and knees in a couple of places, and the marshal insisted that he carry his own rifle. He was determined to prove his point.

After about an hour, we were close enough to shoot. I had heard that Tito was an excellent shot with both rifle and shotgun, and I wanted to see if this was true. I told him to rest his rifle against the trunk of an acacia. He just gave me a hard stare, raised the rifle slowly to his shoulder, took aim, and fired. I heard the distinctive *whump* of a bullet finding its mark. The eland sprang forward, fell over, got up again, and was off at full speed.

I said, "Shoot again." He had quickly reloaded and now fired again. To my relief, the bull, about two hundred yards from us, did half a somersault, fell on its side, and lay still. It was first-class shooting. The marshal was delighted and shook my hand with vigour.

What happened next was some sort of celebratory ritual, new to me but apparently a common practice in Yugoslavia and other parts of Europe. The marshal stretched up to pluck off a small, leafy branch from a tree nearby. Then he took off his hat, placed some of the leaves in the mouth of the dead animal, and soaked the other leaves in the blood oozing from his first shot, perfectly placed through the heart. He stuck the bloodied leaves into the band on his hat and put the hat back on.

He then pulled out a small hip flask and drank a toast to the eland and the hunt. He offered the flask to me as well; its contents were sweet and so strong they made me gasp. The marshal laughed and said, "*Ah*, very good schnapps made from peaches; have some more to celebrate our success."

The Land Rovers had reached us, and everyone was congratulating the marshal on his fine shooting—and sharing his schnapps. The photographer, who had a very powerful telephoto lens, hoped he had captured it all on movie film. We had to pose for some still pictures.

It was already midday, so whilst the scouts gutted and skinned the eland before cutting it up, we moved to a small hill that provided shade and a fantastic lookout. George had packed us a cold lunch plus iced beer and cool wine. He sure knew his stuff. As we all feasted and rested, I called Saidi to find out how he was progressing. He told me that he'd had no luck in finding the lion. I advised him to head off in another direction and to keep a keen eye out for vultures.

I told my group that we were going to look for Big Boy, and I was hoping and praying for a stroke of luck as we motored along. The second Land Rover, carrying the eland, followed our tracks. I did a 360-degree circle without seeing any signs of the great beast. It was time to head back to camp.

Driving past a swampy patch, I suddenly saw some lion on the far side and stopped to check out the male. He was a reasonable tawny-maned lion with two female companions. Marshal Tito became excited and asked if he could shoot it. He stood up through the hatch and took aim; everyone remained dead still. Just as he fired, the lion got up, and the bullet, aimed for the shoulder, hit the animal in the front leg. The lion let out a terrific roar and charged back into the reeds whilst the two lionesses disappeared in the opposite direction.

"That was bad luck," I said, "and now we have a big problem on our hands." We had to deal with a wounded lion in high reeds and a swamp, and we didn't have much time before darkness engulfed us.

I told the marshal that I was going in after the lion by myself. He wagged his right index finger and shook his head. "No, Mr. Eric, you and I will go in together." The vice president was giving orders that the commander and two of his men were to go with us into the swamp. I didn't care for the idea of having nervous, inexperienced people with loaded rifles following me into a thick swamp, especially with a wounded lion to contend with!

I was relieved when the marshal said, "Mr. Vice President, thank you, but only Eric must accompany me, and he must only shoot the lion when it's on top of me. Please, no one else is to shoot, OK?"

The vice president replied, "But what if you get mauled or, worse still, killed? I will lose my job. Please allow my men to go along with you, just in case."

"No, only Eric," Tito replied firmly and started to walk off with his rifle ready.

I shouldered my faithful double, which had two softnose bullets loaded, and set off in front of the marshal. I soon picked up traces of blood,

but judging from the signs it wasn't a serious wound; the lion had a broken front leg. It was getting difficult to see, and I kept my rifle at the ready. Cautiously, we proceeded into the reeds. We were immediately attacked by hordes of hungry mosquitoes, but I had to concentrate on keeping a lookout for our quarry, my eyes straining for the slightest movement.

Suddenly I saw an ear twitch—the lion was peering straight at us through the reeds about twenty paces in front. His incredible camouflage, combined with the fading light, would complicate our problem. I glanced to check whether the marshal was ready before pointing with my finger. I saw his rifle come up just past my left ear; I clicked off my safety and was ready for the charge. Tito's rifle roared, and a huge flash of flames spat from its muzzle just as the lion sprang toward us. The deadly shot entered his brain just above the right eye, and he fell out of the air and splashed into the swamp almost at our feet, spraying us both with smelly, muddy water. I'd been on the point of shooting the lion in full charge, but the marshal had saved me the trouble.

I let out a squeal of relief. My eardrum was singing and hurting from the gunshot, but right then I couldn't have worried less. I was overjoyed that we were both in one piece. Marshal Tito was right beside me, laughing more from fear than delight, I believe! He patted his rifle before slinging it over his shoulder, embraced me, then waved and shouted for his photographer and the others to come and enjoy the mosquitoes and smelly water. They ran into the dirty water, with Madame Broz in front, much to everyone's surprise. Happy that we were safe, she hugged the marshal and gave me a kiss.

I could see that the vice president was still troubled; his eyes were as big as saucers.

Drinks were handed all round and photos taken with a flash; then we hurriedly moved out from the swarms of mossies, which seemed hungrier than ever. My game scouts carried the lion out and loaded it on top of the eland, and we made tracks straight back to camp. It wasn't an enormous lion, but it was a good trophy.

I was exhausted, but my spirits were high, and I was hugely relieved. I sank into a lovely steaming-hot bath, savouring its sheer luxury, and had almost fallen asleep when the dinner gong rang.

Around the enormous campfire that evening we relived the day's exciting events. Neither the vice president nor the Field Force commander had ever seen a hunt like it, and they went on and on, waving their arms as they told and reenacted the story, even dancing and falling down as the lion had done. They would have plenty to tell their mates and families when they got home.

The champagne flowed before and during dinner, as did coffee and liqueurs. I was tired and wanted to speak to my staff about the programme for the morrow. I excused myself and bid everyone a pleasant night's sleep. Lion roaring in the distance was a happy note to sleep on.

It was unusually brisk when I surfaced, shaved, and dressed next morning. All were present as I entered the mess tent, and the birds were singing.

Madame Broz said, "Good morning, Eric. Did you hear the lion roaring their heads off? I was a little bit nervous until I saw the shadow of the two guards walking past our tent. What are we going to enjoy today?"

I replied, "We are going to look for a big old buffalo bull, and hopefully during our travels we will find our main target, Big Boy. Let's eat up and be on our way."

Once again I sent Saidi and his team to search in another direction for a good lion or buffalo. Wildebeest were everywhere, mostly lying down after having been wide awake all night checking for predators. As we came out onto the open plains, I showed my guests a greater bustard, also called kori bustard, proudly strutting along with his tail fanned out and his neck held rigid, almost touching his tail.

"What is he doing?" someone asked.

"Showing off and trying to court that female over there," I said, pointing. I explained that the male of this species was the largest flying bird in the world for its weight, and the males are easy to catch if you chase them into a headwind. I noticed that a strong wind was blowing across the plains, creating dust devils, so I demonstrated what I had just told them. I drove straight up to the bustard, and he took off into the wind. I stayed right under him for a couple of hundred yards, and he soon tired and landed. I jumped out and chased him down in no time flat. A photo shows the marshal and Madam Broz checking the big fellow out.

During our search for an old buffalo, a nice-looking male Roberts gazelle walked across our path. I pointed it out to the marshal, who wanted to add the animal to his trophy collection. He took aim, and the beast collapsed in its tracks.

Just then my radio started to beep. It was Saidi: They had located a very big buffalo bull all alone and sleeping. I got the rough directions, and we began the twenty-mile trek to where Saidi was waiting.

We were going to pass quite near the zebra bait, so I told Bwana Tito to get ready just in case a respectable lion was nearby. It would have to surpass the one he had shot the previous evening.

Marshal Tito, Eric Balson, and Madame Broz examine a greater bustard, also known as Kori bustard. Tanzania, 1970.

We drove up very slowly to the tree where the bait had been placed. No hyena were in view, only a few vultures on nearby trees—a good sign that perhaps either a lion or leopard was guarding the bait or feeding. At first I couldn't see anything, but then I caught a tail swish—a lioness. But she appeared to be alone, so we let her enjoy her meal.

I contacted Saidi to confirm that I was going in the right direction. *"Sawa, sawa Bwana, endelea tu,"* he said. *"Moja kwa moja, huyu nyati dume analala."* (You are on the right track. The male buffalo is lying down sleeping.)

Saidi couldn't speak English, so we always communicated in Kiswahili.

We made good time, and soon I drove alongside Saidi's vehicle. He was all smiles and spoke to his brother; then he pointed to some thickets about four hundred yards to our left. He said the old bull had moved away from the herd and was lying down facing eastward, perfect for a good stalk.

I told Saidi to lead the way, as it was his buffalo; only Tito and he and I were to attempt the stalk. The photographer looked unhappy, so I told him he could come but had to follow exactly behind us and follow my orders, especially if the buffalo made a charge. He shouldered his big camera, and we commenced our stalk.

I could see the buffalo's back and his ears flicking to chase off the biting flies. It was not too hot, even though it was well past midday. There was plenty of cover, so we made good progress, stopping every so often to check the old bull—he hadn't moved.

I selected a big acacia tree as our final destination. I made Marshal Tito rest there for a short while to regain his breath and then asked if he was ready to try a shot. He nodded. I told him I was going to make a slight noise to make the buffalo stand up, and that he must be ready to take a shoulder shot. If the buffalo

ran in our direction, he should keep shooting. Saidi and I would shoot only at the very last minute. He nodded again, and raised his rifle.

I made a roaring sound, which brought the old bull to his feet in an instant, and a second later the gun boomed right beside me. The buffalo spun around and started to run off. I shouted for Tito to fire again—although I was watching through my binocular, I didn't see where his shot had hit. He obliged, firing two more shots in quick succession, and the old buffalo took a nose-dive as I followed up with a shot of my own.

The poor old chap must have been dead before he hit the ground. His back legs were kicking in the air, and then came the familiar

Marshal Tito with his big buffalo. Tanzania, 1970.

death bellow (most buffalo die with a last bellow). I congratulated the marshal on his great shooting. The photographer, as usual, was laughing with the excitement of recording the hunt on film. Saidi shook Tito's hand and said, "*Asante sana, Bwana Mkubwa.*" (Thank you very much, Big Man.)

We checked to see which bullets had caused the damage. The bull had four wounds: I had aimed at the top of the neck and can only assume that one dropped the buffalo at once. Tito's first shot was behind the shoulder but a bit too high, the frothy blood coming from the nose confirming a high lung shot. The two other bullets struck high up in the hindquarters, so all shots had hit their target. The horns turned out to be a fantastic trophy.

We now had only one full day of hunting left. On our drive back to the main camp, I overheard Tito telling the vice president that he would like to spend an extra day in the bush, and apologizing if it would disrupt any official functions that had been planned. So it was arranged that the party would stay another day. At camp, an urgent radio message was sent to Dar es Salaam to alert everyone to the sudden change of plans.

Saidi's vehicle arrived heavily laden with the old buffalo. Elias, the head skinner, went to work on removing the hide for a full shoulder mount, and there would be plenty of good meat for the party to take back to Dar.

George was happy that the guests would spend an extra day; this meant more money and publicity for his business.

The evening meal was as good as ever, and the wine was perfect—not that I knew much about wines in those days. Everyone was relaxed, and conversation was easy as there was so much to talk about. After dinner, as we sat around the fire, a loud roar came from the direction of the zebra bait. I bid my good-nights and said, "That may be our lion, so those who wish to go hunting very early should be ready to depart just before first light."

The roaring continued throughout the long night. I just could not drop off to sleep, wondering if we would find a big lion on the zebra.

Eventually I fell asleep, because the next thing I heard was "*Hodi, hodi?*" (May I come in), and my reply was "*Karibu.*" (Come in.) It was the waiter bringing a Thermos of hot tea. I leapt out of bed, for I had overslept, quickly washed and shaved, downed a couple of cups of tea, picked up my rifle and binocular, and ran to the mess. There I grabbed a couple of slices of toast to munch as we made our way toward the lion bait. I had a good feeling about this day.

When we were some two hundred yards away, I pulled up to check the bait and immediately saw a big lion on the far side of the dead zebra. It was a fine specimen with an impressive tawny mane—not our Big Boy, but a trophy animal nevertheless.

I warned Marshal Tito to be prepared for a quick shot, for I expected the lion to get up and make a sudden dash for the cover in a small gully nearby. I manoeuvred the vehicle to the right to get a better angle for a shot. The marshal was up and had his rifle ready.

Just as I'd thought, the big lion leapt up and started to run. I shouted, "Shoot, Sir!" At the shot, the animal jumped into the air ten to twelve feet and hit the ground stone dead. I never witnessed anything like that before or since.

I told everyone to hang on as I pressed the accelerator to the floorboards and headed toward the lion, whose legs were kicking. Fearing it might have been only stunned, I jumped out, clutching my .470, and ran right up to the animal.

Blood was pouring from the back of the head, and the mane was covered in blood. I knew that Tito's bullet had struck the brain.

I jumped for joy, as did everyone else, and we all patted Marshal Tito on the back and shook his hand. Making a head shot on a lion going flat-out at about 150 yards was truly an exhibition of fine shooting.

The ritual began. Hip flasks of schnapps were handed around as the frustrated photographer tried to get some order so he could take his pictures. Elias and Saidi arrived, and soon they were hoisting the marshal shoulder-high and chanting their lion song. Then they loaded the fine trophy, and we made our way back to camp.

Marshal Tito with his big lion. Tanzania, 1970.

After a good hour's rest and some champagne toasts, Madam Broz said she and her husband would like to remain in camp for the rest of the day. The marshal was more than thrilled and just wanted to relax and reminisce. For me, the pressure was finally off. The remainder of that day was peaceful, though the atmosphere was electric. The vice president came to my tent to congratulate me for making Tanzania's guest so happy. After lunch the marshal asked if he could view his trophies and visit the staff's quarters. Another perfect day was drawing to a close.

As we all sat around the fire, we could see thousands of wildebeest heading in long lines for the small lake. George broke the silence: "I want you all to watch just how stupid those wildebeest are," pointing to where the animals were gathering along the shore. "Just now their leader will try to cross the lake, and I bet you my bottom dollar that when they are halfway across, they will panic and then you will witness complete chaos."

For some unknown reason, this event occurs only during the migration. Herds of wildebeest with their calves decide that they must cross Lake Lagaja, and when they panic, hundreds get drowned, especially the calves. Thanks to George, who had seen this spectacle often over the years, we were all about to witness one of these suicidal crossings.

Sure enough, thousands of animals started to cross the lake. We all ran to collect our cameras and rushed to get nearer before the light got too bad for photography. The noise of water churned up by thousands of legs was so loud that we couldn't hear one another speak. These stupid animals—that's all I can call them—suddenly decided to turn back, which caused untold confusion and a true catastrophe. The leading animals panicked, turned, and started to trample those coming behind. These did the same thing

in turn. Bellows from drowning wildebeest, especially the small calves, were terrible.

With saddened hearts we wandered slowly back to the dining area as the sound of a gong signaled that supper was ready. The silence during the meal was noticeable—events of the past hour had taken their toll. What conversation there was focused on the tragedy that had just occurred.

Liqueurs and coffee were waiting for us by the fire. We sat on one side, where a large pile of red-hot embers kept us warm. The sounds from the lake had died down, replaced by the cackling and laughter of many hungry hyena.

The sunrise of our last day was superb. The marshal was dressed in his city suit, looking very different from the hunter of the previous day. He wanted to speak to me outside. He held out his hand—he had a good, firm handshake—and said, "Eric, I can't tell you how much we have enjoyed this safari. I shall cherish our hunts and the great hospitality that you and your staff have shown us. My wife and I would like to show our appreciation. Please accept this small gift." He handed me a small package.

I heartily thanked him and Madame Broz for the gift and said I would treasure it and many pleasant memories. He then gave me some envelopes containing cash for each of the staff, who had all lined up to say *kwaheri* to our VIPs.

The luggage and guns were already loaded and the vehicles lined up for us to travel the few miles to the waiting Hercules. It took only a few minutes to bid our last farewells. Madame Broz gave me another kiss, and I shook hands with the marshal and our vice president, who thanked me again for such a successful safari. Soon the engines of the Hercules were revving as the pilot taxied to the end of the runway for takeoff. As the Hercules lifted off, we all breathed a sigh of relief that the safari had gone off without any hitches.

George and I still had lots to do, however. He had to work out the safari's costs and give them to me to send to the treasury in Dar es Salaam for settlement. I had to make sure that our two Land Rovers, hired especially for the safari, were cleaned and sent back to Arusha that day. Meanwhile, my game scouts and skinners would oversee the safekeeping and packing of the trophies, which would take a couple of days. The two lion skins and the zebra skin needed special attention: plenty of salt rubbed well into the skins and all fat cut off to prevent the hair from slipping.

I finally had time to open my gift, and to my delight the package contained a beautiful gold watch engraved with Marshal Tito's signature (Josip Broz) on the underside, together with a few hundred dollars, which was a special surprise. I called all the staff to my tent so that I could hand them their *zawadi* (gift) from the marshal. They walked off very pleased and satisfied, for their tips amounted to more than two months' wages.

Later that day I walked down to the lake to see the hundreds of wildebeest carcasses, some floating, others washed ashore. Flocks of all types of vultures and big marabou storks were in attendance, and plenty of jackal and hyena lay all around with full stomachs. I hated to think of the stench that would emanate from all those rotting carcasses in a couple of days. I took some photos for the record, and ambled back with this sad sight embossed in my memory forever.

After breaking camp early the next day, I said good-bye to my friend George and set out for home. At Arusha, Viva was pleased to see me and to hear all about the safari. Not long after, I returned to Ndutu to show Viva and our three sons, Alan, Steven, and Kenneth, where I had hunted with Tito and to meet George. We spent the night at George's camp and enjoyed his company.

The wildebeest were still passing Ndutu by the thousands, and both Alan and Steven snapped pictures with their box Brownie cameras. We were on our way to the Loliondo Controlled Area to check out a suitable camping place for a forthcoming safari for Prince Bernhard of the Netherlands, planned for August.

Whilst we traversed the wide-open Serengeti plains, dodging the wildebeest, which seemed oblivious to our vehicle, the children suddenly yelled, "Hey, Dad, there is a monster black-maned lion over there!" I stopped and trained my glasses on this magnificent beast, and immediately recognized Big Boy. Goose pimples ran down my spine as I started the Toyota and drove closer. He looked at us and then ambled on, striding majestically toward a group of lionesses and cubs sunning themselves nearby. All of us were excited. Alan and Steven took many snapshots. I was annoyed that I had forgotten to bring my camera, which had a big telephoto lens. We watched that magnificent, kingly animal for about an hour.

Some thirty years had passed since I was in Tanzania, but late in 1998 I was lucky to have the opportunity to revisit my old stomping grounds. I found that it had changed beyond my wildest dreams, but I was happy to hear that Ndutu camp is still going and that the wildebeest have surpassed the two million mark.

"Full Charge" *by Mike Ghaui.*

CHAPTER FIVE
Close Calls and Stirring Encounters

Once the dust had settled from the Tito experience and everyone had returned to his normal routine, I received a letter from Coen Geertsema telling me that the 1969 safari to the Selous had been such a success that Prince Bernhard wanted to know if I could arrange another to that part of the world.

I replied that we would be honoured to have PB come on another safari. I booked two blocks running along either bank of the Mbarangandu River, which flows almost through the heart of the Selous Reserve. Brian Nicholson had told me that of all the places in what he called my reserve, he liked the miles and miles of the ever-winding Mbarangandu best of all.

Nicholson also said it was by far the best place to seek a "hundred-pounder" (a bull elephant with tusks weighing at least one hundred pounds on each side) and that he could guarantee the hunter would be in sight of game around every corner—and there were hundreds of corners. "Buffalo and elephant in the thousands" were his exact words. I was itching to see those "wonders," as were PB, Coen, and their buddies Hans and Dr. Stan. The safari was booked for three weeks in August 1970.

I drove with Viva and our three boys to set up the camp on the upper Mbarangandu, eventually arriving after three days of dusty travel. We were thrilled beyond words to see so much wildlife. Once our camp was established, we were able to explore upstream and down.

Brian had told me that this time of year, August–September, was the dry season and that one could motor either way along the river for sixty to eighty miles. But he warned of soft patches here and there that could cause any vehicle to sink right down to its chassis.

I watched out for those soft places as we drove around during the next few days. There were many, many buffalo, hundreds of common waterbuck, plenty of lion, and hordes of elephant around every corner. It was a paradise. Away from the main river, the countryside is covered with *miombo (Brachystegia)* woodland, which is not so interesting and is infested with the dreaded tsetse fly, so we tended to keep close to the river.

My family was sad to leave behind such a wonderland, but we had to return to Dar es Salaam for the prince's arrival. I saw Brian and told him that he had the Number 1 reserve in Tanzania, and long may it last. He grunted, and then a rare smile crossed his face.

Once again, PB and I found ourselves flying toward an airfield some twenty miles from our camp. He was very excited to hear my fantastic reports about our new area. On our approach, I saw my assistant hunter, Joe Newby, driving down the airfield to chase away some buffalo bulls lying there plus many warthog that were on their knees grazing the new growth of star grass along the edge of the strip.

In camp to greet the guests was an old bull elephant that visited every day. You would have thought he was tame, but I warned PB and the others not to venture too close; this was a wild animal and one should not take any chances. They all laughed.

But on this safari we had several narrow escapes and stirring encounters. Let me begin:

Every night we heard the roaring of lion near and far, and numerous pugmarks in the sand revealed their presence. One morning we saw some vultures on a dry tree at the river's edge. Raising our binocular, we saw a lioness feeding on a freshly killed male waterbuck. Hans, who loved to take photos and never once on all our safaris showed a desire to shoot anything, said, "Perhaps she will allow us to get closer for some good snapshots." I signaled behind to Joe, who had Coen and Dr. Stan in the other 4x4, that we would drive closer.

Joe drove us in, then stopped and switched off the engine, which allowed the photographers to work without the vehicle shuddering. The lioness stopped eating and stared angrily at us. Both PB's and Hans's cameras were clicking away. I was ready with my .470 in case she decided she did not like us and charged. She just snarled, though she crouched close to the ground in readiness to

spring. But then she spun around and ran off into some high grass.

I wanted to check the pugmarks around the kill because there was too much eaten for just one lioness. Sure enough, some very big pug impressions marked the wet sand. "Yes, there is a big papa lion around here," I remarked, "so let's be alert and ready." I directed Rashidi and Salum to drag the remains out into the open. I covered them with my rifle while they did this, and PB came alongside with his movie camera to record the scene. Perhaps the big lion would come back to feed.

Joe moved the vehicles to a spot where we could sit in comfort and watch the lion feed, or so I hoped. As he was driving past us, there was an amazingly loud roar to my left, and here came a huge lion at full charge coming straight at PB and myself. I thumbed off my safety and was preparing to shoot when a gun roared right beside me. PB had taken his revolver (either a .45 or a .44 calibre) and shot the charging lion right above its eye, killing it instantly. I was shaken but relieved and turned to shake PB's hand as the others came running over. All were amazed at PB's calmness and accuracy.

Coen said, as he shook PB's hand, "I see you are still a crack shot with your pistol."

PB replied, "I think it is time we all had a cold beer."

As we joined the others, Joe came up and whispered in my ear, "Bwana, that was close!"

The prince lifted his can of beer, pointed it to the lion, and said, "Sorry, my friend, you forced me to do it; we drink to your courage and audacity." And we did.

After refreshments, the lion was loaded and my group drove back to camp so that the skinner could remove and treat the lion's skin so the hair would not slip. As we drove away, hundreds of vultures came flying in from all directions to work over the remains of the waterbuck.

Our old jumbo was in front of PB's tent, pulling up the green grass along the river. The prince took his book and chair to read, relax, and watch his jumbo friend pull up clumps of the juicy grass, bash each clump across his tusks to knock the mud off, then gently place the morsel in his mouth. Nothing could have pleased the prince more than having this old elephant visit every day. These animals were special to him, and this old fellow had long,

curved tusks that must have weighed over eighty pounds each.

Dr. Stan wanted to try for a big buffalo, admitting that it was perhaps his last chance, thanks to his "wonky" knees that gave him so much grief. So this was the next project on our itinerary. Stan could not walk any distance, so we had to find a shootable buffalo not far from a vehicle. This was a problem for me as a senior game warden; the laws then stated, "No person is allowed to shoot within 200 yards of a motor vehicle." But seeing

Prince Bernhard and Hans Gerritsen tucking in to some food. Baked beans and bulley beef and garlic (to keep off ticks) were Prince Bernhard's favorite mid-day snack on safari. Mbarangandu River, Selous Game Reserve, Tanzania, 1970.

that PB had a presidential license, I would be a bit lenient.

We managed to find a big herd of buffalo grazing along the river, with a high bank right above them. This was an ideal situation for Stan. As we moved into position, I saw a fine bull grazing not too far away, but Stan wanted to get closer as he was not a good shot.

The wind was in our favour. Leaving the others on the high bank, I led Stan to a small, dry watercourse near the buff. As we slid down the bank, I had both rifles, giving Stan his once we reached the bottom. I checked that it was loaded and the safety was on and then beckoned for Stan to follow me.

The watercourse turned out to be deeper than I had thought. We were near enough to the grazing buffalo to hear the tick birds calling one another. We could also smell the buff and actually hear them chewing their cud, but we just could not see them. I looked back at the others and saw PB pointing to our left, which meant that the bull was behind us. We retraced our steps until I saw a place where we could creep back up the bank.

As I pulled Stan up, a couple of females passed within a few feet of us but were too engrossed in cropping the turf to see us. The wind was still blowing hard into our faces, which helped. I could not see which buffalo to shoot, so I signaled to the others, and they indicated the bull was sleeping. I positioned Stan behind a small tree and released his safety catch. When I was convinced that he was steady as well as ready, I signaled for them to clap their hands, but they could not figure out my signals. I tried again, and this did the trick.

As they clapped their hands and stamped their feet, there was a stampede. The old bull, stiff with arthritis, took some time to stand up. I tried to point him out to Stan, who was bewildered by the aroused buffalo now running past us both in front and behind. I eventually pointed my rifle at the bull I wanted him to shoot (back in camp we had shown Stan exactly where the vital organs were and told him to shoot for the lungs, a bigger target than the heart).

By the time Stan took aim and fired, the bull had seen us and started to run. I heard the thump of a bullet hitting something, but where he had hit it remained a mystery. Stan said later that excitement and adrenaline caused him to shake so much that he shot to the left.

We waited until the dust had settled before stepping out from behind our little tree. The group joined us. PB said he had lost sight of the wounded bull in the dust, but Coen and Rashidi said it had joined the main group, and Joe backed this up. I shouted for the *chai* (tea), as I wanted to wait at least half an hour before we started to follow up the herd, to give the wounded animal time to die or stiffen up from the wound.

I went with Rashidi and Salum to look for blood sign. We found a few specks here and there but nothing significant. Stan said, "Let's get cracking." I tried to persuade him not to come along—we would have to walk for miles.

"Don't worry about me; I muffed the shot and so must face the consequences," he said with a brave smile, but we all knew he was suffering. The herd had split in two. Joe, Coen, and Salum would follow one part whilst PB, Stan, and I went after the other. Tracking was difficult because most signs of blood were obliterated by the fleeing herd. We did catch a glimpse of it every now and then when the animals stopped to give their calves a rest. Signs of blood disappeared when the herd headed inland into the woodlands, but our task was much easier in the open forest, except when we had to divert around breeding groups of agitated elephant upset by the stampeding herd of buffalo.

The tsetse hammered us mercilessly, but we pressed ahead. At midday, with our water supplies dwindling, I told our group that we would carry on until three o'clock, but then we would have to abandon the search and find our way back to the vehicles.

We worked our way cautiously, checking behind and on both sides, knowing the habits of wounded buffalo. They often ambush a pursuer by making a complete circle and suddenly charging from behind. I was hoping to hear shots from the other group, but no such luck. Poor old Stan was struggling but kept going. I slowed the pace so he could keep up. I asked him if he wanted to go back with Rashidi and leave PB and myself to carry on, but he point-blank refused. Wiping the sweat from his eyes and clearing his spectacles, he said, "If it's the last thing I do, I'll make certain we get that poor beast."

I warned everyone to avoid shooting haphazardly if the buffalo suddenly charged.

Prince Bernhard (front) with Joe Newby and Dr. Stan Furber, cooling off in the Mbarangandu River. The Selous, Tanzania, 1970.

Prince Bernhard used to enjoy the cool waters, spending hour upon hour reading and relaxing. Mbaragandu River, Selous Game Reserve, Tanzania, 1970.

Many hunters have been shot accidentally by overzealous companions faced with a charging animal. Shortly after my little lecture, we heard a snort to our right, and here came a mad buffalo at full charge, intent, I was positive, on taking at least one of us to heaven. It happened so fast: I shouted at Stan to shoot, but he missed. He tried to reload but struggled with the bolt on his .458.

I would fire only at the very last second, to prevent harm to any of us. I have been in this type of situation many times and knew my double had only two bullets, so I saved them for the vital shot. When the buffalo was about forty yards away, still coming full speed, I yelled for PB and Rashidi to shoot. PB raised his rifle and fired,

but his bullet had little effect. He reloaded expertly and quickly fired twice more. Rashidi, too, put a shot into the buff, but it was PB's third shot that stopped the charge. The bull let out a horrifying bellow, splattering us with warm blood from its nose, and turned a complete somersault, landing just in front of us.

"That was very good shooting, Sir. Thank you for saving me the trouble," I said to PB.

Stan murmured, "Thanks, PB—I messed it up again." As he shook the prince's hand, his legs collapsed under him.

Wiping the blood from our faces, we walked over to see where the bullets had struck. Stan's original shot had penetrated the stomach, which accounted for the animal going so far. His second was a complete miss. PB's first shot was perfectly placed in the centre of the chest, enough to kill normally but not enough to stop a charging buffalo, and his second had ricocheted off the horn boss. The third had found the buffalo's brain and dropped it immediately.

Rashidi set off to collect our Toyota as PB and I started to skin and butcher the carcass. Just then we heard voices and saw the others close by.

"What a great sight; who did the damage?" Coen inquired.

"Here's your hero," said Stan, slapping PB on his back.

It was still hot and humid as we swatted at the sweat bees and drank the last few mouthfuls of water. The drone of engines inspired PB: "How sweet that cold beer is going to taste!" As we quenched our thirst with beer, the game guards and drivers loaded the big buff onto Joe's Land Rover, and we were soon on our triumphant way back home.

In camp, PB rushed into his tent and came out wearing his swim trunks and heading for the river, saying, "Who's coming to join me?" Even poor old Stan thought that was an excellent idea.

Beneath a large grove of Borassus palms a few hundred yards upstream of camp was a beautiful deep pool where dozens of hippo dozed and spent most of their day. There were many such pools, some of them former parts of the river but now oxbow lakes, which during the dry months fill up with floodwaters and are usually covered with "floating cabbage," creating ideal havens for thousands of "river horses" (an ancient Greek name).

The hippo is the second largest land creature in the world after the elephant, with some old bulls weighing four tons. They have four large,

curved tusks with flattened, razor-sharp shearing edges protruding from the corners of the jaw. These tusks are sometimes referred to as "poor man's ivory" and are used by carvers in the Far East to produce beautiful art objects.

Despite these enormous, dangerous-looking tusks, grass is the hippo's staple diet. They venture onto land just before or after sunset to walk, sometimes miles, in search of succulent grasses. They use their stubby, fat tails to scatter their dung in all directions during their wanderings, to mark their territory.

Although good-natured, the males of this species can be ferocious fighters, inflicting terrible wounds on one another with sideways slashes of those huge canines. Quite often, such clashes end in the death of one combatant or the other. It is believed that the hippo is the Number 1 killer of humans in man-versus-beast deaths on the African continent. Generally speaking, though, the hippo is not offensive—provided you don't get between him and his watery home.

Almost always, we could hear their loud *haw-haw-haw-haw* and *hooosh* sounds coming from the pool nearest camp. Because some of their paths crisscrossed the countryside right around our camp, the staff made big fires on the outskirts of our tents to keep the huge creatures from dropping in.

Well, for the first two weeks we had no problems from our neighbours, the hippo. Then one truculent old bull decided to stroll through our camp during the early hours of the morning. I was awakened by screams and shouting from the staff quarters and the kitchen. I first thought a lion or hyena had taken one of the staff. A cold shiver ran down my back. Then I thought some "siafu" ants (whose bites are very painful) had attacked the camp. I had my .470 and a torch in my hands as I rushed outside to face whatever it was.

Someone shouted, *"Hatari, hatari, kifaro, kifaro, panda mti haraka!"* (Danger, danger, rhino, rhino, climb a tree at once!) I was amazed at all the commotion and strange noises I had never heard before. Bushes were being smashed, but I could not hear any of the snorts or puffing sounds a rhino usually makes.

The crashing came in my direction. I shined my flashlight and was confronted by a charging tent. I stepped aside as this apparition dashed past me, heading for PB's tent. I could see he had his light on and was up and standing in his tent. I stared in disbelief as the charging tent hit a big tree. Grunts and groans eventually mingled with ripping and tearing as a huge male hippo suddenly emerged from the wreckage. Bewildered, he stared at me and moved around in a daze. I did not shoot, for fear some guests were around. I shouted for everyone to remain in his tent. Replies came from PB and Stan, but nothing from Coen or Joe.

Suddenly Joe was standing beside me clutching his .470 and whispering, "What the hell is going on?" I flashed my light on the hippo, which now was wobbling off toward his pool. I had just told Joe to go and check on Coen when we heard a voice coming from the vicinity of his toilet.

We ran over there to find that poor Coen had fallen in bottom-first. "Please give me a hand out of this mess," he said, holding up his hand—and bursting into laughter. We could not restrain ourselves and began to howl as well. "No, chaps, it is no joke—what happened?" he said, looking ashamed.

"A stupid old hippo got tangled up in the cook tent, but everyone is OK," I replied.

I shouted for the staff to bring hot water to Coen's tent so he could wash, and to make some *chai*. PB had come to join us and was consoling Coen.

"What were you doing, my friend?" he said.

"Well, you will not believe me, but I was sitting on my stick toilet seat just about to drop some bombs when I heard all that commotion. I jumped up, but slipped as I did so and landed in the dump!"

At that we all started to laugh again, and walked over to the mess for some hot drinks. The old cook was so scared that he said he was going to sleep up in a tree for the rest of the night.

In the morning, we found that the old hippo had lumbered into some red-hot embers, making him lunge forward right into the cook's tent. The cook was very fortunate not to have been stomped on; the hippo missed his feet by inches.

Before bidding one and all a peaceful sleep for what little remained of the night, it was voted unanimously, Stan abstaining, that a leisurely walk upstream would be the order for tomorrow.

Since no one was up and about early the next morning except PB, I told him that I was going to check on the hippo. He said that I should wait as he was sure the others would be interested in coming along. Suddenly everyone was interested in hippo—aroused by the events of the previous night, no doubt. Soon the sun was shining through the tree canopy, and I wanted to make a move while it was still cool, so I urged the party along. They gathered up their camera paraphernalia, and Rashidi and Salum plus a couple of porters were on hand to carry the tripods, etc.

As we set off, I said, "Today is going to be dedicated to some of the lesser wonders of this world, our feathered friends, the birds."

Both Coen and Hans were delighted, as both were birdwatchers.

As I explained earlier, the Borassus palm does more than supply a delicious fruit. Many species of birds use its leaves and branches for nesting. The most interesting of these birds, in my opinion, is the African palm swift. This unique little bird glues its tiny nest, made of its own feathers, on the underside of the dried-up palm leaves. Then it glues its tiny white eggs to this lining by using its saliva. How they lay their eggs and get them to stay put is beyond me, because the nests hang vertically. I have studied these swifts for hours on end, trying to figure out how the young hang on once they have hatched, but I still have not found the answer.

At the grove around the hippo pool, we found a nest containing a pair of fish eagles and a hatchling. As we watched, the adults kept on bringing fish to feed the little one. Two palm nut vultures had built their nest nearby in another palm tree, and one of them was sitting on eggs. Other vultures had nests in that same grove. Some lovebirds had taken over an old woodpecker's nest. The lovebirds and parrots have rounded beaks and find it hard to dig out holes in trees, so they rely on the other birds, especially members of the woodpecker family, to do the hard work for them.

We could hear trumpeting ahead, so we made tracks in the hopes of finding elephant drinking and bathing. As we came over a rise on the riverbank, there ahead, coming down the opposite bank, was a very large herd of over eighty head. There were plenty of youngsters and one very large old bull with tusks well over the hundred-pound mark. The wind was in our favour, so we walked to a good, safe position and let PB, Hans, and Coen set up their cameras.

The light was perfect for photography, and the elephant were most obliging and kept us entertained for almost two hours. The babies squealed and frolicked around whilst their parents bathed and threw sand and mud over their parched bodies.

Coen broke the silence and spoilt the serene atmosphere by saying, "PB, there is a nice hundred-pounder for you," and asking if PB wished to shoot it for a museum. I knew immediately what the prince's answer would be, as he had turned down that monster in the Rungwa a few safaris previously.

"Coen, why do you ask such a stupid question? We are watching a wonderful spectacle—why do you want to spoil it?" That was that.

"A most memorable and enjoyable day, Eric, thanks. Your choice was a good one," said PB as he put away his cameras and lit his pipe. Dr. Stan told us he had spent his day relaxing, reading, sleeping, and watching our old friend the jumbo.

PB shot a record southern reedbuck and a most remarkable Lichtenstein hartebeest to cap off another splendid safari. The days came and went, each bringing its thrills, entertainment, and enjoyment.

"Inquisitive Pair" *by Mike Ghaui.*

CHAPTER SIX
Waging the Animal Wars

Conservation is defined as the efforts made by people and countries to preserve or protect their various natural resources—wildlife in this context—from waste or wanton destruction. Ancient records in many European countries indicate that even then, humankind was concerned with its own destruction of what once were rich forests full of wildlife.

During the Middle Ages, laws were passed in Europe to protect fauna and flora. Although these laws were specifically aimed at securing adequate hunting for the aristocracy, they nevertheless helped conserve nature.

On the North American continent, too, there was widespread and haphazard destruction of wildlife toward the latter part of the nineteenth century, the classic example being the almost-complete extermination of the American bison. That tragedy was triggered by the colonization by the white man of the great prairies of North America and by political motivation: the desire to remove the food of the Indians and so break their power—as witness the book *Bury My Heart at Wounded Knee*. It is estimated that between 1870 and the turn of the century, 60 million of these beasts lost their lives to hunters seeking meat and skins.

Almost too late, the United States government stepped in to stop this mass slaughter, and by 1902 it was believed that fewer than one hundred bison remained in the whole of North America. A considerable sum of money was spent on protecting and building up the bison herds, and today more than 50,000 roam the parks of the United States and Canada.

Gradually, the idea of conservation spread, and countries throughout the world passed legislation to establish and define areas in which wildlife would be protected in national parks, game reserves, and forest reserves. Among those countries were Tanzania, Kenya, Uganda, Zambia, and many others in central Africa.

In a young country such as Tanzania, these laws are particularly important because the rich abundance of wildlife continues to be threatened today by a variety of illegal hunting activities, mainly for trophies. Traditional local hunting for family consumption has had little effect on the wildlife herds, with a few exceptions, such as the springbok and black wildebeest in South Africa. Thousands of springbok were shot in the Pareska District and then taken to the towns and sold.

In Northern Rhodesia, now Zambia, the lechwe of the Kafue Flats were subjected to communal hunts by the Baila and Tonga people living on the periphery of these flood plains. During the two to four hunts held there each year, thousands of lechwe were killed under barbarous conditions. Pitman's Report of 1934 records that an estimated 250,000 Kafue lechwe roamed the flats in 1932, whereas figures for 1957 revealed only 30,000 remaining. Other records show that during one of these hunts in June 1957, 1,993 lechwe were killed in twenty-four hours, of which 64 percent were pregnant females. After this, the government passed legislation forbidding these mass hunts. Happily, by 1973 the Kafue lechwe had recovered to near 90,000 and were still increasing. The black lechwe of the Bangweulu swamps in Zambia suffered the same fate, and now they, too, are on the increase.

Traditionally, local hunting in most cases was actually beneficial, for it tended to "crop" or thin out the herds, thereby protecting the habitat. So it was not really the subsistence hunter that the governments were concerned about. Rather, action had to be taken in the field of wholesale slaughter for trophies.

Legislation aimed at protecting wildlife had been in force for several decades in the East African territories. But the increase in world demand for animal by-products made poaching more lucrative, and this led to an increase in illegal hunting.

In recent years, as furs and valuable skins once more became the vogue, world

The work of poachers, using AK47 rifles. There were eight female elephants shot for their tusks, their carcasses left to rot or feed the vultures and hyenas. Ruvuma River, Mozambique, 1997.

Poachers had killed this rhino mother and hacked out her horn, leaving the baby rhino to die. Balson, the prince, and the "gang" were able to catch the baby and save it, in spite of the fact that the tenacious youngster charged them several times and even knocked Balson over. Masailand, Tanzania, 1965.

demand soon exceeded the legal sources of supply. The high prices realized on overseas markets for leopard, cheetah, ostrich, zebra, and crocodile skins, as well as ivory and rhino horn, provided the incentive for unscrupulous dealers in East Africa to cater to the growing demand any way they could, resulting in a tremendous upsurge in the illicit hunting of these species.

Commercially motivated mass slaughter first became manifest in the Tsavo National Park in Kenya during the 1950s. The Kenyan government took decisive action just in time, and in 1956–57 an antipoaching campaign mounted jointly by the national parks, game department, and police virtually eliminated commercial poaching in Tsavo.

Tanzania was determined in her bid to stamp out this nefarious activity. At about this time, I received the letter from the Tanzanian government (see chapter 2). I phoned Prince Bernhard and told him that my work was unfinished in Tanzania—I wanted to smash the poaching rackets that had sprung up in recent months. He was very perturbed about the increase in this illegal business and said he would speak to the president of Tanzania immediately. I did not think any more about that conversation and made arrangements to visit Europe and America in an endeavour to find clients to enable me to start a new life as a professional hunter and guide.

Prince Bernhard invited me to visit him at Soestdijk Palace, and I was honoured to accept. The evening prior to my leaving home,

During the rainy season in Tanzania, many rivers flood. Having no bridges, one has to look for alternative methods to cross. Here Balson's Land Rover is being floated across wrapped up in a canvas. This method proved a great success in crossing rivers, especially when the poachers were not expecting to see a vehicle suddenly appear on their hunting grounds during the rains. By using such methods, Balson was able to catch many poachers. Rukwa Valley, Tanzania, 1965.

I received a phone call from State House, Dar es Salaam, informing me that the president's personal envoy would be at the airport to meet me when I flew into Dar.

During the following three years, 1969–1972, I was assigned, on orders directly from the president of Tanzania, Dr. Julius Nyerere, to establish a network to eradicate the huge poaching rackets that had suddenly escalated since independence. As senior game warden, I set up my headquarters in Arusha, hub of the tourist industry, in the northern region of Tanzania.

My assistant game warden, Musa Mwaimu, and I commenced this almost impossible task, an unending war against the poachers and illegal trophy dealers. We soon discovered that among the masterminds behind these terrible activities were some very influential people. Much to everyone's astonishment and disgust, the biggest culprit of them all was none other than Mama Ngina Kenyatta, wife of the president of Kenya, Jomo Kenyatta.

An article in *Private Eye* magazine sometime during 1973 quoted an article from the *Guardian* newspaper:

> President Kenyatta has pledged his word to have poaching stamped out. . . . Somewhere in the background is the mastermind who organizes collecting points for the "hot" ivory, pays in cash, and transports it to the coast. . . . If President Kenyatta is really determined to nail this mastermind, he only has to utter a gruff rebuke one night before dropping off to sleep, as the chief ivory smuggler in Kenya, and indeed Africa, is Mama Ngina Kenyatta, his lady wife.

How very true those written words were. But nothing—I repeat, *nothing*—was ever done about it. The police and game department officials were too scared to prosecute. I was the first person to find out that Mama Ngina was the big wheel behind the ivory and rhino poaching rackets, but when I went to Kenya with the chief of Criminal Investigations from Tanzania, they tried to kill us. That is another story, which is in a manuscript entitled "Animal War," which no one would print at the time I wrote it in 1971, saying it was too militant, too libelous, and much too political, and that if I wanted it published, I would have to use fictitious names, which I refused to do. So the truth has never been told—until now.

Let me tell you some true stories:

I recall way back in 1966 while I was on relief duties in the Arusha region, a person came to my office one day and asked if it was true that if someone gave the government good *habari* (news) that they would receive a reward in money. I told him this was quite correct, and that if it was really good information, the reward would also be good. His eyes lit up, a grin appeared on his face from ear to ear, and then he whispered that he had this good information, but if he told me, I must promise never to tell anyone who gave it to me. He continued that he trusted the *mzungu* (white man) and that is why he had come to me. I assured him that he could trust me so he must tell me his *habari*. It took him some time to tell me what he had come to say. I could see he was scared stiff. He kept on fidgeting and shifting around in his chair, peering over his shoulder every now and then to make sure that no one had seen him.

He told me that he worked on a lorry, as a "turn-boy," owned by an Arab. ("Turn-boy" is the name given to people who cranked the starting handles of vehicles, and, because hardly any vehicles in the bush had starters, these poor fellows were forever turning the handles.)

He said that the Arab who employed him had refused to pay him enough money for keeping secret what he (the Arab) was up to, so he had come to report.

This Arab, he told me, was a big illegal dealer in rhino horns and to back up his statement he said that the Arab had recently received sixteen large crates of horns from Uganda and was planning to take them to Dar es Salaam that night. I asked him how big the crates were, and where they were at the moment. He did not know as the Arab had moved away from where he had been staying, but he assured me that there were sixteen crates *"Mkubwa sana, bwana"* (very big). The lorry would be leaving Arusha for sure that night as it was already loaded up. He said that the sixteen crates were wrapped around with *gunias* (sacking) and that they filled a seven-ton Mercedes truck to the roof. His story was hard to believe, as these fellows can exaggerate something terrible, but I thought we should take a chance and maybe find a couple of rhino horns. I told him that he must come to my house at 7:30 that evening, and I explained where it was. He agreed and left.

I went over to the police headquarters and asked them for men and equipment to set up a road block along the Moshi road. The officer in charge soon had his men ready. They were under the command of a sergeant who turned out to be an excellent man. I explained to them my plan and how we had to organize this road block. I told the sergeant that he must come along with me, as I wished to take him to the exact spot where they must set up the block. I took him that afternoon and explained in great detail what I wanted them to do; he assured me that he understood, so all was set for our trap.

It was agreed that the road block would be erected only after I had flashed past and given the prearranged signal with my headlights. We had to adopt this last-minute procedure as most of the taxi drivers on the roads in Tanzania had their own code signals to warn any oncoming drivers that there was a police block ahead. By doing this they could turn about and skedaddle before they were caught, as a lot of ramshackle vehicles used to use the roads at night without licenses, brakes, and with goodness knows what other faults. I also told them which hired car I would use and its number, so that no mistakes could occur.

When night came, I made sure that the police had left. Then I picked up the boy who had given me the tip-off, and we drove to mile twenty along the Moshi road. I also took a couple of my own scouts for safety's sake. We did not know exactly when the Arab would come along in his lorry, nor did we know the number of his vehicle, so we just had to wait and rely on this turn-boy. I had also told the sergeant that they might have to wait until the early hours of the morning so they mustn't give up hope or pack up until I gave them the orders to do so.

Time seems to pass incredibly slowly when one is in a situation like this. I kept on glancing at my watch. Luckily it wasn't too cold that particular night, so we could sit with the car doors open, which was a blessing as the pong from my companions was not exactly like Chanel No. 5. Eight o'clock passed. Nine o'clock seemed to take hours to come along, and I was beginning to think that it was going to be another one of those wild-goose chases that we had been on so many times before. Then suddenly a lorry whizzed by, traveling like the clappers.

"Huyo! Huyo! Bwana Mkubwa!" (There he is, Master) shouted the informer excitedly. (In a hue and cry chase after a thief, or a chase after animals, this phrase is often used.)

I started off after him and knew I had to go like hell if I was to catch up and overtake him before he reached the place where the police were. I couldn't believe that his huge lorry could travel so fast. My foot was flat down. The car just wouldn't go (or so it seemed) until I took a quick check of the speedo and saw that we were clocking 95 mph.

I breathed a sigh of relief when the red tail lights of the truck came into view. I was doing well over the 100 mph mark at that point, and the gap between us was narrowing. As I shot past him, I guessed that there were still a couple of miles to go. I kept going without glancing back but could see the reflection of the truck's headlights right on my tail. The swine was traveling at about 85 mph. The bridge loomed up ahead, and I signaled three flashes with my lights. Just as I passed over the bridge, I caught a quick glimpse of people jumping up all over the place.

It took me some time before I could stop and turn around as I was all shaky, excited, and tensed up. By the time I had done a U-turn in the road and arrived back on the scene, there was pandemonium everywhere, with people shouting and swearing all over the place. The air was heavy with the smell of burning rubber. The Arab

This rhino had been wounded by poachers and suffered a slow, agonizing death. The poachers had not yet had a chance to get the horns, which were recovered by Balson. Masailand, Tanzania, 1969.

was letting go in every language under the sun: Arabic, English, and Swahili all mixed up together. He was saying what he was going to do to us all, once he got us in court, etc., as he had nearly had a terrible accident. The police had neither warning signs nor lights for this road block. I told him to dry up before he got a cuff across his ear, but this had little effect.

With all the excitement, I had forgotten about the informer. Suddenly remembering him, and wondering where he was, I ran back to the car but couldn't see him until I looked inside, and there he was, busy trying to hide himself under the floor mats, scared to death.

When things had quieted down and the police had driven the truck off onto the shoulder and cleared away the barriers, the few cars that had meantime accumulated at the scene were signaled to carry on. I asked the Arab what he had on his truck and why the hell he was traveling at such a speed. I produced my identity card and told him that we wished to search his truck. He had calmed down by now and said that of course we could check his truck as he had only his personal effects in the back and that he was in the process of moving from Arusha to his new home in Dar es Salaam.

When the back was opened, it was jammed to the top with big crates covered in sacking. *This looks interesting*, I thought to myself . . . *just as the informer described*. What I couldn't believe was the size of each crate, or at least the ones I could see, as the others were hidden underneath or behind. I told the sergeant to organize his men to unload the nearest crate and open it.

The Arab began to mutter, "*Ah*, Baba, please do not open the crates; otherwise you will spoil the timber of the boxes, which I have had

specially made, as I want to make my house furniture from these boxes once I have removed my belongings."

"*Nyamaza*" (keep quiet), the big, burly sergeant shouted. "If these crates really hold only your personal effects, then you will soon be on your way again."

The sacking was ripped off, and with the help of some tyre-levers, the lid of the box was pried open. Under a layer of dried grass were rhino horns of all shapes and sizes. The Arab was at a loss for words when I asked him what type of personal effects these were. He was arrested on the spot and driven with his truck back to Arusha.

I thanked the sergeant and his men for an excellent piece of work and said that I would see them in the morning. I took off with my men and the informer (who was very happy but who kept himself on the floor until we were moving). I told him that he would be getting lots of money for this case, especially if all sixteen crates contained rhino horns.

First thing the next morning I dashed round to the police station, where I found hundreds of people all jabbering away and very curious. I soon found out why; those sixteen crates were open and the rhino horns were laid out on the floor, ready for the police photographer to take his pictures for the records. I took a couple of snaps for myself at the same time. I was fuming mad by this time as I could see that at least half of these 286 rhino horns had come from the square-lipped rhino (white rhino). This meant that roughly seventy of these rare beasts had been killed just for their horns. What a crime when there were so few left! These certainly came from the Sudan and Uganda.

The case was compiled and taken to court, and the Arab was charged with being in

Balson was startled and concerned to see this enormous lion in the branches of a tree directly above Prince Bernhard's head as they sat in a parked, open-topped Land Rover. He thinks this picture might be the best he ever took of a lion, and considering the circumstances, it is a wonder he was able to take one at all. The driver backed the hunting vehicle out from under the tree, and the lion climbed down and departed. Lake Katavi, Tanzania, 1963.

This "King of Beasts" was strolling across the Serengeti Plains when he was caught by the camera near the famous Olduvai Gorge. Tanzania, 1964.

Eric Balson is pictured with Prince Bernhard's big Rufiji crocodile. Selous Game Reserve, Tanzania, 1969.

Prince Bernhard, Dr. Stan Furber, and Coen Geertsema preparing to cross a small river on a natural rock barrier on the way to set up a fly camp. Ruaha National Park, 1967.

Two male lions out walking among the wildebeest in Loliondo. Tanzania, 1967.

One of the author's safari camps, located in the Katavi Game Reserve in the western region of Tanzania. H.R.H. Prince Bernhard's tent is the one on the right-hand side of the picture, overlooking Lake Chada. Tanzania, 1963.

Eric Balson (right) caught these catfish with a bent nail for a hook and twisted anchor rope for line. Selous Game Reserve, on the Rufiji River, Tanzania, 1969.

Prince Bernhard with his record-book southern reedbuck. Selous Game Reserve, Tanzania, 1969.

Millions of greater and lesser flamingo on Lake Rukwa, Mbeya Region. Great Rift Valley, Tanzania, 1966.

An albino giraffe in the Rukwa Valley of Tanzania. There were actually two albino giraffes in the valley within a few miles of each other. The author spotted them originally by airplane. Tanzania, 1966.

This male elephant was wounded by poachers, and Prince Bernhard finished it off with a bullet to the brain. Selous Game Reserve, Tanzania, 1970.

The lappet-faced vulture, sometimes referred to as the Nubian vulture, is the largest of all vultures and most dominant.

Prince Bernhard's bullet hole can be seen just above the right eye on this big lion. Mbarangandu River, Selous Game Reserve, Tanzania, 1970.

Dr. Stan Furber with his big buffalo. Mbarangandu River, Selous Game Reserve, Tanzania, 1970.

H.R.H. Prince Bernhard with his giant wildebeest; at that time, this wildebeest was No. 2 in the Rowland Ward *record* book. *Beho-Beho Block, Selous Game Reserve, Tanzania, 1969.*

This is the old bull, nicknamed "Our Old Friend," that used to visit our camp. Mbarangandu River, Selous Game Reserve, Tanzania, 1970.

H.R.H. Prince Bernhard with his fantastic impala ram. He shot this animal to feed the hungry lioness and her cubs. Loliondo, Tanzania, 1972.

Prince Bernhard (left), Coen Geertsema, and Hans Gerritsen taking pictures of two old hippos on the banks of a small stream that flows into Lake Chada. Tanzania, 1963.

unlawful possession of these rhino horns, which were valued at that time at £228,800. The accused was found guilty and sentenced to five years' imprisonment. Everyone was exceedingly happy with this sentence. The Arab appealed to the high court of Tanzania and won his appeal on the stupid grounds that "no expert had been called from the game division to identify that the 286 exhibits before the court were actually rhino horn." Can you beat that? The police and game division staff were disgusted, to say the least, and most annoyed at the court's decision. At least the court did not order that the rhino horns be returned to the Arab! The informer got his just reward and came back to work for me when I returned to combat the big racket. I will leave it up to your imagination to work out why the Arab was acquitted.

* * * * * * *

As mentioned, my appointment as senior game warden landed me and my family in Arusha, the fourth largest town in Tanzania, situated on the southern slopes of Mount Meru (14,979 feet) at an altitude of 4,500 feet above sea level.

Back then, Arusha was a busy tourist center and a major starting place for hunting and photographic safaris, with the famous Ngorongoro Crater and Serengeti National Park within easy reach. (The tourism and safari trades dropped off considerably, largely

This picture, taken by the author, shows muzzleloaders, rifles, and bows and arrows confiscated from poachers. Mbeya, Tanzania, 1967.

These 286 poached rhino horns were found in the wooden boxes in the background. Ausha, Tanzania, 1966.

because of the total ban on hunting imposed by President Nyerere on 7 September 1973, a ban that continued into the 1980s).

On my first day at the office, I reported to the regional game warden, James Kahurananga, from whom I received a cold reception. Indeed, he gave me the impression that he knew nothing of my transfer to his station. I sensed his discontent and predicted a lack of cooperation. I outlined the reason I had been sent and voiced my hope that he and his staff would help me to smash this wave of crime.

His first remark did not fill me with confidence: "Why did Dar send you here, when they know that I am doing my best to catch these wicked poachers? Also, I have no office for you and no vehicles to give you."

This made me more determined than ever and also confirmed reports I had heard about this chap Kahurananga.

It didn't take me long to find a small office in a dilapidated old building that had been condemned and was about to fall down. Thanks to my contacts in the Public Works Department, I soon had the place in reasonable shape. Meanwhile, I applied for a government house for my family and me but was told that I had little hope of getting one as there was an acute housing shortage in Arusha. However, John Owen, director of Tanzania's national parks at that time, heard of our plight and came to the rescue. He arranged for us to use a new national parks house until the government allocated us one. Things began to look brighter: I had an office and a house.

Then I thought of a possible solution to my third dilemma—transportation. I had heard from Dr. Owen that Professor Grzimek, director of the Frankfurt Zoological Society and world-renowned for his books and TV shows, was in Arusha. I went to see him, telling him my problems and asking him outright for financial assistance to buy two new Land Rovers.

Prof. Grzimek listened with great interest and replied, "My dear friend, of course. We can always find money for such good causes as yours. Let me know as soon as possible just how much you need, and I will send it as soon as I get back to Germany." What a fine man! The money arrived in a couple of months, and I purchased the Land Rovers.

Believe it or not, soon thereafter I asked the game division for funds to run and maintain the Land Rovers and in reply received this rocket: "Under no circumstances can you have funds for your two vehicles as you purchased them without authority from Dar es Salaam. Please therefore send the vehicles to Dar for the time being."

I refused to send the vehicles as I knew only too damned well it would be the last I would see of them. Instead, I returned them to the agents, Farm Vehicles, and gave strict instructions that no one was allowed to remove them without written authority from me. Somehow, however, someone took those vehicles whilst I was away on patrol (in my own private vehicle) and drove them to Dar. I never got a mile out of them and had the embarrassment of telling Prof. Grzimek that his gift was being put to other uses.

I was beginning to suspect that members of the game division in Arusha were deeply involved in the big poaching racket that I had come to smash. Daily my suspicions grew stronger, nourished by my seeing the same local trophy dealers always hanging around the Permit and Revenue offices. The filthy state of the storage areas there also helped convince me that the people running the game offices had not the slightest interest in their work.

Too, I was receiving reports from professional hunters, farmers, and others of game division Land Rovers loaded with skins and meat, and of shots being heard all through the bush both day and night. These reports suggested that game division staff were busy making illegal money from wildlife.

However, I decided the best policy for the moment was to keep my eyes and ears open and pretend that I didn't notice anything. I kept a careful watch, hoping for a break so that I could catch them all in one fell swoop. During the months of January to April 1970, unknown to the other members of the game division at Arusha, I had been quietly establishing my team of informers. I contacted these men at night and paid them good money for work well done. My police guard, John Singgulubaba (I could never pronounce his name), used to act as a go-between, from time to time bringing me snippets of information from police informers. On moonlit nights, I would tell John to tell an informer to wait for me at a certain dark and lonely spot; then I would pick him up in my car and keep on driving along the Nairobi road until I had his story. I didn't use this method too often, however, for fear of being followed.

I had no funds from the government to pay these informers, so at first I paid them from my own pocket. Once we began to get results and convictions, I could pay them from the fines imposed by the courts or from the sales of confiscated trophies. This system worked well—the informers were happy because they were paid immediately. Formerly, they'd had to wait as long as a whole year before their rewards came from Dar es Salaam.

I had been in Arusha some four months, slowly setting up my secret force of informers,

when an article detailing some of my activities appeared in the *Tanzanian Standard* newspaper dated 30 December 1969. This article came completely out of the blue, and to this day I don't know who was responsible. Repercussions started immediately. The first came, as I had expected, from James Kahurananga, who said that I would be dismissed for releasing this information. He didn't believe me when I told him I had nothing at all to do with it.

"I'll see to it that you are punished for this," he said, and sure enough, on 4 January 1970 Kahurananga summoned me to his office

The author took this picture of a herd of elephants, consisting of between 150 and 170 animals, from an airplane owned by Dr. Hugh Lampery. He estimated that there were at least three bull elephants with tusks well over the hundred-pound mark. Katavi Game Reserve, 1968.

and proudly told me that the head office in Dar had issued me an air ticket and instructions that I leave for Dar that very afternoon. I could tell from his smug attitude that he thought I was going to be fired. I was not in the least perturbed, however; I had only recently been reinstated on the president's orders, and it seemed most unlikely that the powers-that-be would have changed their minds at this early stage.

I arrived in Dar late that evening and found that a vehicle had been sent to meet me and that I had been booked at the New Africa Hotel. At eight the following morning I reported to the chief game warden, who told me confidentially that I'd been summoned because the president and government wished that action be taken immediately to control the burgeoning problem of commercial poaching. From the hotel room I was to draw up a proposal to handle the problem. The proposal would go to the principal secretary, Mr. Kileo, who in turn would take it to the minister.

Before writing the proposal, I contacted Tom Mgondah, senior game warden at H.Q. Tom, an excellent fellow and a sincere friend, would give you his last penny if you were in need[1]. He told me he knew all about the *fitina* (intrigue) directed toward me and that I should watch both James Kahurananga and David Mwakamyamale, who were trying their damnedest to get me kicked out of Tanzania or sent to jail. Tom assured me that the regional commissioner, Aaron Mwakangata; the regional police commander, Mr. Shungu; the regional CID officer, Francis Sabuni; the chief game warden, Mr. Mahinda; and Mr.

Kileo would continue to support me, so I had no worries.

This friendly advice gave me confidence, and I soon completed my proposal and recommendations, which I handed over to the chief game warden on 7 January 1970 before flying back to Arusha that same evening. Here is the essence of the letter I wrote:

Mr. G. J. Kileo
Director of Natural Resources Division
P.O. Box 426
Dar es Salaam

Sir:

I have the honour to submit this short report on the poaching problem, which is causing grave concern to us all. I also submit my proposals for your consideration and onward transmission to our Minister. These proposals are the ideas of Tom Magonda and myself combined, and are designed to remedy this gigantic problem. . . . I hope that this report will help you and members of your committee to come to some definite solutions to this deteriorating situation.

It is quite obvious to us all that this poaching problem and illegal trade in trophies is on an alarming increase. Poaching throughout Tanzania (more so in the northern and Serengeti areas) had increased almost 100 percent within the past few years and, if it is not checked immediately, will certainly affect the whole economy and tourist trade of this wonderful country. I am very happy that a decision has been made to deal with this national problem.

Before proceeding further, I would like to submit for evidence the following facts and

1. During my visit to Tanzanina in 1998, I was told that Mgondah had died, either by poison or by witchcraft. It was sad news, as he was one of the very few honest ones.

figures, which have only come to light during the past few weeks.

We have all read or heard about the shocking reports where poachers recently poisoned a permanent water hole in the Northern Region, killing hundreds of innocent animals and birds. These poor animals, like zebras are forced to water holes during the drier months of the year, and it is here that the thirsty animals are concentrated and are most vulnerable to these horrid poachers.

Recent reports indicate that 75 percent of all water holes in Masailand have tree platforms or pits where poachers sit and wait for these thirsty animals. Many water holes have been rendered useless due to rhinos and other animals dying right in the water after being shot and left to rot. Further reports indicate that the leopard is fast being annihilated. Information received and my own investigations show that an estimated 100 to 125 leopard skins illegally poached are passing through the Northern Region alone every month, most of them going to Kenya. One poacher admits that he had four gangs working for him full time and that each gang operates 60 to 80 traps. These gangs concentrate on leopard, with an occasional rhino here and there. He told me that he spends 4,000 to 5,000 shillings[2] each month to purchase goats, which he uses in his traps. His main areas for operation are the Rift Wall, Olduvai in the conservation area, and Mbulu District right into the Ngorongoro highlands and crater. This man is a big-time operator, handling not only illegal trophies but also gemstones. I am ashamed to report that he claims his two main buyers are Europeans from Kenya. I am at present posing

as a buyer and pretending to offer him more than his other buyers. He is very clever and cunning, but I am sure I will catch him in the end.

I was told by one my informers that another poacher from Singida had recently come to Arusha. I arranged to meet this poacher, who had two rhino horns. I was about to arrest him when he told me he had fourteen more rhino horns at his home. I told him to go and collect them and to come back with them in a couple of days; otherwise, I wouldn't buy them. He came back, and we arrested him with the fourteen horns.

Until recently, only the rhino and leopard were really being hammered, but now I am afraid the zebra is an ever-increasing target for these commercial poachers. Motorized gangs are slaughtering hundreds of zebra weekly in the Northern Region. These poor animals are far more vulnerable to the poacher than, say, the leopard or rhino. Zebra are gregarious and concentrate near permanent water during the drier spells; it is here that the motorized gangs chase these unfortunate beasts for miles, shooting wantonly, wounding many, whilst others die of sheer exhaustion. The poachers only remove the skins, leaving the carcasses to rot or become food for the scavengers.

These and similar reports are coming in daily, and disturbing information has started to come in even from the national parks. Professional hunters are really concerned as Tanzania is famed for its fine hunting and photographing areas. These areas are now being poached extensively.

I am very sorry to have to report that another of our big headaches is the extensive poaching

---

2. These and other figures in this chapter are given in Tanganyikan shillings. In the 1960s and 1970s, seven Tanganyikan shillings were the equivalent of one U.S. dollar, and three U.S. dollars equaled one pound sterling.

done by the armed forces, police, and other government officials. These are the very people who should be helping us to protect the wonderful fauna of this country.

The rest of my report contained a plea for rigorous implementation of a series of detailed proposals calling for increased funding for antipoaching forces (including higher salaries for workers and rewards to informers), increased antipoaching authority for professional hunters, tightened controls over arms and ammunition and over trophies bought at government auctions, and more teeth in the sentencing of lawbreakers.

Unhappily, most of my proposals were never implemented.

I returned to Arusha—much to Kahurananga and company's disgust, since rumours were already circulating that Bwana Balson had been dismissed. I moved to our new house and began to set up my plan of operation.

The following story illustrates how bad things were becoming in Tanzania's Northern Region at that time:

Joe Newby, a professional hunter mentioned in an earlier chapter, was hunting with an American client during January 1970 in the Simanjiro/Lolkisali Controlled Area. Early one morning they were sitting on top of a small hill, scanning the country for a good buffalo, when a Land Rover appeared in a *mbuga* (open plain) just below them. The Land Rover was going like the clappers chasing a herd of zebra. Through their binoculars the hunters could see people standing in the back of the vehicle shooting; several animals fell, and others were left struggling with broken limbs.

"What the hell is going on?" the client demanded. "I thought we were the only guys to hunt in this damn area."

"That's correct," replied Joe, "but it appears we have some guests. Let's go down and see who they are."

They drove up to the Land Rover, which Joe identified right away as a government vehicle; some of the men wore game scout uniforms.

"What do you think you are doing chasing animals and shooting from the vehicle," Joe said, "and who gave you permission to hunt in this controlled area?"

The game assistant in charge, a scoundrel named Christopher Nina, had the bloody cheek to tell Joe and his client to mind their own business, and that they were members of the game division and were carrying out some important research work. This fellow Nina, a very shabby character, said he had been sent to do this so-called research by Kahurananga.

Joe, who was fuming mad, replied, "Important research, my fat arse. What's so important that you have to chase these beasts, shoot twelve and wound I don't know how many more, skin them as fast as you can, and just leave the carcasses to rot in the sun?"

Nina retorted, "I have told you once to mind your own business; don't ask any more questions and clear out of this area. These are my last orders to you."

The client had had enough. He leapt at Nina and was about to let fly with his boot when Joe stepped between them. The client raged, "You bastards are poaching, and you'd better believe I'll get the authorities to lay it on you." And he did just that, reporting the matter to me on his return from the bush.

Joe managed to drag the client away and then headed back to camp, where he said, "Eric

121

Balson would be very interested to know about this incident."

"Joe," the client said, "you go ahead to Arusha to tell Balson, and I will remain in camp with my old friend bourbon to keep me happy."

Joe motored all day over 165 miles of really rough roads to Arusha to see me, told me his story, then drove back through the night to be ready to take his client hunting the next morning.

On hearing Joe's story, I stormed into Kahurananga's office and demanded to know what the hell this fellow Nina was doing shooting twelve zebra. Kahurananga said he would investigate but added that Nina was a good game assistant who wouldn't break the law.

"I have a research station near there," he said, "and what goes on there is none of your business, so please keep your nose out of my work."

The very next day Nina sauntered into the game division office carrying *one* zebra skin, which he took into Kahurananga's office. Nina's tale was that he had shot this zebra, which had been left wounded by Newby and his client. He also reported that the hunters had sworn at him, a government servant, while he was doing his duty.

Kahurananga said, "You see, Balson, your professional hunter friend seems to be the one at fault."

"I have never heard such utter bulls--- in my whole life," I said angrily, walking out of that office before I really lost my temper.

I was fast discovering that the problem of poaching and illegal sale of animal products was a cancer whose tentacles reached into the highest levels of the Tanzanian government.

An especially vulnerable area was the procedure for importing or exporting trophies. It was almost jokingly simple for authorities to falsify certificates of ownership or export permits, allowing thousands of trophies, especially zebra skins, to leave Tanzania illegally.

It was very difficult for me to prove that this chicanery was going on. Through intrigue and more than a few dangerous episodes, I was able to determine that the "big fish" in the poaching pool included Kahurananga; David Mwakamyamale, the game division's permit officer[3]; and none other than the well-respected Saidi Kawaha, senior game assistant and brother of Rashidi Kawaha, vice president of Tanzania! Those names were included in a letter I wrote to Mr. Shungu, the regional police commander.

At this stage of the drama I thought it best to ask Mr. Shungu for some protection, as I had already received a couple of threats by phone. I had the phone removed from my house, and that night two armed policemen came to guard my house. I prepared myself as well: I had been issued one .38 pistol, and my friend Brian Nicholson loaned me another, a .38 automatic. If these chaps meant business, at least I wouldn't be caught napping.

Mr. Shungu also assigned to me a police corporal named Dominic, who was alleged to be a crack pistol shot. Shungu suggested that this man travel with me and work as my assistant and bodyguard.

I had previously told Shungu that I was intent on catching a big-wheel poacher/seller, and that I would not give up until he was

---

3. On my visit to Tanzania in 1998, I heard that Mwakamyamale had died of AIDS. I thought to myself, *bloody good news.*

Myles Turner, deputy chief park warden of the Serengeti National Park, and Balson did a combined antipoaching exercise in the Loloindo, Klien's Camp area. The picture you see here shows some of the thousands of wire snares they found and destroyed. Myles and Kay Turner's son, Michael, is sitting on the snares.

behind bars. An informer had told me of a person who had fourteen leopard skins and twelve rhino horns for sale, and that he would sell them only to a *mzungu* (white man) from Kenya. This seemed an ideal situation for me to pose as a buyer, which I did occasionally. I passed the word that the *mzungu* from Kenya had arrived in Arusha and wanted to buy all this man's trophies. Through my informer, I arranged to meet this man at night on the Nairobi road. His name was Saidi and he worked for a "big boss" who lived on the slopes of Mount Meru. I told him I would only do business with his boss and no one else. He said that they had been caught twice before and were reluctant to trust me. But finally, after several meetings at different rendezvous, I met the big wheel. He told me politely that if I split on him and he was caught by the police, he would personally cut my throat with a blunt knife. This made me even more determined to catch him.

After two weeks of bargaining, I persuaded this poacher to show me the trophies and his hideout in the forest. The day was fixed, and Dominic and I drove to a certain spot and parked the car. The stooge, Saidi, was there to meet us. Saidi led the way on foot. It was beginning to get dark, and we hadn't the faintest idea where we were going. Both Dominic and I were armed, and I had told him we might be ambushed on the way through the forest. Mist was settling in the valleys, and a cold nip was in the air. We had prepared ourselves with thick clothing and overcoats. We walked along a winding, never-ending path that passed through countless banana plantations, our faces cold and wet from water dripping from the overhanging leaves.

After a good hour, we left the plantations behind and entered the forest. The path was dim, so we had to stay close to each other. What an eerie feeling it is to walk in a strange forest in pitch darkness, not knowing what lies ahead. After about a mile, our guide stopped and gave a low whistle, a signal to alert others that we were approaching and not to shoot us.

The path ended where a huge overhanging bush blocked our way. Saidi told us to get down on hands and knees and follow him. We crawled a few paces, and then found a big fallen tree in front of us. He signaled us to climb up onto a branch that he had already scaled. We followed carefully until we were on the main trunk on this gigantic supine tree. The moss on it was damp and very slippery.

Suddenly Dominic lost his footing and fell off the log, landing somewhere in the dense undergrowth below. He let out an almighty howl and hurriedly climbed back up. He assured me he was OK but explained that he had fallen slap into the middle of some stinging nettles.

We soon reached the hide, cunningly concealed beneath the base of the big fallen tree. The big wheel was there to greet us. "*Karibu* (come in)," he said. The hide was not very big,

and it smelt like an outhouse. I nearly honked my ring when I got inside. One soon became used to the smell, but the bloody smoke from the fire had my eyes smarting and watering as if I were crying; I wondered how I was going to last the night amongst this lot.

I asked where were the trophies we had come all this way to see. Saidi was detailed to go and fetch them (they were never kept in the same place the men used for sleeping). Whilst Saidi was gone, we were offered some of the local *pombe* (beer) and *bhang* (marijuana). I declined both. Dominic took a couple of swigs from a large beer mug and appeared to be quite content.

The hide seemed well used: There were two beds made out of sticks and grass, a few pots and battered tin mugs, a couple of homemade stools, and bits of torn clothing and old blankets hanging from the roof.

I asked the big wheel how many men worked for him, and he said he operated five teams who did nothing but trap leopard. "I have about three hundred goats that are used only for trapping," he said. "During the day my men tend the grazing goats and look for places to set up traps. Each team operates in a different locality." Places he mentioned were Manyara National Park; the forest around Mto-Wa-Mbu; the forests at the foot of the rift wall at Kitete, Olmoti, and Monduli mountains; Ngorongoro Crater highlands; and the Oldeani forests right down into the conservation area at Endulen. He told me he exported from sixty to eighty leopard skins and twenty to thirty rhino horns *each month*.

Saidi and another man came back with the trophies; the skins looked to be in good condition and were well salted. I asked how it was that the skins were not marked with any bullet holes or spear marks. He explained this in great detail: Traps were constructed out of logs in the shape of an upside-down V. The entrance to each was left open, with a door suspended above. To this was attached a small tripwire; when the leopard entered the trap to grab a goat, it touched this wire, triggering the door, which slammed shut behind the animal. Goats used as bait were tied so that they could not escape and would call for the rest of the herd, attracting leopard and hyena.

"When my men find a leopard in the trap, they light a small fire to heat up their sharp spears. One man goes in front of the leopard to attract its attention whilst another grabs hold of its tail. Then a spear is pushed right up the anus of the leopard into its stomach, and it soon dies, hence the lack of marks. *Marifa mzuri sana* (very good method)," he concluded.

You bloody, fornicating bastard, I thought to myself. *I wish I could stuff a red-hot spear up your arse to see if it really is* marifa mzuri sana.

With fourteen leopard skins and twelve rhino horns right there in front of me, I felt like taking out my pistol and shooting all three poachers right there and then, but I wanted to catch as many as possible. We agreed upon a price after much haggling: 800 shillings for a leopard and 40 shillings per pound for the rhino horn. The final transaction would take place the following evening.

He would wait for me at 8:00 P.M. beside an old cattle dip just outside a hellhole called Ngare Mtoni. As I approached the dip, I was to flash the car's right front blinker, slow down, and do a sharp U-turn. Dominic would open the door, whereupon the poachers would throw in the sacks containing the trophies. I would hand over the money through the offside window so that no one would see the receiver. Saidi would be there with the big wheel, and I was to come with only Dominic.

Just prior to our parting, the big wheel asked for some money so he could pay porters to help carry the trophies to our meeting place (a distance of about six miles). I gave him two hundred shillings in ten-shilling notes; all of their serial numbers had been recorded by the police.

Boy, was I glad to get away from that place, with its mingled smells of beer, sweat, *bhang*, and smoke, mixed with stale farts; those bastards could fart like zebra!

All was set. Another car, full of police, would drive right on my tail without any lights. In my own car I would have three men who would hide on the floor, and as the door was opened they would jump out and grab both poachers.

At three minutes to eight I started off along the main Nairobi road, driving slowly with the other car close behind. As I approached the meeting place, I told the police in my car to lie low. When the dip came into sight, I started to flash my right blinker, slowed almost to a stop, and did the U-turn. As I did this, Dominic opened the back door as well as his own. There were the two poachers with the sacks ready. They were just about to load them into the back of my car when the three chaps back there leapt out, together with Dominic, and grabbed the culprits.

It was all over in seconds. The pair were handcuffed and put into the back of my car with a policeman and Dominic. On the way to the police station, Mr. Big Wheel took out a cigarette and asked the policeman to light it for him as his other hand was cuffed. He appeared too calm and collected for my liking.

At the station they were searched. Big Wheel still had most of the shilling notes I had given him the previous night, tied in a dirty old hanky. The two gunnysacks were emptied onto the floor. One held only dried-up banana stems folded to the same size as a leopard skin. The other contained twelve pieces of wood carved in the exact shape of rhino horns. They would have fooled even an expert in the dark. I swore under my breath. Little did he know that the bag I was going to hand him contained only pieces of paper bag cut up to the size of notes.

Big Wheel was laughing at us and demanding to know why we had arrested him. He said he was going to sue the government for wrongful arrest. Then I asked Corporal Dominic to check the numbers of the notes I had given Big Wheel the night before, and of course the numbers tallied.

When the case came up in court, we were able to charge him only with obtaining money under false pretences, and I was able to play for the Magistrate recordings of most of the meetings I'd had with the accused prior to his arrest. I had carefully installed in the boot of Viva's Datsun a small tape recorder and hidden the microphone in the roof. You should have seen the accused's face when he heard himself talking. I am happy to say that he and Saidi were locked away for a year—but we had the last laugh.

I went back with police and game staff to try to locate their hideout but never could find the place. We did hear from the locals around there, though, that the poachers had given up killing leopard because a *kali mzungu* (fierce white man) had just come to Arusha who had special *dawa* (medicine) that could catch all those who broke the law.

After many such episodes over the ensuing months, I became disheartened, disgusted, and depressed by all the bribery, corruption, and political chicanery that were eroding Tanzania's wonderful wildlife resource. Finally, I drove to Dar es Salaam and handed in my resignation.

Just before my decision to leave Tanzania, Robin Brown, who worked for a television network based in Great Britain, wrote me to ask if he could come to Tanzania to do a documentary on the poaching. The government gave him permission, and I escorted him and assisted in the production of his documentary—also called *Animal Wars*—which told at least some of the story. Robin Brown wrote about me in his book, *Bye Bye Shangri-La*. When I read his story, I felt honoured that at least someone had recognized what I had battled to do. He wrote:

Eric Balson launched an incredibly brave clandestine operation to try and save Tanganyika's wildlife from what was turning into a holocaust of poaching. In the next ten years it [the poaching] accounted for at least 75,000 elephants, an illegal cull from which the Tanzanian elephant population has never recovered.

He went disguised and alone into the mountains at night, posing as a buyer. He sat in mountain caves bartering with poachers for leopard skins, killed by the repulsive method of a heated spear in the anus to avoid damaging the skin, and went on doing it long after word got around that there was a secret agent at work. On another trip he took a load of ivory to the coast in an attempt to trap an Arab dhow captain he knew was running illegal ivory and rhino horn out of the country.

He set up a network of informers who would call him at night at his house in Arusha. These agents were often "reformed" poachers themselves and would refuse to come anywhere near the house, forcing Eric to see them in the dark. Any one of them could have been an assassin.

At the same time, Eric used game department records to demonstrate that thousands of skins, ivory, and rhino horns were being laundered through Tanzania using stolen export permits from Kenya. One of the people implicated was the prime minister's brother. Twice, cars were used in attempts to run Eric down. He kept two armed guards at his house, night and day, and never went anywhere without at least two handguns. Hence to meet the bravest champion of animals I have ever known, Eric Balson.

As Viva and I packed up to leave our beloved Tanzania and head for new pastures in Zambia, some of the headlines in the newspapers read: "Tanzania's war on poachers," "Wildlife threatened—the lives of millions of animals," "Illegal trophies sent to Kenya," "When will the killing stop?" "Poachers on the rampage in the Northern Circuit," and on and on and on. I could fill many pages of this book from the four scrapbooks I kept filled with cuttings about this horrid illegal trade.

I left that magnificent land with tears for its fauna and flora. Few of my partings from workplaces tore my heart quite like leaving Tanzania; it seemed that loyalty counted for nothing anymore.

"Charging through the Mud" *by Mike Ghaui.*

CHAPTER SEVEN
On the Wilderness Trail with Norman Carr

In 1972, as we drove across the border at Tunduma into Zambia, I felt a huge burden drop off my back and was ready to face my new challenge. I had secured the position of managing director for an American organization, Wildlife Conservation International (WCI), to supervise the management and development of the newly gazetted Lower Zambezi National Park. Management of the park for twenty-five years had been entrusted to WCI by President Kaunda of Zambia.

By some coincidence, the house we rented had been built by the brother of the legendary author Norman Carr, and because of this we met up with Norman. When Prince Bernhard heard that Viva and I knew Norman, he wrote asking if I could arrange both a safari to the then-famous Luangwa Valley and a personal meeting with the author. He had read some of Carr's books and had had to cancel at the last minute a safari planned with Norman. The prince had also written a foreword to one of Carr's books, *The White Impala*.

Among Norman's other books was *Return to the Wild*, which describes how he reared two male lion cubs he found orphaned and returned them to the wilds. I think I am right in saying

that Norman was the first person to "walk with lion," many years before Joy and George Adamson did. Another of his books carries the title *Valley of the Elephants*, which relates his feelings about the Luangwa Valley, where he was buried alongside some of his best friends.

Viva and I grew very close to Norman, and whenever the opportunity arose to visit with him in one of his camps along the Luangwa River, we would jump at it. Our eldest son, Alan, worked for Norman for some time as an assistant guide, taking tourists on foot safaris. PB wanted to meet Norman and walk with him and our gang on one of his foot safaris.

So I made arrangements for our August 1973 safari to the Luangwa Valley and set up our camp just north of Norman's Chibembe camp, situated on high banks above the river. Viva and our three sons helped with the preparations and building the camp. We had to build a grass fence around most of the camp to stop the elephant and hippo from walking through. Once the work was completed, we had a few days to "play" and do some reconnaissance, getting to know the area.

It was beginning to get really dry, which made the Luangwa River a walking mass of wildlife everywhere one looked. Some of the larger pools

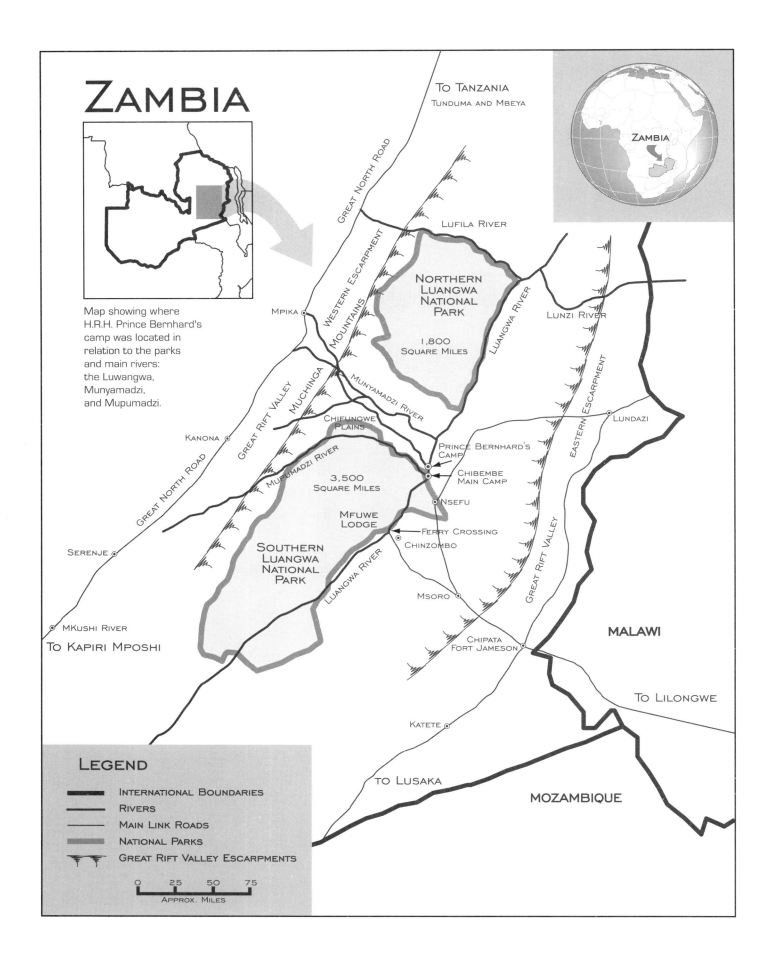

ZAMBIA

Map showing where
H.R.H. Prince Bernhard's
camp was located in
relation to the parks
and main rivers:
the Luwangwa,
Munyamadzi,
and Mupumadzi.

ZAMBIA

TO TANZANIA
TUNDUMA AND MBEYA

GREAT NORTH ROAD

LUFILA RIVER

WESTERN ESCARPMENT
MOUNTAINS

NORTHERN
LUANGWA
NATIONAL
PARK

1,800
SQUARE MILES

LUANGWA RIVER

LUNZI RIVER

MPIKA

MUCHINGA

GREAT RIFT VALLEY

MUNYAMADZI RIVER

CHIFUNGWE
PLAINS

KANONA

MUPUMADZI RIVER

3,500
SQUARE MILES

EASTERN ESCARPMENT

LUNDAZI

PRINCE BERNHARD'S
CAMP

CHIBEMBE
MAIN CAMP

MFUWE
LODGE

NSEFU

FERRY CROSSING

CHINZOMBO

SOUTHERN
LUANGWA
NATIONAL
PARK

SERENJE

GREAT NORTH ROAD

LUANGWA RIVER

MSORO

GREAT RIFT VALLEY

MALAWI

MKUSHI RIVER

TO KAPIRI MPOSHI

CHIPATA
FORT JAMESON

TO LILONGWE

KATETE

TO LUSAKA

MOZAMBIQUE

LEGEND

▬▬	INTERNATIONAL BOUNDARIES
—	RIVERS
—	MAIN LINK ROADS
▬▬	NATIONAL PARKS
⋏⋏	GREAT RIFT VALLEY ESCARPMENTS

0   25   50   75
APPROX. MILES

A large crocodile is working on his hippo supper, while others are about to join in the feast, just outside the Luangwa Game Reserve, Zambia, 1973.

created during the rains were drying out, and thousands of birds could be found feeding on the fish trapped in these pools. Marabou storks would wait until a yellow-billed or woolly-necked stork would catch a catfish, then make a charge and steal the wriggling fish from its long beak. One could spend hours just watching their antics.

We had to return to Lusaka, for Prince Bernhard was due to fly in. I had to check that the chartered planes were ready to fly the gang into the Mfuwe airstrip, about forty miles from our camp at Chibembe, which was located just outside the park's southern boundary.

All went according to plan, and our vehicles—and Norman Carr—were on hand to meet us. After all the handshaking and

introductions, Norman invited PB for a drink at the Mfuwe lodge. On the way to camp, we were stopped by a breeding herd of elephant going to the river to drink. PB was in his element, watching his favourite animals. We arrived, and PB, as always, was most complimentary about the camp and his tent's view.

What perfect weather we had throughout that safari! We walked many miles, with the knowledgeable Norman keeping us all informed about the animals and the history of the valley. On some days we encountered as many as forty black rhino. Today, thirty years later, there is not *one* left, all fallen to the guns of poachers. *Catastrophe* is not a strong enough word to use. The same goes for the elephant; thousands succumbed to poachers' bullets, but today one can still find a few pachyderms that survived the onslaught.

One day, during a foot safari along the river, we saw hundreds of crocodile swimming upstream. Norman informed us that probably a hippo had been killed by another hippo— during the night we'd heard a furious battle taking place upstream.

Not a mile farther on we watched some vultures circle and then swoop down toward the river. On closer examination we saw the swollen body of a hippo floating slowly downstream and a couple of lionesses walking on the sand following the carcass, hoping it would come toward the shore. Lion hate to get their feet wet.

As we waited and watched, some of the croc started to arrive, and the lion took to the bush, scared of these vicious reptiles. This is no wonder, for some of the croc exceeded fifteen feet in length and probably weighed in excess of a ton. They were huge. In fact, I had seen a bigger crocodile only once, the one I told you about earlier that attacked our tyre and boat.

Norman suggested that we try to pull the hippo closer to shore and then build a hide out of brush and grass so PB and the others could get spectacular photos of the reptiles eating.

Well, there were no volunteers for that chore, so we just waited until the carcass grounded itself. This happened in a very opportune place, near a high bank. So the rest of the day was spent in building the hide, and our movements did not disturb the hundreds of croc waiting close by for decomposition to commence, which would occur by the following day.

Very early the next morning, we set out for the hide before the elephant started to come down to drink. Norman warned us to watch for hippo, which would be returning from their night's feeding. After an hour's brisk walk, we crept behind the blind. We peered through the holes left in the grass wall, large enough for a telephoto lens to protrude, and were astounded at the number of croc trying to get their share of the dead hippo.

Let me expand on the natural history of this ancient creature. The most extraordinary characteristic of the crocodile is how it has managed to survive from prehistoric times to the present day. It still retains archaic features that link it with the gigantosaurians—yet thanks to evolutionary adaptation, the croc is considered to be among the modern reptiles.

Some ninety million years have elapsed since the croc's enormous fifty-foot ancestor, *Phobosuchus*, ruled the earth. This reptile was worshipped and mummified by the ancient Egyptians and to this day is sacred to some tribes in Papua New Guinea and elsewhere.

There is no questioning the fact that this "flat dog," as the croc is sometimes called, is a fascinating and important creature from a scientific standpoint. The awesome sight of a group of these monsters with their huge jaws agape, sunning themselves on a sandbank, sends cold shivers down one's spine.

The crocodile cannot move its upper jaw; only the lower jaw is articulated. Thus it lacks the snake's ability to open the mouth wide enough to swallow prey much larger than itself.

These dreaded reptiles have some special features. For example, their sensory organs are so highly developed that when the creature submerges, special valves close the nostrils, nictitating membranes lubricate and protect the eyes, a thick opercular flap seals the ear openings, and another muscular flap forms a barrier at the rear of the mouth cavity so that water cannot enter the throat when prey is seized underwater.

The crocodile species are incapable of chewing; their sharp teeth are used chiefly for grasping their prey firmly prior to swallowing it.

Croc are capable of storing food temporarily in the muscular pouch suspended from the lower jaw. When they are feeding on large, decomposing carcasses, they grab a chunk of skin or meat in their strong jaws and twist over and over until the morsel breaks away; they then swallow it whole, for they cannot chew. Fish, turtles, ducks, geese, and other small creatures are also swallowed whole. Crocodile propel themselves through the water with serpentine body movements. The head is always pointed in the direction in which they wish to travel, and each sideways swish of the tail has to be counterbalanced by a movement of the rest of their body to the other side.

Croc are often seen basking in the sun with their mouths open, which helps regulate their body temperature. Heat loss by evaporation and radiation through the mucous in the mouth enables these reptiles to maintain their body temperatures at acceptable levels. Their temperature-regulating system is more characteristic of mammals than of other reptiles.

During mating season, the males have been heard to roar, making sounds like distant

Prince Bernhard with his 16mm Bolex cine camera on Norman Carr's safari (Eric Balson in background). Luangwa Valley, Zambia, 1973.

This black rhino is about to charge the author and his party. When the rhino charged, they stood their ground and hid behind some large acacia tree trunks; Balson threw a rock at the rhino as it dashed past, and it got such a fright that it ran off, snorting.

thunder; the female may emit an occasional higher-pitched roar in response to the male, but otherwise they remain completely silent. Of course, as the breeding season approaches, there are fights between rival males over females or to defend territories.

The morning sun was just rising above the trees by the time the cameras were ready to commence shooting. The water around the hippo carcass was boiling with crocodile twisting and turning in their efforts to tear off chunks to swallow. PB's 16mm Bolex was churning away, as was mine. Coen and Hans were busy clicking away and changing spools. Those croc that had full stomachs were basking in the early morning sun; as we watched, blacksmith plovers rummaged about

inside their open jaws in search of leeches, pieces of meat, or small invertebrates. It appeared that these were the only birds allowed to do this. Other species of birds— including Egyptian geese, storks, ibises, herons, and ducks—were tolerated nearby but not permitted to pick the mouths.

Watching this primeval scene, an observer couldn't help but wonder how the crocodile has managed to survive for thousands of years when almost every other creature from ancient times has long since perished. During the past century, archaeologists and other scientists have found fossil remains and artifacts that have opened the door on prehistory so that today we have a much better understanding of the Jurassic age and beyond.

The "stage" before us was an endless source of interest and entertainment. And as if that wasn't enough, an old bull elephant walked along the opposite bank and proceeded to show us how strong he was by pushing down a huge acacia tree as if it were a mere fence post. Amazing. I myself have tried to push over huge trees with a D8 Caterpillar tractor and had great difficulty in doing so. Elephant have to spend three-quarters of each day foraging for food. This old bull was having a tough time finding food within reach of his trunk, so he just shoved the tree down and had ample food for the time being.

Eight hours passed in a seeming wink of an eye. We completely forgot that we had to walk back to camp before dark.

How peaceful it is just to sit and relax after a hard day's trek and have the privilege of watching a magnificent kudu bull suddenly appear. He had likely spent most of the day resting or sleeping under an evergreen Natal mahogany tree. This species of tree, in my opinion, is the best in the African bush for shade and to shelter one's tent or fly camp. You must be aware, however, that snakes often hide in its green canopy to ambush small birds that also flock to this tree to hide from raptors.

As the kudu made his way gingerly to the water's edge, a pair of white-headed plovers dive-bombed him and then flew to an open space and performed all kinds of antics to divert the intruder's attention from their nest. Before the kudu drank, he surveyed the murky water in front of him, knowing that perhaps a big croc could be waiting for him to begin drinking before grabbing his snout and dragging him into the water. In fact, this majestic beast decided not to drink but instead walked back up the bank and started to pick up the sweet-scented flowers that had fallen from a sausage tree. Just then a lion roared on our side of the river. The kudu looked up and listened, and when he was satisfied that all was clear, he continued his search for flowers. As the sun set behind us, the kudu disappeared.

Along the larger rivers in eastern and southern Africa during July–August, it gets pretty nippy once the sun drops. So we gathered around a roaring bonfire to talk about the plans for a long "wilderness trail" trek over the next few days. Norman Carr was the first, to my knowledge, to inaugurate this type of walking safari.

Thanks to the invention of the four-wheel-drive vehicle, a journey that used to take a month on foot can now be accomplished in a day or two. One soon forgets how peaceful and revealing it is to travel on foot rather than in a noisy, smelly motor vehicle, from which almost every animal flees on sight. One of the main reasons for PB's safari, besides having the opportunity to meet and travel with Norman on a wilderness trail, was to savour something of the glamour, excitement, and atmosphere of the "real Africa" as it used to be.

I had heard and read a lot about the Munyamadzi River; some said it was even better than the Mbarangandu in the Selous. I doubted it. So I had suggested to Norman that our wilderness trail safari with PB include the Munyamadzi, so we could judge how it compares with the Selous' Mbarangandu. And so around the campfire it was voted unanimously that this would be our plan for the morrow. As Norman bid good-night, he said, "Tomorrow morning we leave at the crack of dawn, so have a good sleep as we have a long walk ahead of us."

I snuggled beneath crisp, clean sheets listening to the water murmur over small boulders in the river, combined with the strange choir of frogs and hippo interrupted by the *prrrup-prrrup* of the scops owl. In the distance I could hear the call of the *fisi* (hyena). No African night is complete without this nocturnal symphony. I thanked the dear Lord for giving us such a wonderful world to live in and enjoy.

One of the best-known calls of the wilds of Africa is that of the Cape turtledove. It is usually the one you wake up to. Its *kuk-cooo-kuk* or softer *coooc-currr* is a peaceful accompaniment to your morning tea or coffee. Here on the Luangwa, one is hardly ever out of hearing of the *hur-hur-hur-hur-hur* of the Egyptian goose, followed by its honking *ha-ha-ha-ha-ha* as it takes off. These birds are usually seen in pairs and are said to mate for life. These sounds and the honking of the hippo serenaded us as we set off on our wilderness safari that crisp morning.

Our walking pace was leisurely. I took up the rear, my .470 cradled in the crook of my arm or slung over one shoulder. I formed a sort of backstop, as Coen and Hans were forever stopping to check on a new bird to add to their list. They would get excited, chattering like kids with a new toy, when I agreed that "You can add that one to your list." PB was up in front with Norman, who would stop every now and then to show PB something or for PB to kindle his pipe.

Our game guards followed behind, escorting the porters carrying our camp equipment. The cooks carried only their own personal effects. Norman had told them where we would camp, so they packed up the camp whilst we went ahead.

We saw many family groups of elephant, a few black rhino, plus two large herds of buffalo. It is difficult to count these large herds because they are constantly on the move amidst a great deal of dust created by hundreds of hoofs.

At the junction of the Munyamadzi and the Luangwa, Norman called a halt to explain about the vultures, which were spiraling in ever-increasing circles, gaining height without flapping their wing, just soaring on the thermals. These creatures have phenomenal eyesight, which they use to watch for other vultures suddenly folding their massive wings and "stooping" toward the ground. As mentioned earlier, this behaviour indicates that something is dead or dying and means *chakula* (food) for the big birds. It attracts every other vulture within miles, and soon the sky is alive with three or four species of vultures, all dropping out of the sky onto the target.

To me these fascinating creatures are a source of interest and joy; others think of them as repulsive carrion scavengers. They play a vital role in the ecosystem. They can be very aggressive when hungry. On a sandbar not far from where we sat, many vultures squatted with their wings outstretched, absorbing the sun's rays. Also enjoying those rays were half a dozen huge crocodile with their mouths open.

The Munyamadzi was crystal-clear in comparison to the dirty Luangwa, churned up by perhaps thousands of hippo upstream. None of us could resist the enticingly cool, clear waters after our six-hour walk during the dry heat of the day. No ladies were present, so no protocol was called for; we all threw our clothes over the bushes before splashing into the warmish water naked as the day we were born.

The companionship and contentment on our walk are difficult to explain. One has to experience them to know what I mean. Here were five people joined together by the lure of the wilds, walking in the wilderness and watching nature at its best.

Norman said, "I can hear our carriers talking—let's get ahead of them or we will miss out on the game animals that usually come down to drink at this time of the day." Scrambling to our feet, we followed the leader, watching ahead for any signs of the Big Five. Many puku and waterbuck lay about under the large *Acacia albida*, commonly known as the winterthorn or apple-ring tree. *What a serene setting for a movie,* I thought as we strolled along.

Suddenly, to our left I noticed a big old elephant bull standing on his hind legs with his trunk at full stretch, trying to pick off some apple-ring pods from the high branches.[1] We headed toward him in the hopes of getting good pictures. The wind was in our favour, and we approached within fifty yards, far enough off so as not to disturb him. Norman announced that we were nearing our fly-camp site for that night, so we could relax, watch the old jumbo, and wait for our rear-guard to arrive, which didn't take long.

The cooks had the fires going and our beds and nets were in place as we sat on stools watching a troop of baboon making their way fortress for the night. Flights of cattle egrets were winging to their roosting trees as the evening faded away into darkness.

One cannot take wild animals for granted. Not far from where we camped, an eccentric but brave lady, Mary Gough, had been killed and eaten by either lion or hyena a couple of years before. No one will ever know the exact cause of her death as she always traveled alone, and she was found several weeks after what must have been a terrible death. Her biggest mistake was to be so trusting toward wild animals.

The next morning we were awakened early by the cooks with a nice hot cup of tea. Over breakfast Norman said we would walk upstream for several miles to our next fly camp,

sited in a lovely place just beneath the Muchinga Mountains. We would sleep there one night and then cut across country on the third day to the Mupamadzi River, which we would then follow downstream back to base camp at Chibembe.

Again leaving the game guards, cooks, and carriers to break camp, we set out with Norman leading the way. A fresh breeze cooled us as we headed upstream toward an escarpment. Red lines across the surrounding mountains and columns of smoke rising into the sky showed where the inevitable bushfires were ravaging the countryside. That morning we moved along at a brisk pace whilst it was still cool, for we had a long way to travel and, hopefully, plenty to see. This was elephant and buffalo country; the elephant calves and old bull buffalo, especially, loved to rest on the cool, wet sands during the heat of the day.

The silence of the woods was broken by the rapidly repeated notes of a greater honeyguide. These remarkable little birds have the unique ability to eat beeswax, and they rely mainly on man and the honey badger to provide this special diet. By using calling and dive-bombing tactics, they can actually lead native honey hunters or a honey badger to bees' nests in hollow tree trunks or rocky outcrops. Once the nest is broken into or axed out, the honeyguide gets its share of wax whilst the hunters get their honey. These birds get very agitated if you fail to follow them, and their chitter-chatter gets monotonous after a while—so much so that you have to throw a stone or stick to chase them away.

Some local honey hunters believe that if you follow a honeyguide, it will lead you to a lion and to your death, so they hate this little

---

1. See the illustration by Mike Ghaui on the title page of this book.

bird. Another interesting habit of the honeyguide species is that they are parasitic in their breeding habits, depositing their eggs in the nests of barbets and woodpeckers.

I spotted some movement in the short grass, and then saw the head of a lion. We moved up the riverbank to higher ground and could now see two lionesses feeding on a waterbuck. We approached carefully, hoping not to scare them away, but some vultures took off, making the lion run off a short distance. They turned to face us before snarling and vanishing into the long, yellow grass.

We paused to make certain the coast was clear, then slid down the embankment and walked toward the carcass. I noticed sudden movement from what we had thought was a dry log washed up during the floods. The log became a gigantic croc. It stood up, stretched, and started to run toward us. I don't think it was charging us, only trying to chase us from the food.

I switched my .470 to my left hand and picked up a piece of driftwood with the right. The big croc opened its jaws, and I placed the chunk of wood into that gaping maw. The jaws immediately slammed closed, snapping that heavy piece of wood as if it were a toothpick. I transferred my double into both hands and hightailed it like a wild thing back to my mates, who were in fits of laughter. I think PB captured it all on movie film. The croc plodded back to its hidey-hole in a small, deep pool covered with floating Nile cabbage.

As we continued our journey, birds flew everywhere, searching for the last of the inland pools, which were drying up very fast. Thousands of fish were stranded and gasping for oxygen as their gills and mouths became clogged with the thick, muddy water. This is why the birds flock to these pools, also called pans: There is so much food.

This feeding frenzy occurs only at this time of the year, and as the water dries up, the fish become more and more concentrated until the water turns into a boiling cauldron of liquid mud. That is when the fish-eating birds arrive, which is what we were about to witness. The scene was set for a dramatic performance, and our cameras were ready to roll

I had seen all this before in Tanzania, but this was the first time for PB and the others. A pair of fish eagles, operating out of a nearby tree, would swoop down, grab a struggling fish with their powerful talons, then fly off, labouring to gain height to get back to their lookout perch. The pelicans seemed to work in unison; they would swim along in a line and then, as if given a signal, all would duck their heads underwater with their flat beaks open, resurface with wriggling fish in their pouches, and swallow them alive. Meanwhile, the yellow-billed storks moved in smaller groups along the banks with their beaks open underwater, disturbing the muddy bed with their feet to chase fish between their beaks. Most of the fish in these pools were catfish, and if they were too big to swallow sideways, the storks would throw them into the air and catch them headfirst.

Some people are bewildered by where these fish come from year after year. Some African tribes believe that *Mungu* (God) sends them from the sky. But what really happens is that a few catfish—or barbel, as they are sometimes called—manage to dig a hole in the mud and seal themselves in during the dry season, leaving a small air hole with a porous seal through which oxygen can flow. Interestingly, this species of fish can remain in a dormant state until the next rainy season. They have rudimentary lungs and can breathe air, whereas all other species of fish depend entirely on water passing through their gills from which they extract oxygen. This was all explained to PB, Coen, and Hans whilst they enjoyed the show.

During this entertainment, I noticed the game guards and their party pass by en route to our next fly camp. Norman suggested that we stay put there and give the staff time to get everything in readiness for our arrival. PB replied, "What a wonderful idea. This is perhaps a chance in a lifetime and is too good

an opportunity not to take full advantage of. The only snag is that I am running out of film."

A bit later, we noted with admiration that the staff had our fly camp set up and working as efficiently as if it had been established for weeks. The cooks were busy preparing supper but had tea ready for anyone who wanted it. Seats were set up around a portable table with a clean tablecloth, and the mess servants were walking around with presupper snacks. I know I have said all this before, but it was mind-boggling to have this level of creature comforts in the bush of darkest Africa.

Hans Gerritsen, Prince Bernhard, and Eric Balson (with Norman Carr in the background) enjoying an early morning breakfast in the bush. Banks of the Munyamadzi River, Zambia, 1973.

After an especially delicious meal washed down with a fine wine, we made for the campfire, a homely but fine place when shared with true and trusting friends. Over the past two weeks we had spent many hours together, and our fellowship had grown stronger. PB received no challenges at either draughts or gin rummy, as he was without doubt the champ at both games, so bed was the next best alternative.

At dawn, the deep, resonant *Ooom, ooom, ooo-ooom* of the southern ground hornbill echoed against the escarpment, followed by the alarm call from a flock of helmeted guinea fowl, a raucous, staccato *Kik-kik-kik-kaaaaaa,* a perfect start for the day.

After a hearty breakfast served around the campfire, we shouldered our *vyombo* (things), such as cameras and rifles, and followed our leader, Norman, who set course for the Chifungwe plains some twelve miles away. The air was brisk, so Norman set a fast pace. I was amazed at how PB, Coen, and Hans kept up with him. On nearing the edge of the plains, we observed a white "cloud" flying low over the high-standing *Hyparrhenia* grass. That cloud of cattle egrets could mean nothing less than a big herd of buffalo on the move. Soon we heard their bellowing and grunts.

The grass, about eight feet tall, made it impossible to see them, but the cattle egrets hovering above the herd indicated that no more than a hundred yards separated us and that the buff were advancing directly at us. We either had to retreat or find another route. This was easier said than done, for Norman was following a well-worn elephant path and the grass on either side was like a wall.

By chance I noticed an enormous anthill to our right and signaled for Norman to follow me. That anthill could not have been more conveniently situated at that precise moment. As we climbed it, the egrets began to fly down and settle on the backs of some buffalo, which meant that the herd leaders had decided to rest.

An hour slipped by without much action except for the occasional bellow from a hungry calf wanting to suckle; no doubt his mother was lying down. Then the wind decided to change direction, and I could feel it on the back of my neck instead of in my face. This often happens in midday. Loud grunts, groans, and bellows erupted from just ahead; the buff fled panic-stricken, and the egrets flew into the air and followed the herd.

We scrambled and slid down from our hill and walked out onto what looked like a small football field with dung heaps, some still steaming, all over the place. The herd must have numbered over two hundred head, judging from the droppings and flattened grass.

Walking through high walls of grass is never a pleasurable pastime, especially when it's getting hot, but when the tops of some palm trees loomed ahead, we knew that the Mupamadzi River was close at hand.

Whilst we soothed our hot feet and cooled off in the water, we watched with glee as family groups and single old bull elephant came and went. You could sense an aura of timelessness here. Norman broke the serene silence: "I hope that our vehicles are waiting for us at the prearranged place; otherwise we have a very long trek ahead back to Chibembe." We eased out of the water and dressed without drying, which would help keep us cool for a few miles.

It is most frustrating to trudge along while thousands of small mopane bees buzz in your ears and eyes. For some unknown reason, there seemed to be many more than usual. PB's fly-swish, working overtime, and plenty of smoke from his pipe helped keep the nuisances at bay. I had broken off a leafy branch and was trying to do the same.

Despite the confounded bees, we were all admiring the peacefulness when a loud trumpet from the opposite bank heralded a small group of elephant. I shook my little handkerchief, which I'd filled with fine wood ash from the campfire that morning, to test the wind. The elephant had picked up our scent—they were stretching their trunks skyward, feeling for our wind.

Norman said he thought he recognized the matriarch and knew her to be very aggressive toward humans—he had had a few encounters with her on previous safaris. He suggested that we give her as wide a berth as possible, especially because one of the females had a tiny baby only a couple of days old. Females are most protective of very young offspring because their little legs are still wobbly. Our better judgment told us to backtrack and do a lengthy detour.

That detour took us through a devastated woodland. Hardly a tree was left standing, and even those few bore the scars of an overpopulation of elephant. This type of habitat destruction can eventually lead to the starvation of hundreds if not thousands of elephant. Such a disaster occurred in the Tsavo National Park in Kenya, where a heavy concentration of elephant, combined with a drought year, wiped out literally thousands of these wonderful animals.

A couple of Thornicroft giraffe stood looking at us as we made our way through this maze of knocked-down or uprooted trees. These lovely animals, tallest in the world, are predominantly browsers, and their fate also stands in the balance, for without trees to feed on, they will perish. That would be another catastrophe, for they are unique and endemic to the Luangwa valley in Zambia.

Resuming our course along the riverbank, we were pleased to see two Land Rovers waiting for us at the prearranged meeting spot. Soon aboard, we drove the last few miles back to Chibembe and all the comforts of modern camp life.

The day of our departure back to civilization was nigh. As always, we were sorry to leave this delightful wilderness and our comfortable camp sheltered by the giant thorn trees on the banks of the river. It is always a solemn moment when one bids farewell to the bush and recommits to the hustle and bustle of a gregarious society.

"Acacia Island" *(bull elephants) by Mike Ghaui.*

CHAPTER EIGHT
The Artist and the Elephant

I first read about Guy Coheleach in a magazine put out by the Audubon Society. He had done some beautiful bird paintings for them, and I, being a keen bird man, was impressed with his style and the magnificent detail he could render. You had to look very closely to determine that his works were paintings and not photographs.

During my last months with the Tanzanian Game Department, I received a letter asking if I could recommend a suitable candidate for a director of a wildlife operation soon to be founded in East Africa or Zambia. To cut a long story short, I ended up being one of the finalists for the post. I flew to San Francisco for the interview with the trustees of Wildlife Conservation International (WCI), and was chosen to be its director in Zambia. I would run an international wildlife park on the lower Zambezi River opposite the Mana Pools Park in Rhodesia.

It was to my Lower Zambezi Park that Guy Coheleach came to study the majestic African elephant. He had been invited there by Brick Stange, president of WCI, to photograph and sketch the largest and most powerful land animal on earth.

Guy told me soon after our first meeting that he was going to emulate the successful initiative of another artist, David Shepherd. David was the first painter to donate an original painting for sale or auction, with the proceeds going to the preservation of the Bengal tiger. David's *Tiger Fire* raised thousands of dollars (as mentioned earlier in this book). Guy wanted to do the same for the African elephant, but he had never been to Africa before and had seen elephant only in zoos and circuses. He wanted to experience the feeling of stalking as close as possible to one without putting his life or anyone else's in danger, so a safari was planned for my park. Guy would be shown the ropes and, it was hoped, get the material he needed to complete his project. He told me that he had never drawn or painted a wild jumbo and was excited and raring to go.

I organized everything, and in a short while Guy, Brick, and I were on our way to the Lower Zambezi Park, a few hours' drive from Lusaka, capital of Zambia. The weather was perfect for photography as we traveled toward our main camp along a rutted and bumpy bush track that paralleled the Zambezi River.

This was tsetse-fly country. The bite of these large, tough flies is painful, and most people swell up as if stung by a bee. Tsetse are attracted to dark colours and to the dust created by herds of moving animals and moving vehicles. I have seen the spare tyre on the hood of a Land Rover totally covered by the little blighters. We were dive-bombed by hundreds of these pests as we drove along. Luckily, none of us was allergic to their bites. One has to give the tsetse a heavy slap, for they are difficult to kill. My game guards used to catch them and remove their proboscis or pull off their head.

A tsetse bite can transmit the dreaded sleeping sickness, trypanosomiasis, which can be fatal to humans and more so to domestic stock. Wild animals are immune, as are mules. Early settlers in eastern Africa had most of their cattle and horses die from the disease. Eradication of the tsetse was tried, first by shooting the game on which it fed and clearing the bush, and later by aircraft spraying.

The wildlife was plentiful, and we soon spotted a beautiful male kudu with a harem of females. A little later a huge herd of Cape buffalo was sighted. Seeing the first of the Big Five whetted our appetites for more. Guy was especially excited, as this was his first time in the real *bundu* (bush). Brick had hunted in Africa before.

Our first herd of elephant caused us to stop for a closer look through binoculars. There were some very young calves in amongst the giants. As always when babies are present, one must practice extreme caution and avoid disturbing the herd, for the females can become very nasty when protecting their offspring. Guy took a couple of photos and wanted to get closer, but I declined, telling

him we would have ample opportunity to see many more ahead.

Brick, who had hunted in Kenya, Tanzania, and Zambia, mentioned that Zambian game warden Johnny Uys had a unique method of dealing with an angry elephant. Brick was convinced that the method really worked. I knew Johnny Uys very well, but I was always extremely dubious of his theory that banging two small sticks together would always stop a charging or enraged pachyderm. Johnny considered himself a connoisseur of elephant mannerisms and moods. I once told him that he was dealing with wild animals and not tame or zoo animals, but he just laughed and stood by his method.

A couple of years after he left Zambia, Johnny was guiding a group of tourists on foot through a park in Zimbabwe. As the group crept behind bushes and trees to get closer to some elephant for photos, a female elephant suddenly charged without warning. Johnny took his two sticks and banged them together. It did not work. The cow kept coming and killed him and could well have taken the lives of some of the tourists as well.

I mention the incident because the same thing nearly happened to Brick and Guy, despite my continuous warnings to Brick never to try Johnny's method as he or someone else would get hurt or possibly killed.

We came across several lone bulls with their askaris, younger bulls that roam with the older ones to protect them and learn from their habits. We climbed down from the vehicle several times to photograph and for Guy to make his sketches. I always had my .458 rifle ready, just in case of a charge or other emergency. One can never be too cautious in the bush. Brick wanted to approach much closer, but I refused to allow it.

Incidentally, a war of independence was going on then in Rhodesia, and this park was on the front line. Many buffalo were shot and some wounded by the freedom fighters. One had to assume that wounded, dangerous game was wandering around the park, especially along the riverbanks, where forage and water were easy to come by. I can only assume that the events about to unfold were the result of gunshot wounds, or maybe the elephant was just sick and tired of having humans molest him.

It was midday, so we decided to proceed to our main camp for lunch. On arriving, we saw five young elephant bulls drinking and feeding on the riverbank just below our mess. This was a perfect opportunity for good photos and for Guy to study these splendid beasts.

After a scrumptious lunch, which Viva had prepared for us, I told Brick and Guy to remain in the building or at least not stray farther than the open veranda, and that I would be back in about an hour. I took my Land Rover to the staff quarters to deliver the monthly rations and collect monthly reports. The game guards told me that the five young bulls were always around the camp and that they couldn't do their work properly because one of the bulls would always chase them. The staff quarters were located about six hundred yards from our main camp.

Whilst we chatted, the unmistakable, chilling trumpet of an enraged elephant came from where I had left Brick and Guy. I ran to the Land Rover, grabbed my .458 Winchester, and ran flat out toward the sound, loading as I went. I raced past the dining-room open mess, and a premonition prickled through me when

I saw that Brick and Guy were not there. I heard another furious trumpet, and there, about three hundred yards ahead, I saw an elephant chasing a person. I closed in much sooner than I ever thought possible, as they were coming toward me.

Guy could really sprint, but the young bull was fast gaining ground anyway. I fired a shot into the ground just in front of it, which did not slow the charging beast at all. This charge was for real: The bull's ears were squeezed tightly against its body, and its trunk was curled up under its jaw. Time for Guy was running out, and I had only a few seconds to prevent a tragedy.

Guy was about fifty yards from me when he turned around and, in a futile attempt to protect himself, threw his movie camera into the face of his charging adversary. He was knocked down by its outstretched trunk, and the elephant now stood almost on top of Guy, who lay motionless beneath his six-ton attacker.

I was now only ten yards or so from the battleground. The elephant was about to kneel on his victim to provide the coup de grâce, crushing Guy to death and possibly impaling him with a tusk.

I aimed my rifle at the tiny cavity that protects the football-size brain. A split-second before I pulled the trigger, I realized that a brain shot might well drop the hulk right on top of Guy, probably killing him, so I raised my aimpoint.

Let me explain. I found from experience that an elephant that is shot in the brain almost always sits on its backside then either stays there as in a type of half-sitting position or rolls over sideways. But I have shot many elephant in full charge with a frontal brain

145

shot, and they just fell over forward, their front legs collapsing, their momentum taking over. I also witnessed one of my best game scouts, Redmore Nyondo, being crushed by an elephant. The elephant had knocked him down and was about to kneel on him when another of my game scouts, who was standing nearby, shot the enraged elephant in the brain. Sadly, it fell on top of Redmore and crushed him to death.

The elephant's front legs were bending to kneel on Guy. In a split second I raised my aim to place my bullet into the "honeycomb" structure that surrounds the brain. This, in theory, meant that the elephant would fall sideways, sit on its haunches, or collapse forward. I prayed for the latter not to happen. Luckily as my bullet hit the bull, he fell over sideways and then sat on his backside, trumpeting, not knowing what had hit him. I was thankful to see the elephant sit down, much like a boxer getting a solid hit, rather than falling on top of Guy.

The animal was dazed and struggling to regain its feet. Guy was almost knocked out from the terrific blow he had received in his back from the charging elephant. I shouted, "Get the hell out of there!" Guy just looked at me with glazed eyes and was speechless. I didn't blame him—not many folk have gazed up at an elephant and lived. I ran up and dragged Guy out from under the dazed elephant with one hand, clenching my .458 in the other. How I managed to do this, I will never know, as Guy weighed in the region of 200 pounds. Surely some "Super Power" took over and gave me the strength to enable me to virtually throw Guy out of the way. Then I turned to face the elephant, which had recovered its footing and was going around in circles trying to get oriented.

I pulled Guy farther away and had a good look to see how badly injured he was. I thought he might have died from sheer shock. He was at least breathing, although his face was as white as aspirin. The elephant, still wandering around in the general area, gave a gurgled squeal and took off in the opposite direction. *Thanks for small mercies,* I thought, relieved that I didn't have to kill the poor beast.

Now, what had happened to Brick? Was he already dead? Terrible thoughts go through one's mind under such circumstances. Guy was motionless, but at least his eyes were open. I shouted at him, "Where is Brick?" He pointed in the direction of the river.

My game guards, hearing the shooting, had come running to see what the commotion was. I gave Guy a drink from my water bottle, sat him up against a big acacia, and told him I was going to look for Brick. He smiled and waved—no words would come from his lips. He was in a state of shock. I instructed two scouts to stay with Guy and took the two others with me to look for Brick.

I began to shout Brick's name, still not knowing his whereabouts or condition. Suddenly, from a small hole in the riverbank, the scouts and I heard a croaking whisper, and there was Brick, shivering, his eyes almost popping out of their sockets. We managed to pull him out; he was speechless, but able to hobble back to where Guy was resting. Guy at least smiled when he saw that Brick was alive and kicking.

"Dear God, thank you so very much for saving us," Guy managed to whisper, "and Eric, thanks to you I am still in one piece."

Misty-eyed, Guy and Brick hugged one another for a long time, and I'd guess that during the dead silence that followed, they were praying. Both had been very lucky not to have been killed. Brick, I found out right then, could not run at all; he suffered from painful gout and could hardly walk. I give him full credit—he was in pain long before he left Lusaka and endured the pain in silence.

"What the hell were you trying to do?" I asked them.

Brick was the first to reply, apologizing for his mistake in leaving the camp and taking Guy right up to the elephant. He had still believed in Johnny's trick, and was amazed when it failed.

I told them that we had better head back to Lusaka so that Guy could have a thorough check-over by a doctor. As we drove along, we saw the aggressive young bull standing with

Guy Coheleach presenting a painting of a greater kudu to Eric Balson, San Antonio, Texas, 1973. The inscription reads "To Eric Balson, to whom this intrepid, but foolish, artist owes his life." (Photograph by the late Zavell Smith)

his four buddies. He was taking mud from the bank in the tip of his trunk and trying to place it on the wound. Maybe boxers should use mud! A few days later, I returned to check on his whereabouts and condition. My game guards had kept a close track on the bull's movements and told me he was feeding and appeared well.

The doctor found that Guy had suffered no broken ribs or bones but would have terrible bruises. We all sighed with relief, had hot baths, and I tucked into a good meal. Brick and Guy were still too shaken to eat; all they wanted was bed. Guy was black and blue the next morning and very sore and found it hard to move.

Brick asked what I thought would have happened to Guy had I not been there. I related a couple of gory elephant-versus-human stories. Both men listened from the edge of their chairs.

"Heard enough?" I asked, and they both nodded.

"One more question," Guy said. "How can you tell whether an elephant's charge is a bluff or real?"

"That just comes from experience," I said. An elephant begins its charge, I explained, with the head held high and forward as it searches for the enemy. Its ears are pushed tightly against its body, and the trunk is curled under its lower jaw, ready to lash out and knock the adversary to the ground with a mighty blow. Just prior to delivering the blow, the elephant lowers its head. The charge is usually accompanied by a terrifying trumpet or scream, which is enough to scare anyone. Once its enemy is down, the elephant usually drops to its knees to impale the victim with one of its tusks. Then it will either toss the victim into

the air with its trunk or throw him on the ground. I saw this happen to one of my best scouts, who was killed instantly. The elephant may also kneel on its victim and crush him to death, or may simply trample him into pulp with its huge front feet.

Brick and Guy were departing the next day for the United States. Guy had been so very close to an elephant that he would likely know all kinds of physical details from an unusual angle—so long as the trauma didn't erase them from memory.

There is a sequel to this story. A year later I was a guest speaker at a Game Conservation International meeting in San Antonio, Texas. Guy Coheleach was to exhibit at the same convention. It was a special evening, and the guests were enjoying a lavish dinner in a large banquet room when, unannounced, the lights went out. An elephant trumpeted, and a picture came up on a big screen showing Guy being chased by an elephant. The movie included all the film that Guy had taken right up to the moment he decided it was time to flee for his life (and just before he threw his camera at the charging jumbo). The lights came on, and Guy was standing on the stage with a microphone.

"Ladies and gentlemen, sorry if anyone was startled by what just happened. As you have seen and heard, I am lucky to be alive and speaking to you all tonight, and I want to show my appreciation and to say thank you to a person who saved my life. Eric, could you please step up and say a few words to everyone gathered here tonight?"

I felt proud as I walked up next to Guy. He shook my hand and hugged me, and then someone came onto the stage carrying a big framed painting. Guy handed it to me and said,

"Just read the inscription, and accept my everlasting gratitude." Guy Coheleach presented me with an original painting of a greater kudu with an inscription that reads, "To Eric Balson, to whom this intrepid, but foolish wildlife artist owes his life."

"Sizing Up" *(buffalo bulls) by Mike Ghaui.*

CHAPTER NINE
Fearsome Creatures, Real and Imagined

Let me begin this chapter by saying that I am one of the last old-time game wardens–professional hunters still alive and kicking from the colonial era when the British were in control of eastern Africa—Kenya, Uganda, and Tanganyika. At this writing, I am now in my seventy-third year and, "touch wood," still blessed with good health and energy.

As far back as I can remember, I have loved the bush for its peacefulness, its diverse and abundant fauna and flora, and its fantastic sunrises and sunsets; the African bush is a Shangrila that, once savoured, is never to be forgotten.

Among those great hunters and explorers who felt the same way were Frederick C. Selous, John "Pondoro" Taylor, Dr. David Livingstone, Henry Stanley, Martin and Osa Johnson, Ernest "Papa" Hemingway, John Hunter, Karamojo Bell, George Rushby, Constantine Ionides, and Alan Tarlton, to mention just a few. In their day, sightings of herds of six hundred elephant or three thousand buffalo were commonplace. Now, sadly, these are only dreams of years long gone.

Those early hunters and settlers used wagons drawn by mules, horses, or oxen, porters to carry their loads on shoulders or heads, and small boats and dugout canoes to journey by

water. By contrast, today's hunters move about in four-wheel-drive vehicles with power winches, use Global Positioning System devices to determine exactly where they are at any given time, and fly to isolated areas in the relative blink of an eye. I am afraid that this modern world we now live in will bring an end to the wildlife that the early explorers, hunters, and settlers and my own generation had the privilege to live with and enjoy.

The number one cause of poaching in both Africa and Asia is poverty mixed with greed. Grasping for wealth will, in the long run, be the death knell for the rain forests and their fauna and flora. Poaching and habitat destruction will cause thousands of species to become extinct.

I have worked with the rural people in both Africa and Asia and know their feelings and thoughts on wildlife. The ordinary peasant farmer sees the wild animals only as raiders of their precious crops, killers of their livestock, and competitors for the vast grazing lands. They feel that they can derive direct benefits from these "nuisances" only by killing them for food and money. The stressed-out wildlife authorities of these nations have so far been unable to convince and educate these poor people that the wildlife resources will bring benefits to them in the long run.

In my opinion, there is only one solution: Humankind must learn to live with and support wild animals in a mutually beneficial relationship. Whether this can be achieved, only time will tell. I only hope and pray that it can be achieved soon, or it will be too late.

All this came home to me during my last visit to my beloved Tanzania in 1998. The wildlife that I and others had devoted a third of our lives to protecting had been mostly destroyed since my departure in the early 1970s. I visited areas that used to teem with elephant and buffalo and could not believe the paucity of wildlife.

The poignant memories evoked by that last visit and the voluminous personal notes and records I reviewed in the course of writing this book stirred up in my mind some special episodes involving native Africans and the large animals that were part and parcel of their daily lives. Here are a few:

Following the Honey Hunters

After the tragic plane-crash death of Bill Moore-Gilbert, my fellow game ranger (as we were known in those days), I took over his duties. This meant that I was now looking after the Western and Southern Highlands Provinces of Tanganyika (now Tanzania), an area of over 100,000 square miles.

My duties often involved traveling vast distances, and I had to plan these "safaris" well in advance. I would try to take the shortest routes to my destinations, and I soon became

an expert at using the old roads or tracks pioneered by the Germans when they occupied and oversaw German East Africa at the turn of the century (early 1900s).

I was amazed at how many of these early German routes had been abandoned or neglected when the British took over after WWI. I was also amazed to find that the Germans had built many district headquarters miles out in the sticks. All of those old German buildings were constructed like forts or castles, mainly, I believe, for defensive purposes. Outstations like Singida, Kondoa, and Tabora all had fortresses.

I was on one of my many journeys from Mbeya to Tabora, negotiating one of those old German tracks. As my game scouts were cutting up and removing one of the hundreds of broken trees that had been pushed across the track by elephant in past years, some old honey hunters appeared from nowhere. They were miles from their camp and many more miles from their village.

Whenever I was in new country, I always liked to meet such old men as these, for they knew the local bush intimately and could tell me many stories about it and give me some rough ideas on the numbers of wildlife that inhabited the *miombo* woodland. Honey hunters usually located their camps near permanent water, which they needed to process their honey and extract the wax. I asked these men to climb aboard and show us the way to their camp.

Their leader, a very old man with a graceful and pleasant look to his face, was only too happy to take us there, especially when he found out I was *Bwana Nyama*[1] (Mr. Game). He jumped into

1. *Bwana Nyama* actually means Mr. Meat, but for some reason, before and during my era, game department officials and wardens were called Bwana Nyama.

the front seat beside me. As we twisted and turned to avoid the many fallen trees, he told me that they were being harassed every night by lion and that one of their friends had vanished a few weeks earlier and was believed to have been eaten. Their camp was far off the track, and it was late afternoon before we finally arrived after some very rough going.

The old man thanked me for bringing them home before the lion commenced their *ngurumas* (roaring); with their heavy loads of honey, they never would have made it back before nightfall.

He handed me an enamel bowl filled with fresh honey to show their gratitude and said, "*Lazima leo, hawa simba ta sikia sauti ya bunduki ya Bwana Nyama.*" (Surely today, these lion will hear the noise of the game warden's gun.) I asked what he meant.

He replied, "*Kila siku hawa simba na nguruma karibu kabisa usiku kucha, usiku wa leo, wewe sikiliza*" (These lion roar close by every night; tonight you listen carefully). He continued, "*Sisi wote na hofu sana kwa hawa simba sababu wao napenda kutafuna watu*" (All of us are afraid because these lion like to eat people).

Let me explain further. Early explorers and settlers in Tanzania who wrote about their adventures often mentioned the beliefs of the local people, giving details of lion killing and eating humans. I myself have had firsthand experiences with lion that became man-eaters (I will relate these later on). Most interesting of all, when I was stationed in the Singida District during 1955–1958, I heard and read many stories about the "lion-men of Singida." At first I thought it was a joke, but I soon found out that a cult actually existed (more about this later also).

These honey hunters really believed that the lion were sent there to kill them. They were terrified to venture into the bush alone, so they would go in groups of five to eight, which they believed were safe numbers.

I assured the honey hunters that I would protect them from the lion, especially if the animals were man-eaters. These gatherers wandered around the woodlands following the honeyguide birds and gathering honey from hollow trees or from hives they made themselves from bark that hung from trees.

My staff and I set up our tents not far from the natives' tree encampment. Most honey gatherers made their bush camps by interweaving the branches of big trees growing close to one another, creating a strong barricade against lion. They also built three fires, which burned all night. One was situated in the middle of their fortress to keep them warm, another at the rear of the camp, and the third, usually the biggest, in front of the entrance.

Whilst they kindled their fires, Rashidi had ours crackling away, mainly to cook our evening meal and to heat water for my bath. A good hot bath when it is cold makes me sleep like a log. We were treated to a beautiful sunset of orange, apricot, and assorted grays and blacks. Far off, an elephant trumpeted.

No sooner had I settled down to enjoy my dinner than an almighty roar erupted from a male lion right near our camp. My game scouts rushed for their rifles whilst Rashidi came and placed my .470 against a small tree nearby. The honey hunters' eyes lit up with excitement—or fear. I just laughed. I love the roaring of lion; it makes you realize that you are in the African wilds.

I must say, though, that in all the thousands of nights I have spent under the stars in the African bush, I have never heard lion roaring like they did that night. Roars were erupting from 360 degrees around us, almost nonstop. How many lion I shall never know.

None of us had much sleep that night; everyone was up and huddled around the fire. I didn't really mind, because it gave me plenty of time to pick the brains of those old-timers. I asked them if they had seen any signs of poachers or vultures, and they said no, though they had investigated the carcass of an old buffalo, which had helped make some lion fat and happy.

During my many years in the bush, I hardly ever found honey gatherers indulging in poaching; mostly they relied upon lion kills for their *nyama* (meat). In the late 1960s and 1970s, however, many poachers used the guise of honey hunters to hide their main objective: killing elephant for their "white gold," as ivory became known. I learned a lot about that particular topic during the next couple of days from those old men.

In the morning, the strangest thing happened. I had set up my shaving mirror on a small tree and was looking into it when I had to blink twice to be sure what I was seeing. Reflected in my mirror was a big lioness followed by a huge black-maned male walking straight toward my back.

I froze, then reached for my .470, which I had nearby. None of the others had seen the lion, so I told everyone to remain still but to keep on talking. The sight was too much for a couple of the old men, who dived headfirst for the entrance of their fortress. The lioness was ten yards from me when she stopped, switched her tail, put her nose in the air, urinated, and continued on her journey. The big male, following on her heels, let out a terrific roar, sniffed where the female had urinated, then walked by with his teeth bared and his nose in the air, typical behaviour when a female is in heat.

I breathed a sigh of relief, but not for long: Suddenly three more lion, all young males, came into view, and one of them looked annoyed, for his tail was really twitching. I sat down but had my trusty .470 Rigby in hand, thinking what a funny sight this was: I sat with my face covered by shaving soap, clutching my rifle, with three male lion looking straight at me from a few yards off.

Then it happened—so fast that I had only enough time to shoulder my rifle and fire. The twitchy lion apparently decided that he was going to take his frustrations out on one of the old guys and sprang at him as he made a dash for his fortress. The lion misjudged his charge and landed on the side of the entrance, clinging to the trees with his front paws and tearing at the branches with his teeth, growling all the while.

I shouted, and the beast suddenly stopped and stared right into my eyes from about ten yards away. I could see he was turning to make a spring at me. By the time I shoved the safety catch off, he was already airborne, snarling with his mouth half-open. I let him have both barrels at almost point-blank range. The momentum of his charge was stopped in midair as both my softnose bullets hit his chest, and he hit the ground, dead but still kicking. The two other males took off at the sound of my gunshots.

I quickly reloaded. Luckily the shirt I had carried out had spare ammo in the pockets, and it's a good thing because just then Rashidi shouted, "*Angalia, Bwana, huhu dume simba na rudi!*" (Look out, Master, that male lion is coming back!) I didn't want to shoot the animal, so I fired into the ground just in front of him. Dust and bits of grass splattered into his face, making him jump into the air and take off toward the female. I believe he had come back just to see what all the commotion was about.

I noticed Salum talking to Rashidi and pointing to something. He aimed his .458 and fired, and then I saw what he was shooting at. Two more males had come quite close to their tents, so Salum had followed my lead, firing into the ground and making them dash off.

After the pandemonium faded, a couple of the old men plucked up enough courage to emerge from their fortress and almost stumbled over the lion lying right there. They started to clap their hands and dance around the corpse. The others joined in, singing over and over, "*Asante sana, Bwana Nyama, leo sisi tu lala mzuri.*" (Thank you very much, Mr. Game, today we will sleep in peace.)

Their leader questioned why we didn't shoot all the lion. I explained to them that I'd shot the lion only because it had charged. Otherwise, I would have let them pass by; they were only doing what was natural, following a lioness in heat.

I stayed in the area that day to allow my skinner to do his work. My scouts and I took a long walk to see how these old men went about finding the beehives in hollow trees. I was fascinated by how they would follow the honeyguide birds, which would actually entice the men to follow them by using a combination of high-pitched chattering and the act of spreading their tails to highlight their white tail feathers so you could see them easily in the woodland.

As you approach the honey, the bird really gets agitated, making a *chee-tii, chee-tii* sound followed by a shrill *trrrreeeee*, telling you that the hive is right there. Then they fly around and around, waiting for their reward: some comb with bee larvae and beeswax therein.

We must have followed those tiny birds twenty miles that day, zigzagging all over the woodlands. I was intrigued by their antics, and

impressed by those old honey gatherers, who wore only a small loincloth twisted around their waist and tucked between their legs.

Once they found a hive, they would start a small fire under it, using some dried elephant dung with green leaves or grass on top to make plenty of smoke, which they said made the bees *lala* (sleep). One or two of them would climb the tree with a smoldering bunch of twigs and place it either in or right under the hive entrance. They almost always had to enlarge the entrance to allow their arms to fit in and pull out the combs. As they did this, hundreds of bees would swarm around and sting them all over their naked bodies, but it seemed to have little effect on the raiders, and the stings did not swell up. It was a tough way to earn a meager living, and I take my hat off to those courageous old men.

We must have found twenty-plus beehives that day, so those poor fellows had very heavy loads to carry back to camp. They enjoyed eating the bee larvae along with the honey, so they carried the entire combs back with them. After extracting the honey and eating their fill of larvae, they began the task of preparing the wax. This they did whilst telling their yarns around the campfire. Much to my disgust, I was presented with some combs with larvae. "*Maziwa ya nyuki, tamu sana*" (milk of bees, very tasty), they said, laughing when I wriggled my nose at the very thought of their delicacy. I did, however, manage to eat some, and it tasted quite good if I closed my eyes and crunched away blindly. It was even better when I ate it with fresh honey.

Despite being pressed for time, I decided to spend another day with these serene and innocent people. What a contrast from the arrogant thugs one often meets in the cities and bigger towns. Too, there was plenty of fresh sign of elephant and big herds of buffalo, plus we saw some lovely sable antelope during our walks. And we could tell that many lion were nearby, usually a good indicator of an abundance of the creatures lion eat.

That evening, whilst the old men did their chores around the roaring fire, lion stories were told and retold, the chatter occasionally broken by periods of dead silence, when we all listened to the real thing in the far distance. The stories continued late into the night, long after I had retired to the comfort of my bed.

Bigfoot and Death by Witchcraft

Allow me now to tell you a couple of stories relating to tribal superstitions and beliefs that I encountered during my tour of duty as a government servant in Tanganyika (later Tanzania).

Once, Prince Bernhard and I were out in the middle of Masailand tracking a big elephant whose huge front-foot prints we'd found earlier that morning in the soft mud at a natural water hole. Those foot impressions will remain locked into my memory forever. Why? Well, in all my days of hunting and tracking these huge beasts, I never saw another elephant with feet that size. They measured twenty-eight inches in length. Viva could sit down with room to spare in the impression of one front foot. Our experienced tracker, too, said he had never seen such a footprint; he was just as anxious as we were to catch up with the elephant to see the huge tusks the animal must have been carrying.

As we were following Kunduki, our Wandorobo tracker, I noticed that he would never point directly at a track; he would always walk over it, stop, and, still looking ahead, close his

hand and point with his clenched fist backward at the track. He explained that it would bring you bad luck if you pointed directly at the spoor or track of an animal you were following. If we were lucky enough to shoot this elephant, he told us, he would remove the tusks, because he was a *fundi* (expert) at the job, but would never look at the nerve as he was withdrawing it from the tusk.

Let me explain about the nerve. Every elephant tusk contains a nerve that fits tightly inside the tusk's cavity—like the roots of our teeth. The nerve is usually about one-third the length of the tusk. In a big tusk, say a hundred pounds or more, the nerve is about thirty-six inches in length, conically shaped, and consists of soft, jellylike matter. It has to be removed or it will rot and spoil the tusk. Usually, the person who cuts out the tusks also twists out and removes the nerve. It is at this stage that the "puller" would look away; otherwise the spirits of the dead elephant would "*sumbua wewe kila siku*" (torment you every day). They truly believed it would happen.

We eventually caught up with the big fellow after tracking about four hours—we calculated that we covered approximately three miles an hour, so we had walked some twelve miles. It was getting very hot, so the ponderous creature had decided to rest in the shade of some large acacia trees. The old devil was fast asleep—we could hear his snores quite plainly—and rocking back and forth with his enormous penis touching the ground. We kept our distance, downwind some hundred yards, until we could determine the size of his tusks.

He was indeed a giant, so we were expecting to see enormous tusks. But when we eventually got a good look, we were astonished to see he had NO tusks whatsoever—he was what we called a "*budi*," a tuskless elephant. Both Prince

Bernhard and I were happy that it was so; in fact, even if the bull had carried heavy ivory, PB said he would not have shot him, because he was such a special jumbo. We left him peacefully sleeping with his head leaning against a big tree.

Interestingly, a couple of years later, whilst I was visiting PB at his holiday villa in Italy, I noticed that he had named his boat *BUDI*. He told me that he had enjoyed the encounter with that big-footed jumbo so much that he named his boat after him. I thought this a marvelous gesture.

Speaking of superstitions and beliefs, here is a story that will make you wonder. It occurred on one of Prince Bernhard's safaris in the Selous Game Reserve. After we had been in the bush for a week, my head game scout, Rashidi, came to see me in my tent early one morning. He brought along my second head scout, Salum, to verify his story, which went something like this:

One of the skinner's helpers had told them that he was going to die that day. When they asked him why, he told them that he had not awakened with an erection that morning, so he knew he was about to die.

Dressing quickly, I went to see the man. I found him sitting up with a queer look in his eyes. I took his temperature; it was normal. His pulse felt perfect, and he said he didn't feel sick at all, but knew he was going to die. I told him not to be foolish, but he insisted that the *uchawi* (witchcraft) had been cast upon him by a *mchavi* (a witch or wizard of either sex who practiced sorcery). Again I tried to convince him otherwise, but he was adamant that his day had come. I gave him some Andrews Liver Salts, which we used for upset stomachs and as a laxative, and was quite refreshing when drunk whilst it was still effervescing.

Usually any type of medication given under these circumstances works well, but not in this man's case. Apparently, after the prince and I left camp to go down to the Rufiji River, his condition grew worse. He suddenly started to scream, went stiff, and died in that position. I had left instructions where we would be and told Salum to fetch me immediately if there were any problems. As we lunched on the banks of the Rufiji, Salum drove up to inform us that the poor man had passed away.

It was a very awkward situation for me as I had to write to the district commissioner and the district medical officer explaining what had occurred. I felt like a fool telling these learned men that one of my staff had died as a result of witchcraft. Even PB and his friends could not believe it. The prince said to me that evening that his friends back in Holland would think he was pulling their leg.

I had to arrange for the body to be sent to Morogoro, some three hundred miles away, because it was the headquarters for the area where we were camped. An official autopsy had to be carried out by a doctor in order for a death certificate to be issued. Well, the chief medical doctor's final report said that no visual diseases or aliments had been found and concluded that the man had died of unnatural causes and of his own free will due to his beliefs in witchcraft. Can you believe that?

Prince Bernhard felt sad about the death and left me some money for the man's wife and family. The wife was very appreciative and told me to thank the *Bwana Kingi* for his *zawadi* (gift).

The Elephant Lady and the Hyena People

This all happened in 1956–57, soon after Viva and I were married and whilst I was still working for the Water Development Department of Tanganyika and acting as an honorary game warden. I was stationed in the Singida District and charged with helping to build an irrigation scheme for the local villagers living around a big dam called Miangi Mungaa. The district commissioner, a tall, thin man by the name of Ian Norton, came one day to explain to the villagers who I was and what the government was going to do to help them. Two local chiefs sat on either side of him.

"*Jambo watu wote*" (Greetings everyone), he began. He told them I was the *Bwana Maji* (Mr. Water) and that I had been sent by the government to build canals that would carry water from Miangi Dam to their *shambas* (fields). Ninety-nine percent of the villagers were extremely happy, but one disgruntled old man kept saying he didn't want us to build the canals—he only wished to be left alone in peace. Unfortunately, his *shamba* was right in the middle of the proposed project and his demands jeopardized the entire scheme.

Of course, all the other villagers shouted him down; they wanted the water to help grow their row crops and their banana and sugar cane plants. When the meeting was over and the officials had left, I was thinking, *What on earth are we going to do with this person?* when out of the crowd stepped a distinguished-looking old woman with a wrinkled but pleasant face. She smiled and beckoned me to follow her.

Tucked under her arm was an old rooster, which she said was a present from the villagers for my newborn son, Alan. She walked to my car and placed the rooster on the floor in the front. Its feet were tied together so it could not run away.

Then she turned to me and said, in her language, "It will not do, the words of that old man—he is crazy." She said she would speak to her friends, the elephant, and tell them to come

and destroy his crops. "So don't you worry," she said, "the elephant will probably kill him."

Well, one day an uncanny thing occurred. A herd of elephant led by an old matriarch passed right through all the other *shambas* without pulling up any sugar cane or touching any banana trees (a delicacy for these large animals) and headed straight for the old man's *shamba*. In a couple of hours, they trampled and knocked down his huts, destroyed his grain bins, and then stayed there eating the maize before calmly walking out in an orderly manner, again following the matriarch and again without eating or badly trampling anyone else's crops.

Very strange indeed. Was this a coincidence, or can you believe that someone had called up and spoken to those elephant? It makes you wonder. Having lived in Africa most of my life and listened to countless stories around many campfires, I believe that some sort of magic exists. It gives one a strange feeling to think that others may have such powers.

In having to deal with hundreds of complaints about herds of elephant destroying crops and grain bins, I never saw anything like what happened near Miangi Dam. I went to survey the damage the next day. There must have been at least twenty elephant in the herd, and they almost exactly followed the villagers' small footpath on their journey into and out of the fields.

The poor old man never gave us any more trouble. In fact, he was splendid to deal with after that incident. I felt sorry for him, for he and his family had lost their entire year's food supply. So I made arrangements, via the district commissioner, for enough compensation to tide the family over until their next harvest—which was a very good one due to the fact that the irrigation project was a great success.

Our game-warden friend Bill Moore-Gilbert used to reside in a small outstation known as Manyoni, one hundred miles from where we lived. He had heard of the elephant "doing their job" and came to visit me to see if there was any truth in the story. He wasn't a bit surprised and went on to tell me some strange stories of the "hyena people," the Mbugwe and Wagogo tribes. The tribes had a number of witches, men and women. Each was said to own one or more hyena, which lived in their houses and which they would ride at night all over the countryside, visiting other witches to indulge in obscene orgies.

Some months later Bill told me and a few of his other friends that he was going to have to cull some hyena in and around the Dodoma township, where the local residents had made many complaints to him about these night prowlers killing their domestic animals and pets.

Whenever Viva and I visited Dodoma to do our monthly shopping, I remember seeing hyena running all over the place, especially after nightfall (but I never saw anyone riding on their backs). I had heard much about the "hyena people" business and just laughed it off as a joke. But do you know, on the night that a group of us, led by Bill, went out in different directions to look for these animals, *not one hyena was seen,* let alone shot? As we drank coffee later at the government guest house where we stayed, Bill told us that someone must have warned the hyena people to hide their "pets," and that's why we never saw any.

A few months later, another friend of ours, Herbie Raynor, who was drilling boreholes around Dodoma, told us that one night he'd had to shoot a hyena quite close to his home. Next morning he and his wife Barbara heard a terrible wailing, went to investigate, and found an old woman lying on the hyena corpse. She shouted at them, "Why did you shoot my husband?" They left her to drag her "husband" away and bury him. No wonder hyena are feared and hated by many of the other tribes.

The Lion-Men of Singida

Talking about victims, let me tell you a story about the "lion-men" cult of Singida. This, too, happened whilst Viva and I were stationed at Miangi Mungaa. I was called by the matron of a big mission hospital, about four miles from our home, to see a victim who claimed he was the victim of *"mbojo,"* the name given to the so-called "lion-men," who, it was said, were invisible to all but the sorcerers who controlled them.

The mission was operated by an order of nuns known as the Medical Missionaries of Mary. The hospital's doctors and nurses, mainly from Ireland and Europe, were afraid and yet very skeptical about the stories of "lion-men," for they had dealt with many badly mauled and mutilated patients in the past. The matron wanted me to interrogate a new "lion-men" victim immediately, in case he died. His rescuers had carried this man many miles to that particular hospital because it had a good reputation for curing people with such injuries. I was intrigued to find out more about this so-called cult and hear the man's story, so I rushed over to the hospital.

The sister who showed me to the victim's room said she believed his wounds were caused by a man-eating lion rather than a "lion-man." The man's wounds had been treated, stitched, and dressed to prevent gangrene, which can set in very quickly if the person has been attacked by a real lion. He was a young man in his mid-twenties, and though he was still in shock, I was amazed at how strong he appeared despite his condition. It has never ceased to amaze me how much pain can be endured by people who have been attacked in the bush by hyena, lion, hippo, and elephant. I will relate a couple of those stories later on.

Here lay a man with over two hundred stitches closing his bleeding wounds, still able to smile and willing to tell his story. This was in 1957, when the local peasant people were still primitive, apathetic, and full of superstition. These lion-men killings sometimes turned out to have been done by real lion that had turned into man-eaters for some reason. Many other cases turned out to be murders in which the perpetrators had tried to disguise their evil deeds by covering the victim's body with deep claw marks made to look like those of a lion. That's what had happened to this young man, whose story went something like this:

He believed that the "lion-men" were real, for he had been told by both his father and grandfather that these mythical creatures captured young children and took them to secret caves, where they brought them up so they never saw daylight. They were dressed up in lion skins, and their hands and feet were actually stitched into the form of lion's paws. They were completely brainwashed to believe that they were indeed real lion and so must behave like lion. They learned to walk around on all fours and eat raw meat of humans and other animals. They were allowed to venture out only at night and were used by their "owners" to kill people and eat their private parts.

This victim had managed to survive his horrific ordeal only because he screamed as his testicles and penis were being clawed off and eaten. Luckily for him, his "lion-man" was a

novice at his trade and had not pierced his victim's heart with a sharp-pointed homemade knife, as the ritual demanded, but instead had only punctured his left lung. Some villagers who were returning from a drinking party heard his screams and rushed to investigate (something they would hardly have done had they been sober; most villagers are very scared at night).

Later, those villagers told police that they had seen a lion running from the scene, and they took the police to where they had found the man. The police told me that they had seen footprints that resembled those of a lion, but the victim swears that he saw a person dressed up to look like a lion, and he added that he knew who was trying to kill him. He gave the name to the police, who went and arrested the suspect and his accomplice (apparently the murderers had hired a "lion-man" to carry out their dirty deed).

A trial was held, and the two suspects were found guilty. The murderers had paid the lion-man the hefty sum of fifty shillings (about U.S.$17 in those days). Why? Because the victim had reported the men to the police for abusing his mother.

It also transpired during the trial that the guilty parties did use a person dressed in a lion skin, but the police could not bring that person to court because he was certified as mentally deficient. I believe the final outcome of the case was that the two culprits were sentenced to jail for several years and the mental person was sent to an asylum for treatment. The poor victim survived, thanks to the excellent care he received at the mission hospital. Sadly, he lost his reproductive organs.

Over the years there were many such incidents and court cases involving these so-called "lion-men" of Singida. I was told that during the height of the cult in the 1940s, some two hundred killings of humans took place. Most were proven to be arranged, deliberate murders. But the villagers still insisted that they were "lion-men" killings.

An old friend of mine was assigned to trap or shoot lion that were getting out of hand throughout the Singida and adjoining Kondoa districts. He told me that in one year alone, 1947, he led an intensive campaign and accounted for thirty-eight wild lion. *Bwana Rufiji* was his nickname (real name de la Bere Barker), and he was a fine hunter and bushman. The theory goes that with so many wild lion about, they had difficulty finding their natural prey, so they soon turned to killing people or livestock.

Some authorities and anthropologists suspected that "straight murders" were committed by arrangement with "wizards," who then hired assassins to carry out the actual deeds, pinning the blame on the "lion-men." Perhaps, but there is still a lot left unanswered, even to this day, about this strange cult.

"Old Boys" *by Mike Ghaui.*

CHAPTER TEN
Where Have All the Mighty Tuskers Gone?

Are all the mighty elephant gone? Has the gene pool for giant tuskers vanished forever? Ever since hunters began shooting elephant, their main targets have been big bulls carrying heavy ivory. Read any book written in the nineteenth century by an African hunter or illegal trader in ivory, and inevitably you will see mention of elephant tusks weighing more than one hundred pounds each.

During the height of the safari years, from the 1950s through the 1970s, hunters would travel from all over the world to eastern Africa—to Kenya, Uganda, or Tanganyika (later Tanzania)—to seek the Big Five, elephant, rhino, buffalo, lion, and leopard. In those days it was a hunter's dream to bag a "hundred-pounder." Safaris run specifically for such purposes were organized by professional outfitters. Such safaris would bring in plenty of foreign exchange from license and hunting fees and so were welcomed by the governments of the day.

During the colonial era, these three countries had efficient regulations that kept strict control on all safari operators, their professional hunters, and the numbers of animals allowed to be shot by any one hunter. Sadly, soon after these East African countries attained their independence

from British rule, an almighty surge in poaching and illegal hunting commenced, a subject I have touched on elsewhere. Thousands of elephant and rhino were slaughtered, including hundreds of big tuskers.

This, in my opinion, was the major cause for the decline in the elephant populations and the demise of the hundred-pounders. The politicians who ran these countries were undoubtedly the main culprits, for most of them were involved with this illegal activity. To get the real inside story, read *Ivory Crisis* by Ian Parker and Mohamed Amin.

Scientists, conservationists, and many others from all walks of life, including myself, are alarmed at the number of large male elephant that have been killed—over 95 percent by poachers and the remaining 5 percent by legal hunters. Our main concern is the loss of the gene pool: It will take decades of protection for the gene pool to build up to the point at which mighty tuskers will be seen wandering the wilds once again.

Let me tell you a couple of hunting stories involving hundred-pounders. But before I do this, allow me to give you a little background on why I myself became interested in wildlife generally and elephant in particular.

My first sightings of wild elephant occurred on the semiparched plains known as Ngaserai, which the ponderous creatures crossed heading for the "Masai furrow," which carried clear water from Mount Meru across those arid plains. That area will be cited again in my epilogue, which speaks of a particular day forever etched in my memory.

After the tragic death of my father, killed in action during WWII, my elder sister, Eileen,

Eric Balson (left) and Game Warden Ndolanga with four enormous tusks that were confiscated from poachers who had shot elephants somewhere in the Selous Game Reserve. The taller pair weighed 168 and 167 pounds; the outer pair weighed 152 and 150 pounds. Game department warehouse, Dar Es Salaam, Tanzania, 1971.

my younger brother, David, and I had the privilege of having a second father. He was the late Alan Tarlton, known as *Bwana Nyoka* (Mr. Snake) of Kenya, an outstanding hunter and naturalist. Uncle Blinkie, as we called him, taught me many fascinating things about the fauna and flora that surrounded us.

He took me out on my first real elephant-hunting safari as a present for my thirteenth birthday in August 1943, and from that day on I was always fascinated by these amazing animals. Alan told me stories about the brave and famous Waliangulu elephant hunters (who preferred to be known as the Wata). He had hunted with them in the Embu District and learned how they used their potent poisoned arrows to kill their prey.

Alan showed me the shrubs from which the Wata obtained the ingredients to make their *ourbain* poison. Wood and pieces of bark were mixed with the roots and berries of the *Ackanthera schimperi* tree, chopped up, and boiled for hours. To this they added roots of the beautiful desert rose shrub, which contains potent cardiac glycosides. Once these ingredients had been boiled for a long time, the pulpy materials were discarded and the thick, gluey, tarlike residue was boiled once more and then was ready to be applied to the arrows.

To test their product, the Wata would catch some poor unfortunate creature like a lizard or frog and prick it with a large thorn impregnated with the poison. If it died almost instantly, the poison was good. Uncle Blinkie explained that this Wata poison could kill a big bull elephant before it ran three hundred yards from the place it was shot. The powerful poison affected the nervous system, which controls the heart muscle, and the victim died of a heart attack. Amazing!

Also in my youth, I happened to meet Howard Hill and Bill Negley, well-known archery hunters from the United States. I think I am right in saying they were among the first to shoot the Big Five with bow and arrow—without poison. They told me how amazed they were that those Wata hunters could draw back their big bows, which had pulls of between 120 and 150 pounds. I can't even imagine having strength like that; I now do a lot of bowhunting, and I find it hard enough to draw my bow, set at a fifty-five-pound pull.

As I grew older, I finally realized my dream of becoming a game warden, and as I went about learning the tricks of the trade, I had the good fortune to work with many professional hunters and their influential clients. During the course of such meetings, whether in my house or office or in their hunting camps, inevitably the subject of huge ivory cropped up.

Hunters and poachers alike wanted to shoot a hundred-pounder. The very lucky hunter who obtained "Great Ivory"—tusks weighing over 120 pounds each—suddenly became a celebrity. The term "hundred-pounder" had a magical attraction, and the ultimate hunting thrill was shooting, having the pleasure of touching, and bragging to others about such mighty tusks.

I clearly remember a young district officer named Brian Tulluck who was lucky enough to shoot an outstanding elephant in western Tanganyika. When he came to see me in Tabora, he was so excited about his triumph that he ran into my office and said, "Come and see what I have got!" He led me to his pickup and said in his excitable manner, "Just look at them! Place your hands around their girth and endeavour to pick them up—guess how heavy they are." He took them down from the vehicle. I was most impressed and shook his hand in congratulations. I could only just lift the bigger of the tusks. They were almost a perfectly matched pair. As I recall, they weighed in at 188 and 186 pounds (I stand to be corrected on these weights, but they were definitely in the 180s).

To conclude this little story, Brian's wife had just given birth to a little girl, and they agreed to name her Kishandra after the valley where he shot the massive tusker.

A Texan's Bragging Rights
(1969–1970)

Professional hunter Bill Ryan, a close friend, introduced Viva and me to one of his Texan clients by the name of Robert Zerega, known to all as Bob. It transpired that Bob wanted desperately to shoot the biggest and best hundred-pounder (typical Texan) and had traveled to Africa to achieve his goal.

After several safaris without success, he decided that he was going to emigrate and settle in Kenya, where he hoped to become a resident and therefore qualify to hunt without the services of a PH (visiting hunters had to hire one).

Bob considered himself a good hunter and purchased all the equipment he needed to fulfill his dream. He organized his own safaris and, with trackers and other helpers, ventured into the wilds of Kenya seeking his big elephant. Viva and I happened to be visiting Kenya, and Bob invited us to supper at his new home on

Robert "Bob" Zerega with a very large elephant. The author believes the tusks weighed in at 168 and 166 pounds, but stands to be corrected. N.F.D., Kenya, 1970.

the outskirts of Nairobi. With Viva navigating from the map Bob had given to us, we eventually arrived just before dusk. Whilst Bob and I talked hunting, his wife Gloria showed Viva around their new home.

Bob asked me what chances I thought he had of getting his hundred-pounder. I told him that each giant tusker was 99 percent luck and that he would have to walk at least one hundred miles. He laughed and said he never believed in luck and didn't believe it took one hundred miles to shoot a good elephant.

He asked me how I had arrived at the figure of one hundred miles. I explained that I had been hunting for many years, both as a hobby and also in my work, and that for every good elephant over seventy pounds that I had shot for myself, I calculated that I had walked at least one hundred miles.

"Well, I beg to differ with you, Eric. I hope you don't mind."

I shrugged my shoulders and said, "Just you mark my words."

Several years went by, and apart from exchanging Christmas cards, we saw very little of each other. This was mainly because I was working in Tanganyika and Bob in neighbouring Kenya. But on one of his Christmas cards he wrote, "The more I hunt, the more I am beginning to believe your words, but I am still trying to prove otherwise."

A couple of years later I heard that Bob had had some problems with the game department over shooting a big elephant after official hunting hours and that the tusks had been confiscated. Soon after this happened, Viva and I were sitting at the New Stanley Hotel's Thorn Tree Café, the most popular place for Kenyan professional hunters to meet their clients. You could not sit there more than a few minutes without seeing someone you knew. We had been talking about Bob, and just then he appeared. I waved, and he came over, pleased to see us. He kissed Viva and shook my hand vigorously before pulling up a chair and sitting down.

He and Gloria had gone their different ways, and both had remarried. He had sold his house and bought an apartment near the middle of Nairobi. He was excited and could not wait to give us the good news that he had just won his case about those big tusks and now could collect them from the game department. He showed us photographs of his trophy, and I must say I was impressed with the size and symmetry of the tusks. Rarely does one find such big tusks so perfectly matched.

He put out his hand to shake mine, saying, "Eric, you are a *fundi* (expert); I have to admit that I must have walked hundreds of miles after elephant before Mr. Luck handed me this unbelievable trophy." He went on to describe to us what had happened.

He heard that some big elephant had been seen outside the Tsavo National Park in the upper Tana River area, in an open area where licensed hunters could shoot. He headed for the place before others hunters did the same thing. He found a Somali herdsman taking his cattle and camels to water and got some good information from the man. The herdsman said he had seen one very big elephant a few hours back—"*Mkubwa saaaaana*," he said, emphasizing the final word to show that it was a *really* big elephant. He also said he would take him to the place. They agreed on a fee, and that if the elephant was as big as he made it out to be, Bob would give him a *zawadi* (a very big present).

Nightfall was approaching, so they agreed to meet at first light. Bob had bathed and was sitting around his campfire dressed in a *shuka* or *kikoy* (loincloth), which a lot of men wore at night in East Africa in place of pajamas, and a jersey. He was sipping bourbon when his cook came running over to tell him, "*Tembo mkubwa anakuja!*" (A big elephant is coming!)

Bob rushed into his tent and came out with his fancy rifle, specially made for him by his friend Roy Weatherby. The cook pointed to a dark object about seventy-five yards away. Bob could see the outline of an elephant but not its tusks. Deciding that he and his staff were in immediate danger, he aimed at where he estimated the vitals were and fired two shots in quick succession. The elephant let loose a horrific trumpet, spun around, and charged off, just missing the tracker.

After a few minutes, the tracker came to tell Bob, "*Wewe na kwisha kupiga yule tembo mazuri sana, kwa sababu yeye ana fariki.*" (You have shot that elephant very good, because he has died.) The tracker wanted to go and look at the elephant, but Bob, admitting to me that he was nervous just in

This was the first "hundred-pounder" the author shot, east of Morogoro in Tanganyika (now Tanzania) in 1954. The tusks weighed 108 and 110 pounds. Balson was short of cash in those days and sold the tusks for U.S.$1,000, the equivalent of over eight months' salary for someone working for the British government for $120 a month.

Balson was courting his wife-to-be, Viva, at the time this photograph was taken in 1954. He was out hunting with Viva and her sister when they were charged by the elephant in very thick bush. He shot the elephant at a distance of only five paces.

case the animal was not dead, told his men that they would go in the morning.

Bob also admitted that he broke down and cried when he saw the size of the enormous tusks. He couldn't believe his eyes or his luck. However, the area game warden came to his camp and, when he heard the circumstances, told Bob that the tusks were being confiscated because the kill had been made after government regulation time.

In court, Bob Zerega's lawyer argued that the elephant had been shot a few minutes before the end of legal time, just after sunset, and that Bob had shot the animal in defense of life and property. The magistrate found in the defendant's favour, and Bob was once again the proud owner of the tusks, which I believe weighed 168 and 166 pounds, respectively.

Later Viva and I were invited to his apartment, where we met his young wife and admired his big tusks. They were among the finest I had ever seen, and I have seen many hundred-pounders. We drank plenty of champagne that evening to celebrate "Mr. Luck."

Although I did shoot a couple of hundred-pounders for myself during my many years in the game department, the myth that game wardens had the perfect opportunity to shoot trophies simply was not true. Game department employees were forbidden to shoot any elephant for their own gain during the course of their duties, except during their annual two-week leave, and this was strictly monitored and adhered to.

I will not relate any of those hunts, though I will tell you that my two hundred-pounders were sold to help pay for our children's education (our salaries were amongst the lowest paid to government officers). I will, however, show you pictures of my elephant trophies.

Two Rogues to Remember (1996)

I am now going to jump ahead some twenty-five years to 1996, to describe an experience I had in Mozambique, a country bordering Tanzania. I was offered a fantastic job, drawing up and implementing a five-year development plan for the Niassa Game Reserve in remote northeastern Mozambique. Grupo Madal, a company with many interests in that country, had signed an agreement with the government to financially assist in the management of this unique area for a period of five years. The long-term objective of the project was to ensure that the wildlife-rich and scenically spectacular parts of that country would be preserved and protected from destruction after some twenty-five years of wars. I completed my development proposals and submitted them to the government in October 1996. I am happy to say that my plan was a success. The president of Mozambique visited the area and was so impressed with what he saw that he doubled the management period from five to ten years. This was great news for me.

I present the above information just to set the scene for readers. Let me continue.

When I first was flown into this remote area, we landed on an airstrip built and used by the Portuguese who administered that country for many years. Then a fierce struggle broke out, and after some years, the Portuguese decided they had had enough and handed the country over to its rightful owners, the indigenous Mozambicans. They had earned the right to rule and run it their way.

The biggest snag to all this was that because of the wars, thousands of villagers around Niassa had run away across the mighty Ruvuma River to seek safety in Tanzania. There they remained for some twenty-five years before returning to their homeland.

During those twenty-five years of war, the region's elephant had not really been poached or even legally killed. Neither army shot at the animals for the simple reason that the shooting would have revealed them to their enemy. With the local inhabitants gone and the armies shooting only at each other, the wildlife, especially the elephant and the buffalo, increased beyond anyone's imagination. For example, when I was flown over the vast area and briefed, I was told that the elephant there numbered approximately 750. I could see immediately, from my years of experience in adjacent Tanzania, that this number was grossly understated. That figure had come from some "boffins" sitting in IUCN headquarters in Geneva who had no real idea how many elephant there really were. After six months of studies in the field, I found that at least 10,000 elephant lived in the region. You can imagine what an impact so many would have on the *shambas* (cultivated gardens) in which the newly returned villagers were trying to grow their crops.

Soon my biggest dread was realized: Reports started to pour in of elephant killing

170

people or destroying their food crops. I wrote to the authorities suggesting that we move some villagers, but they were reluctant to do so, preferring not to hassle these poor people—"even if you have to shoot the elephant" said the reply. Well, this caused a big headache for me and my bosses because now we had to come up with a solution. It was protect the people and their crops or shoot the elephant. Whilst we were trying to come up with a workable method, several bad accidents and near fatalities occurred.

We eventually came up with a solution, an expensive one: All villages and their gardens would be protected by electric fences. The idea had been very successful on a Kenyan game ranch called Lewa Downs, owned and operated by the Craig family. Ian Craig was my immediate boss and also the chief coordinator for the Niassa Project. It was he who had come up with this idea of electric fences operated by huge solar-powered batteries.

But before we could get the fences installed, one particular big old elephant went on a rampage around an isolated village miles from nowhere. He and a smaller companion were not at all scared of the local inhabitants and would nonchalantly roam about the *shambas* and huts in broad daylight. When the villagers threw stones and other missiles to try to chase the elephant away, the pachyderms, especially the old *mzee*, would charge at their tormentors, actually chasing villagers right into their huts.

This is the chief's brother's house, which the old "mzee" destroyed. I am pointing to the destruction and the chief. It was acts such as this that made the old "mzee" a threat to the village and its people. Naulala Village, Niassa Province, Mozambique, 1997.

It became such a frightening situation for those defenseless people that the village chief walked some eighty miles to report it to the district administrator and myself, demanding that the elephant be destroyed immediately. I could not go, so I sent two of my game guards right away to the village. I told them not to shoot the elephant with their shotguns, which would only wound the beasts and enrage them more, but rather to try to scare them away by shooting over their heads. I told the chief to return to his village with the guards and that I would follow as soon as I had spoken to my bosses over the radio.

Every day I radioed Ian Craig at Lewa Downs, but I had to wait until our scheduled 6:00 P.M. call-up time. The guards and I had established an efficient radio network, and I told them to keep me informed of the latest developments.

That very evening I received an urgent message from the game guards saying that the old *mzee* and his friend had knocked down some grain silos, killed the chief's brother, and almost killed one of my guards. I reported to the district administrator that I was proceeding immediately to the scene, closely followed by the government game warden, Antonio Abacar, in his own vehicle.

Tusks from another killer elephant that Balson shot; they weighed 104 and 99 pounds. Singida, Tanzania, 1956.

I was very concerned by now that the game guards did not have weapons suitable to kill elephant. They had only shotguns. Antonio and I had the only heavy rifles.

The administrator told me that he had spoken to the governor of Niassa Province, who had ordered drastic action to protect the villagers, including killing the troublesome elephant if necessary. The next step would be to send the army in to deal with the matter. I told him not to worry, that I was already on my way and would keep him informed by radio.

Ian Craig told me by radio to do whatever was necessary to keep the peace and to keep the army out at all costs. As you can imagine, having the army come in and try to deal with a situation in which they had no training or experience would have created complete chaos.

It had taken the old chief two and a half days to walk the eighty miles from his village to report the trouble, and during that time, the situation had grown from serious to critical. One old man had been killed, and the elephant were getting even more aggressive.

On my arrival, I asked the senior game guard what had happened. He related this story to me in great detail: He and the other guard had waited at opposite ends of the small village, which consisted of no more than twenty flimsy huts, for the elephant to emerge from a nearby *kichaka* (thicket). Just as the senior guard was explaining the plan to the villagers, one of them pointed and said, "*Hatari!*" (Danger!) Emerging from the bushes right behind them was the old *mzee* with its companion right on its tail. The people disappeared into their huts.

The senior guard said the big elephant came quite near him, but the wind wasn't right and it couldn't find him. When the *mzee* came within twenty paces, he fired a first shot over its head.

The elephant stopped dead still, its trunk stretched high into the sky. He reloaded and fired a second shot, which brought an immediate and chilling trumpet and a full charge. The guard just managed to plunge through the doorway of the nearest hut, but the elephant gave another trumpet and tore the thatch off the roof. The two men inside plus the guard made an express exit through a small hole at the back of the mud hut just as the whole house was pushed over by the enraged elephant.

The smaller elephant, which had smelt or seen the three running away, charged after them. They entered another hut, but the old *mzee* came on the battle scene once more and demolished the second hut. Again the temporary occupants vacated through a rear door and headed for a third hut close by, with the young elephant in hot pursuit. Believe it or not, a fourth hut became involved before the terrified men decided to do a vanishing trick and headed for the thicket, leaving the elephant creating havoc behind them.

They ran at least a mile before stopping to take stock of the situation. They could hear people screaming and banging drums at another village a few hundred yards toward the river. Heading there, they found nearly all the occupants from the first village, including their chief.

I reached the trouble spot around 10 o'clock that night. I had problems in finding the right village, but eventually I saw both game guards in the headlights. The senior guard greeted me with, "*Jambo, Bwana Mkubwa, wale tembo mbaya saaaaana.*" (Hello, Big Man, those elephant are verrrrry bad.)

Had I known the elephant would turn into killers, I never would have sent the game guards out alone with only shotguns. Man-eaters including lion, leopard, and hyena can be frightened away or killed with a slug-loaded shotgun, but not a killer elephant.

Some villagers had seen the elephant running toward the river, so I left my vehicle there but removed the battery, which I needed to operate my 750,000-candlepower spotlight. The chief gave me some helpers to carry the heavy battery, and we set off toward another small village where we heard drums and people shouting—probably to chase away the rogue elephant.

These tense and excited villagers welcomed us and said the elephant were in their maize fields on the banks of the river. "*Hapa hapa, karibu kabisa*" (Right here, very close), one old man whispered. The moon was hidden by clouds. I urged everyone to be silent and listen. Soon we heard twigs snapping. The moon emerged from behind the clouds, and we could see the maize shamba on a small flood plain right below us. A large anthill was close by, ideally situated. I signaled for silence by putting my finger to my mouth, then climbed the hill, sat down with my elbows resting on my knees, and raised my 10X40 binocular. Two dark shapes turned out to be two elephant some one hundred yards away, much too far to shoot. I wanted to make absolutely certain that these were the killers.

It was well after midnight. The elephant were feeding along very slowly. I thought I glimpsed a big tusk but couldn't be sure. Suddenly they decided to come our way. I clambered down, hitched up the spotlight, and showed the game guard how to switch it on once I gave him the signal. By this time the elephant were almost below us, but the big one, whose massive tusks were shining a little in the moonlight, was not in a suitable position for a good shot. I waited, only too aware that once the spotlight was switched on, hell would break loose.

As mentioned earlier, government game warden Antonio Abacar (I called him Alpha Alpha, and he called me Echo Bravo), was assisting me and carried a .375. Our head game guard, whose name was Kapten, had an old .375. So we had enough firepower. What really worried me was that my companions had never before faced such a dangerous situation at night.

I spent a few minutes giving them precise instructions. They must both shoot at the smaller elephant, leaving the big one to me. They must *not* shoot before I did, and *under no circumstances* were they to run away. I also told the villagers not to run away; they must come and stand behind me. "*Ndio, Bwana*" (Yes, Sir), they said, nodding their heads. I could see and feel the tension in all those around me.

Finally the old bull was in position for a shot. I gave the signal, and the intensely bright beam illuminated the elephant below. The big bull let out a bloodcurdling trumpet and spun around so fast that my shot did not hit his vitals. As I reloaded, the second elephant let out a trumpet and charged straight for us.

Well, the poor chap who was holding the spotlight dropped it and ran away, followed by all the others—except for Alpha Alpha and Kapten, who fired at the smaller elephant. I shouted for them to follow me onto the anthill, a very large one that had enough space for us all. As I reached the top, I saw the old bull trying to climb the steep bank right below me. His trunk was at full stretch, searching desperately for us.

Again luck was on our side: He could not climb up, which enabled me to get another couple of shots into his chest. He tumbled over backward, screaming, but rolled over and was immediately up on his feet again. I shouted to the two others to shoot at the smaller elephant, which was milling around as if lost. Luckily, the moon plus the glare from the spotlight lying on the ground gave us sufficient shooting light.

All three of our rifles went off simultaneously, huge red flashes spouting from the ends of the barrels. The bulls were confused as well as badly wounded, but they took off down the embankment, screaming in rage and pain, and were swallowed up by the thick bushes on the opposite bank.

There was a deadly hush for a couple of minutes. Alpha Alpha broke the silence, saying that he thought our days had come to an end.

Then Kapten had his say: "*Hi ni mara ya kwanza kuwinda usiku kama hii, mbaya sana,* *kweli leo Mungu na tunza sisi.*" (This is my first time to hunt at night like this; it is very bad; truthfully, the Lord looked after us today.)

By now the others had returned, and I must have looked angry, because the poor fellow who had dropped the light stepped forward sheepishly, picked it up, and mumbled, "*Tafathali, Bwana Mkubwa, mimi na kosa, niwie rathi?*" (Please, Master, I made a mistake, forgive me?)

"Of course I forgive you—it is I who made a big mistake."

They looked at me with astonishment. I explained that I never should have put their

This is the elephant that killed a local villager near Lake Rukwa. Balson and some of his crack shot game scouts eventually caught up with him and killed the big fellow. His tusks weighed 102 and 99 pounds. Mbeya Region, Tanzania, 1968.

lives in danger by trying to shoot the elephant at night. On the other hand, I wanted to kill the rogue animals to protect the local villagers, plus I did not want the governor to send in the army. This seemed to reassure them, and the laughter began. Before setting off back to camp, I told everyone that we must be ready at 5:00 A.M. to begin the dangerous task of tracking the wounded animals.

I felt sick at heart: Why hadn't I done a decent job and killed the elephant right there? Then I reasoned that it had been some twenty-five years since I had killed an elephant, these circumstances were very different, and I did not have my trusty .470 Rigby, only a strange .458 bolt-action. This made me feel a little better.

On the journey back to camp, the others were laughing and pulling the leg of the unfortunate fellow who had dropped the spotlight. "*Nani woga?*" (Who's afraid?), they teased. I soon stopped that nonsense by telling them that all those who had run away were *wogas* (afraid). There was dead silence for the rest of the way back to camp.

Alberto, my old cook, had hot coffee brewing and some supper ready for me, but I told him I was very tired and asked him to set his alarm for 4:30 A.M. I fell into bed, but tossed and turned the few hours of the night that remained, thinking of those wounded elephant on the other side of the river. I prayed that they would die and not suffer. I was up and ready to go before Alberto brought my pot of tea.

By five we were all assembled where the action had taken place the night before. There was sufficient light to see blood. We soon found plenty and followed it down to the water's edge. It was evident from the tracks that the smaller bull was dragging his front leg. Crossing the stream, we followed their tracks in the sand and

on up the steep bank and into the dense riverine vegetation. There were splatterings of blood on the bushes, but not enough to give me confidence that we would find the elephant dead. I whispered to Alpha Alpha that things didn't look good; he just nodded.

As the vegetation got thicker, we came upon some droppings. I stuck my finger in and was pleasantly surprised that they were hot. This told me that the elephant were moving very slowly, for we had covered only about three hundred yards since climbing the riverbank. Just then Kapten tapped my shoulder and, without speaking, signaled to his ear and pointed to our right. He had heard noises. We stopped and listened for a good five minutes, then heard a low *phhhrrrrrrr*. I told everyone to remain right there and to stand behind some big tree trunks; I would go alone to take a look.

As I made my way very cautiously through the undergrowth, I was scared. The adrenaline was pumping, and sweat poured down my forehead. I had to take another route, not the one the elephant had made, because I had to get downwind of them. There were neither movements nor sounds.

The entwined undergrowth was too thick for me to make any headway without arousing my quarry, so I got down on my belly and wriggled very slowly along. This was nerve-wracking—I was on my stomach, and if the elephant smelt or heard me, they could trample me before I could shoot them. It was impossible for me even to sit up, which made me think, *Balson, you are a stupid fool. You are asking for trouble. Maybe you should turn back.* These thoughts made me even more nervous.

After a breather, I decided to continue. I had caused this situation, and now it was up to me to finish it off. Just then I spotted a movement not ten paces ahead. Eventually I made out a foot of an elephant. The adrenaline really spurted now. I held my breath, fearing that it was too loud, then let it out slowly. I could hear muted rumblings and the soft flapping of huge ears. This told me that they were resting and cooling themselves.

I was trying to figure out a plan of attack when I noticed that if I moved a few paces to my right, I might get a better chance for a shot along a relatively open path made by other elephant or bush pigs. Painfully slow wriggling brought me to an opening through which I could see the *mzee* standing with his head drooping forward. I could see his left shoulder clearly for a heart shot, but under these circumstances I needed to drop him stone dead with a shot to his tiny brain. With a heart shot he could run, even though clinically dead. More than a few hunters have been killed by animals that were dead on their feet, shot in the heart. So I had to wait until he turned his great head to allow me to place the coup de grâce. I still could not see the smaller one; he was hidden behind the *mzee*.

I said a small prayer for my shot to go straight to the brain. I planned to run up and stand behind the body of the dead elephant, using it as a barrier and hoping for a chance to shoot the smaller one as he charged or ran away. I was most worried that the wind would suddenly change. I slowly but surely eased into a kneeling position. It seemed to take ages. I raised the .458 and slid off the safety just as the old fellow turned enough for me to get an angle to his brain. But it was an acute angle, so I had to be 100 percent accurate.

I fired. As I scrambled forward, I saw him crumble and fall on his side with his legs stretched out toward me. I reloaded as I ran, but the damn cartridge jammed. I was able to pull it out and chamber another, all whilst trying to dodge his kicking back legs. There was a shrill trumpet from the second elephant, because I was able to get a glancing shot at his brain as he dashed away. There was a gurgling type of trumpet as he fell sideways and finished up leaning against a tree trunk, stone dead.

My shirt was wet through from sweat, and I began to shake with cold, or maybe fright. My knees were shaking so much that I had to sit down, and I waited a few minutes for my nerves to steady before yelling for Antonio to come with the others.

There was much hand shaking and plenty of "*Loo, loo, loo, loo*" (a word uttered in wonder or pleasure) as the men stroked the tusks and lifted the tail and touched the feet. And many, many repetitions of "*Mama wee, mama wee, mama wee*" reflected the villagers' surprise, for some of them had never seen an elephant at close quarters, let alone such an enormous specimen.

I pointed to the other elephant, and the others went to see. I walked around to take a close look at the tusks of the old *mzee*. A cold shudder ran down my back, and my arms broke out in goose flesh. I felt ashamed and sad at having to destroy such a magnificent beast. Stroking his eye, which was staring at me, I said, "I am very sorry, my old man," and felt trickling on my cheeks.

I wiped the tears away and wandered over to the second one. He lay with his head facing skyward as if asleep, and I fervently wished he were sleeping instead of dead.

When the villagers heard the shooting, they came to investigate, led by their chief. They were overcome with joy that the killers had been dealt with. They had meat aplenty, and the remainder was dried and sent to schools and hospitals throughout the district. The administrator, pleased that the troublemakers had been dealt with, reported the good news to the governor.

As for those superb tusks, I hope that they are in the Mozambican museum. I had the skull cleaned and preserved for posterity and educational purposes, believing that this animal likely was one of the last big tuskers that roamed Mozambique at the turn of the twentieth century.[1]

My main duty there had been accomplished, but I remained for a while to supervise the enormous task of butchering two elephant and to show the villagers how to smoke and cure hundreds of pounds of meat. At the kill site, gore and guts were everywhere. Many village women were gesticulating with their arms and making a yodeling sound across their rolling tongues. They love to do these dancing antics when they are happy. The two game guards had done a marvelous job of setting up huge, sloping platforms on which hundreds of slices of meat were already spread out in layers I had given strict instructions that no one was to attempt to cut out the tusks or even go near the heads of the elephant. My game guards would construct a platform in a big tree nearby where they could sleep and chase away any lion, leopard, or hyena attracted by the smell of the carcasses.

The next morning I meandered from my camp back to the "elephant graveyard." My sensitive nose soon picked up the strong smells of woodsmoke and roasting meat. As I clambered up the now well-worn footpath, I came upon a mass of men, women, and children armed with homemade axes and knives dashing in all directions. Some carried strips of meat whilst others busily hacked away at the huge bodies, now grossly disfigured and diminishing rapidly as lumps of meat or fat were cut off.

There was a continuous din; people were laughing or singing away as they laboured at their chores. Others squabbled and shouted at each other over a choice morsel. Everyone was reveling in this *kirimu ya nyama* (feast of meat). Surely not many white men have witnessed this sight.

As mentioned earlier, I was highly pleased that the government of Mozambique accepted our management proposals to extend the existing Niassa Reserve to protect the fauna and flora, especially one of the largest concentrations of elephant left in Africa today. However, the subsequent return of the refugees to their motherland destroyed the comparative peacefulness of the elephant's domain and implanted in the animals a new sense of apprehension and wariness.

Elephant have long memories, and easily learn that man is their main enemy. I know from firsthand experience. Many years ago, whilst I was on my patrols in Masailand in Tanzania, I would camp below a big granite outcrop that overlooked a permanent water hole in the midst of a dense thicket. Each morning I would climb to the top to watch the sun rise. Almost any day, no matter what the

1. When I arrived in Kenya a year later, I was asked by many hunters what it was like to shoot a hundred-pounder. Many of them believed that no big elephant still roamed the bush. But those enormous tusks weighed 110 and 106 pounds, respectively. At Christmas 2000 I received a card from a dear old hunting friend who said that he had recently spoken to another hunter who had seen those very same tusks in Niassa. That hunter had "stretched" the weights, saying that they were 120-pounders.

*This is the gaboon viper (*Bitis gabonica*). One can see what a striking reptile it is. (No pun intended!)*

Eric Balson (left) confiscated these huge trophy "hundred-pounders" from an Arab poacher in the Western Province. They weighed 114 and 112 pounds. He found the smaller pair (shown lying on the ground) on a dead elephant, presumably wounded by a poacher, in the bush. Pictured on the right is Brian Stronach, another game warden. Sumbuwanga, Tanzania, 1964.

Prince Bernhard, Eric Balson, and Norman Carr at Mfuwe Lodge. Luangwa Game Reserve, Zambia, 1973.

A fine black rhino, an animal almost wiped out by poachers in most parts of Africa. Ngorongoro Crater, 1971.

A sunrise over Lake Katavi. Tanzania, 1966.

This cheetah simply posed for Balson, as if to say "Please take my picture." Loliondo Controlled Area, Tanzania, 1969.

Black rhino in the Ngorongoro Crater, before the Masai and other poachers started to kill them. Tanzania, 1961.

Two large, male greater kudu quenching their thirst in a hole dug by baboons in a dry riverbed. Ohorongo Game Ranch, Namibia, 1990.

This mighty tusker seems positively ghostly as it slips through the bush. Banks of the Rungwa River, Tanzania, 1968. (Photograph by Viva Balson)

This young askari fell against a tree, which collapsed under its weight.

The South African subspecies of giraffe, Giraffa camelpardalis apenensis. *Mfolozi National Park, Zululand, Natal, South Africa, 1992.*

The author holding the tusks from the old mzee, *1997. They were thick and solid ivory, and the nerve cavity was short, which added to the weight of the tusks. They weighed 110 and 106 pounds but would more than likely weigh about 105 and 100 pounds after a drying-out period of sixty days.*

Ahmed of Marsabit was protected by presidential decree and was guarded night and day until his death. (Photograph by the late Peter Jenkins, an old school friend of the author and fellow game warden)

Whilst on a 14-day leave in Mpanda, Balson shot his biggest elephant; the tusks, weighing 128 and 118 pounds, are shown here.

The old honey hunter. Note the homemade ax, his prize possession, over his left shoulder. The axes are usually hand forged from motor vehicle springs.

A young bull elephant looking for food. The Rift Valley, on the shores of Lake Rukwa, Mbeya Region, Tanzania, 1965.

This is the author's look-out rock in Masailand, from which he used to watch herds of elephant each day, quenching their thirst and rolling in the mud. The rock is still there, but, alas, most of the elephants have been poached.

A superlative picture of Mount Kilimanjaro

Dr. Wolf-Eberhard Barth (right), a senior forester in Germany, came to Ohorongo to teach Eric Balson how to work with the Hanoverian hounds. The kudu in the picture was for demonstration purposes, to work the hounds. It was later used for staff rations. Also pictured are Balson and Artus (Balson is on the left).

This is the Lugenda River, bordering the Niassa Game Reserve, in the dry season. This was the area in which the old mzee *used to live. Mozambique, 1997.*

Balson with the old mzee. *The author reports that he was still shaking when this picture was taken. Mozambique, 1997.*

time, from that outlook rock I would see at least one elephant at the water hole, drinking, rolling, or wallowing in the mud.

Several years later I revisited that lovely, secluded place. After sitting and watching that water hole for an entire day, I saw *not one* elephant come to drink. I could hear them trumpeting, squealing, and breaking trees, and I saw plenty of droppings as I walked through the bush along their well-trodden paths. What was going on?

I soon discovered that some lousy poachers had found that water hole, the only one for hundreds of square miles that held water all year. It appeared that the poachers had built a flimsy platform in a large tree on the edge of the water hole. I found two dried-up carcasses of elephant that had been shot right there. Soon the elephant had learned to come to drink only after dark. Poachers are too scared to sit out at night; they are really afraid of lion, which can climb up the trees after them.

Because of such acts, elephant are rarely seen in daylight hours these days. They have become nocturnal, eating and drinking at night, resting and sleeping in dense thickets during the daylight hours. Thank goodness there are still a few national parks and other sanctuaries where these ponderous animals can still be seen going about their daily routines in peace.

Crash Course in Dangerous Game (1963)

The College of Wildlife–Mweka was situated at the foot of Mount Kilimanjaro (highest mountain on the African continent), a fantastic location to say the least. Its purpose was to train future game wardens, and students were selected by most East African countries, including Ethiopia, Sudan, and others as far south as Botswana, to attend a two- or three-year course. This was the first college of its kind in eastern and central Africa. My ex-boss, Tony Mence, once chief game warden of Tanganyika, was at this time chief administrator of the college.

He phoned me one day in Mbeya, where I was stationed as senior game warden for Tanganyika's Southern Highlands Province, to ask for advice. Did I know of a good place for his final-year students to complete their practical examinations, for which each had to shoot an elephant and a buffalo? Prior to receiving their diplomas, they had to prove themselves against dangerous animals.

I told Tony that a few days earlier I had received, via bush telegraph (a runner), a letter from the chief of a remote village in the Rukwa Valley called Rungwa West, and that I was at that very moment organizing a month's safari there to do some control work on both the elephant and buffalo populations, which had increased so much that they had to be reduced. This gave me a good opportunity to train some

of my newer game guards in this dangerous aspect of their duties. I told Tony that I would welcome his students' assistance in dealing with herds of marauding elephant and buffalo.

Tony replied, "That is wonderful news, Eric. I shall call a staff meeting just as soon as I put down this phone, and commence preparations right away for a three-week safari to your area for all those students—about thirty."

I must point out here that the instructors at Mweka were mainly ex-professional hunters or ex-game wardens, including experts like Pat Hemingway (Ernest Hemingway's son), Frank Poppleton, Gil Child, Tony Mence himself, plus two forester-game wardens from Germany.

I explained to Tony the shortest routes to our meeting place, a small village that had a game department outpost plus a small landing strip, for it was soon to become a game reserve. I informed him that it was now the rainy season, and that it had rained so much during the past three weeks that the eighty-mile bush track from the village to Inyonga was completely flooded. We would have to prepare ourselves for a tough trek. We might even have to walk in.

Tony just laughed and said, "Eric, my old pal, don't worry; we have ten Unimogs [special rough-terrain vehicles with four-wheel-drive and heavy winches both front and back, made by Mercedes Benz], plus we have our own Mercedes mechanic, Blackie Swatzmann, and he is a real *fundi* (expert). So rest assured that we will reach Inyonga and Rungwa West."

All went according to plan. Viva and I and my crew met Tony and his group along the edge of the airstrip. Tony had flown in with his Super Cub. It rained again that night, and all rivers were in full spate, some spilling over their banks.

On the Mweka Safari, one of the Unimogs got completely stuck in the mud. Not even a winch could pull it out, and the vehicle had to be jacked up and logs placed underneath it to extricate it. The vehicle was stuck in the quagmire for eight hours.

Our travel to Inyonga was a five-day ordeal of plowing through black *mbugas*—areas of terribly sticky soil that is almost impassable when wet and dries out into huge ruts and cracks. Every night it poured, and each day we could travel only about ten to fifteen miles, thanks to those dreadful *mbugas*. We must have winched our way along for miles across those hazards, but we finally made it to Inyonga on the fifth day.

An old chief at Inyonga told us he had his own elephant problems, so our group split up. Pat Hemingway, Frank Poppleton, and half the students stayed fairly close to Inyonga, whilst

Gil Child and I and Blackie Swatzmann headed for Rungwa West.

The going was good along an old ridgetop road engineered by the Germans, and it took us only a couple of hours to travel the sixty miles to the top of the Rift Valley escarpment, where I knew of a fantastic campsite on the banks of the Rungwa River just before it plunged over the rift and flowed into Lake Rukwa. It wasn't long before our tents were up and the cooks had their fires going.

After lunch, all available hands helped cut down a few trees and branches overhanging a flat section of road, to widen it so that Tony could land his small plane. We built a small, smoky fire to show Tony which direction the wind was blowing so he could approach upwind. A flat, low plume of smoke would mean it was blowing too hard and Tony would have to return to Inyonga. All went well, and Tony touched down. I must say he was an excellent bush pilot.

Before the large group had split up, I agreed to give a pep talk to the students. It went something like this: "Some African animals are respected mostly for their size, such as elephant, hippo, and rhino; some, like lion and leopard, for their stealth and courage; and others, such as kudu, sable, and gazelle, for their incomparable beauty and grace. But

hunters, like you are about to become, must be warned about the legendary *Bwana Nyati* (Mr. Buffalo). He has earned the status of one of the most dangerous, if not *the* most dangerous, of all animals because of his aggressive nature, especially when wounded."

They all began to shuffle about as if to say *We've heard all this before at Mweka,* but I continued. "No other herbivore carries a more fearsome reputation than the massive bull buffalo. He has inflicted many casualties on his main enemies, lion and humans, often with fatal results, so don't say you haven't been warned."

Some of the students nodded; others just smiled. I went on, "Old, solitary males—usually weighing fifteen hundred to two thousand pounds, truly imposing specimens of

This is that big elephant that we saw from the air the previous night near Revuka Village. Niassa Game Reserve, Mozambique, 1998.

nature—have reached their maximum physical development and find it difficult to keep up with the herds. So each one adopts his own lifestyle, confining himself to his own little territory where there are succulent grasses for his nocturnal grazing, plenty of shelter from the hot midday sun, and, if possible, a convenient watering place and a muddy pool where he can sleep for hours, cool off, and keep the biting insects at bay. Today, my friends, we are all going together to meet the chief and introduce ourselves to the villagers." We wandered down the steep road to the village.

Our normal daily routine was to patrol the bush, following the spoor of elephant or buffalo that had raided *shambas* the night before. Most students, when it came their turn to shoot, performed admirably, dropping their buffalo or elephant without any hassles. One or two animals were wounded, and we had to follow up and put them out of their misery. And that's where this story really begins.

On the fifth day it was student Ismail's turn to shoot. We were soon on the trail of some elephant that had eaten an entire patch of sugar cane belonging to the chief's brother. It was early morning, heavy dew lay on the grass, and following the herd was simple, for they left a wide, trodden path for us. We entered some tall thatching grass (so called because most villagers used it to thatch their huts), and then even taller elephant grass, or phragmites, which grows along the riverbanks.

We came across some elephant droppings and tested their temperature by inserting a finger deep into the stuff. It was cold, which told us the animals were miles ahead. So I hastened the pace in the hopes of closing the gap.

I was leading the pack, followed by Ismail. As we rounded a corner, there, staring us in the face, was a huge old bull buffalo. I stepped aside and signaled for Ismail to shoot the buffalo in the middle of its chest. He was fumbling to push off the safety catch on his .458, and I think he was suddenly overcome with fear.

Just as he lifted his rifle to shoot, the old buffalo wheeled around and started to run away. I shouted to Ismail not to shoot, but it was too late. His rifle roared, and I heard a dull thud as his bullet hit its target, goodness knows where. Ismail was trembling, trying to reload.

I signaled for all to sit down and rest for at least half an hour. I walked forward to check for blood, but did not find enough to indicate a lethal hit. I returned and said, "Well, chaps, remember my words on that first morning? We now have that wounded buffalo on our hands and must follow it up." There was dead silence all around, except for some baboon barking in the distance.

Eventually we moved forward. I went ahead, with the others close behind. I hated walking in front of people with loaded rifles, but this was something we had to train them to do.

We soon came out of the high grass into a clearing. At the edge I stopped and sat down, signaling for the others to do the same. I was thinking that Ismail's bullet had entered the stomach and punctured a lung, because what little blood I had seen had a slight pinkish tinge to it and some was pinkish and frothy. After a short rest, I called them all around me and told them what we were going to do. Their facial expressions revealed their concern. Because the wound was likely not a deadly one, it would take a couple of days for the buffalo to succumb, but after an hour or so he would be very sick and stiff, so we would sit there and wait.

A troop of baboon was frolicking in some fig trees. The leaders suddenly stopped and sniffed the ground about them whilst others stared intensely into the bed of reeds along the river's edge. Because of the steep banks, I could not see what they were looking at, and it was some five hundred yards off. Soon their leader gave a loud *Waugh*, and they rushed back up the trees.

I guessed they had smelt blood and perhaps even seen the buffalo. I hoped so, but I did not let anyone know my feelings. Instead I told the students how these primates form a protective bond with impala and bushbuck. The graceful game animals have a subtle sense

of smell that can detect the approach of the baboon's main enemy, the leopard. The baboon, in turn, call out their loud alarm signals from lofty positions in the trees. So each species alerts the other in plenty of time to take evasive action.

The students were interested in this and now appeared more relaxed. In fact, one said, "Thank you, Sir. This is animal behaviour that they did not teach us at the college."

I explained to them that from here on we would have to be constantly on our guard,

An enormous baobab tree, the biggest the author ever found. He refers to the baobab as an "upside-down tree" since its branches look like roots sticking skyward.

especially from behind. "Make no mistake," I said, "buffalo are cunning creatures. Most of the lightly wounded ones that I've had to follow worked their way around and charged from behind. We have the wind in our favour, but I will use my little bag of ash to test it as we move along." I shook my handkerchief filled with fine wood ash. The wind carried the powder behind us. They nodded their understanding.

"Now I want you all to check your rifles to make sure you have solid bullets and *not* softnose bullets in the breech." This they did quietly and again nodded.

"An enraged buffalo in full charge is a sight to remember—if you survive. He comes out at you like a rocket, and you must keep your nerve and stand your ground. Otherwise you could find yourself flying through the air or, worse still, impaled on his horns. *Never* run away."

We headed toward the baboon, and I pointed at something down in the reeds about sixty paces off. A wide elephant path led down the bank, and it seemed that the wounded buffalo had followed that route. At thirty paces, I saw some tick birds fly into the air just as a black flash darted out of those reeds. It was our buffalo. With blood covering his face and chest, he was coming straight at us.

To a novice, a charging buffalo must seem like approaching death. I shouted for Ismail to shoot, but nothing happened. I quickly looked around, and not one of those students nor my two game guards were nearby; all I saw was backsides heading in the opposite direction.

By now the bloody-faced bull was at fifteen paces. I managed to keep my cool: I raised my .470 double, aimed at the base of his massive horns just above his eyes, and pulled the trigger. Just as I fired, he dropped his head a fraction

and my bullet ricocheted off his thick boss. He was right in front of me, lowering his head to toss me or knock me over, when I placed a bullet into his brain. Before I could jump aside, his heavy, hot, bloody body hit me just as he collapsed onto his knees. He did a somersault—knocking me over and landing clean on top of me, all the while bellowing and kicking in his last death throes.

I lay still a couple of minutes, trying desperately to get my breath. The buffalo must have weighed almost a ton. Warm blood sprayed all over my face and ran down my neck and up my nose, which made me sneeze. I felt a terrible pain inside and thought that the blow must have broken some of my ribs. I prayed as I lay there.

I then heard Ismail, who could speak a little English, say, "My God, what do we do now that Mr. Eric is dead under the buffalo?" The others had gathered around and were "Ummming" and "Ahhhhing," probably shaking their heads. I couldn't see. I played dead, just to hear their reactions.

I did not know if I had any broken bones, but I was finding it more and more difficult to breathe under the hulking, mud-encrusted body. Finally I had to shout, "*Mimi ta kufa sasa hivi kama ninyi hawesi kuondoa kabisa hii nyati!*" (I am going to die right now if you don't do away with this buffalo!)

I wouldn't have believed eight men could lift a dead buffalo and throw it to one side so fast. They lifted me up, hugging me and feeling me all over as one of my game guards said, "*Polepole, Bwana Mkubwa, kweli ni dume kabisa.*" (Be calm and never mind, Big Man, truly you are a real he-man.) Words like this were commonly used to soothe or encourage a victim after a shock or accident.

I was trembling with anger, or maybe relief, but then began to laugh. I flexed my arms and legs to make sure I was in one piece, then checked my Rigby to see if the stock was broken or the barrel bent. I was relieved to find it OK. I gave them a smart dressing down for running away, before telling them what had happened. They smiled, and each one shook my hand.

We turned the dead buffalo over to see where Ismail's shot had entered. It had traversed the stomach and passed into the right lung.

I radioed base camp for a driver to bring a Unimog to collect the meat. After the choice morsels were removed, we dropped the rest of the carcass at the old chief's house, which brought a broad smile.

The remainder of that safari went largely according to plan. Each of the students filled his tags, the entire group killing fifty-three elephant and sixteen buffalo. All received their diplomas. The student leader wrote me a thank-you letter, as did Tony, who said it was the most successful and interesting safari he had experienced.

Before I forget, I must tell you about my friend Phillip Nel. Phillip had just flown in with our monthly supplies and mail. It was always a fun time when he was around—he was so full of life and was nearly always happy. Only very occasionally would he be "off colour," and that's when he had had one too many. Then his character changed completely and he became aggressive. But that was a very

A picture of my dear friend, Phillip Nel, playing the fool. Little did we know that two months later he and his lovely wife, Jane, would be killed in a light plane accident. What a loss of two wonderful people.

186

small fault. Ninety-nine percent of his time he was a lovely, happy person.

One day we were out on a walking patrol, to try to see if we could find a big bull elephant we had seen the evening before from the air. As usual we walked down the Chulezi River, checking for fresh tracks that were easy to see in the wet sand, but also to be safe from any land mines left over from the bush war. We soon came to the point, which I had observed from the air, where we would turn inland and follow a well-defined valley that had huge Acacia albida trees, whose apple ring-like seed pods were a delicacy cherished by bull elephants.

We walked very slowly up that park-like valley, seeing many splendid bushbuck, male and female, darting off into the undergrowth as we approached. There was some fresh elephant dung here and there, but not too many signs of other game. As we came around a corner in the small stream we were following, there ahead of us was our big bull elephant, rubbing himself against a tree stump. To get a better view, we manoeuvered to our right. It was then that we discovered that he was actually masturbating against a stump of the *ilala* or vegetable ivory palm, his enormous penis nearly touching the ground, squealing soft noises in his delight. Unfortunately, the wind changed before I could capture his antics on film; he smelled us and, after a couple of trumpets and mock charges, took off at full speed in the opposite direction.

I shall always remember that day, because Phillip collapsed to the ground with laughter until tears of joy ran down his cheeks. He stood up and said, "Hell, Bwana Eric, I have never seen such a giant penis in my life, have you?" I thought he was referring to the old elephant; then it suddenly dawned on me that the stump really looked like a giant penis.

After a short while we had gathered our composure. Phillip insisted that we have our pictures taken with that phallic-shaped stump. We showed these pictures to all our friends as they didn't believe us. Tragically, not two months after this picture was taken, poor Phillip and his dear wife Jane were both killed in a light plane crash. What a sad ending for two charming people.

Ahmed of Marsabit

The most famous and probably the most photographed and written-about elephant in recent times has to be Ahmed, the great bull of Marsabit Park. Many conservationists and others were thunderstruck in 1973, when President Jomo Kenyatta of Kenya issued a presidential decree protecting a single, living animal. The decree made Ahmed famous overnight. He was guarded day and night until he died.

Many naturalists and other observers believed his mighty tusks weighed some 170–180 pounds a side. But all were proven wrong after his death: The tusks scaled only 148 pounds per side—a perfectly matched pair. This was probably due to the fact that he was a relatively small animal, measuring less than ten feet at the shoulder. Other big bulls stand eleven to twelve feet at the shoulder.

"Prize Possession" *by Mike Ghaui.*

CHAPTER ELEVEN
Terror Times Two

Let me tell you about a lion's roar. Few things are more difficult to describe. I think that the lion has three types of roars. First, he grunts, usually when hunting. Second, he lets go with an angry and bloodcurdling roar when he is charging. The third is the throaty roaring for which this species is universally known. The roar grows in volume and then gradually dies away but is repeated over and over, indicating, I believe, satisfaction after the animal has killed.

And when you hear that second type of roar, see those flaming yellow eyes bearing down on you, and know that you are the prey, you *will* be transfixed.

Soon after I took up my duties in 1965 as a senior game warden in southern Tanganyika, the commissioner of the Chunya District informed me that he had a major problem: lion were killing and eating men, women, and even children, and could I do something about it immediately?

I assured him that I could, and would be there by tomorrow. Most of the killings had taken place around a small village called Luika, near the once-famous Saza gold mine. Viva's father used to work for the mine, and she

reminded me that she had been born in a tent on the edge of Chunya airfield. Her father, Rudolf, had sent for an airplane to take his in-labour wife to Mbeya hospital, but by the time the plane arrived, Viva was already born, with her dad acting as midwife. Naturally, Viva wished to accompany me for old times' sake. Her family had lived in that area for many years, her parents operating a thriving fishing business on Lake Rukwa.

We stayed at an old derelict camp of the PWD (Public Works Department, which we used to call the Piss and Wind Department). The three small whitewashed buildings still had their corrugated iron roofs intact, but all the wooden doors and windows had long since been pilfered. At least we had four sturdy walls and a roof over our heads.

As we settled into the biggest of the three buildings, the local *jumbe* (chief) arrived, bringing us some chickens and eggs, a gesture of welcome. He told me that over the past three weeks, lion had killed and eaten five of his villagers, one man and four women, plus many goats and dogs.

I asked him how many lion he thought were responsible. *"Mengi saaaana"* (very many) was his stern reply. He said the lion usually walked right past where we were camped, and warned us to be careful, especially as we had no doors or windows.

I questioned him further. He said it had been four days since the last person was killed—a woman cultivating her garden close by the village. They had found only pieces of clothing covered in blood; the rest of her apparently had been devoured completely.

It was getting dark, so the chief said, "Kwaheri" (good-bye) and went on his way, wanting to reach home before nightfall. Two of his warriors were with him, carrying sharp spears. Most of those people who lived away from the cities or towns back then were terrified to walk around after dark, due mainly to stories passed down from generation to generation about lion killing and eating people.

Viva and I occupied one building whilst our cook had another and the third was for my game scouts, including Rashidi and Salum, and our driver, John. We barricaded our doorways with large tree trunks especially cut for that purpose. The windows we left open. We heard lion roaring, but they were miles away.

We had to wait for the man-eaters to strike again before we could place our traps or baits, but we did not have to wait long. Early the next morning two villagers arrived to report that another old woman had been killed whilst waiting in her *shamba* (garden) to chase away monkeys trying to steal her maize. I had half-expected, half-dreaded the news. Viva said she would stay behind—she didn't feel like seeing a mutilated corpse.

Rashidi came over to tell me that there were some fresh lion pug marks on the road right there by our camp. I took a look, and we came to the consensus that two lion had come

from across the Luika River, crossed a bridge, and passed not twenty paces from where we'd been sleeping. A cold shudder ran all over my body. I took Salum with me but left Rashidi to stay in camp with Viva.

On our arrival at the isolated garden, the victim's son pointed to a small, open-sided hut where the family would gather for their main meal at midday. He said, "*Simba na kamata mama yangu kule kule karibu ile nyumba kidogo.* (The lion caught my mother there, close to that small house.)

Salum and I found pug marks right away, and as we approached the hut, we found signs of struggle; bits of torn clothing lay about, and there were blotches of dried blood everywhere. This is where the lion had pounced upon their victim, ate some, and dragged the remainder into the high grass.

I told the two villagers to wait there whilst we followed the drag marks, but they shook their heads and asked if they could hide in my Land Rover. They were scared stiff, and I couldn't blame them. The drag marks were not easy to follow in the long grass, but the splashes of blood on the vegetation showed us the way. Soon we flushed the lion, only hearing their growls and grunts as they dashed through the grass ahead.

Seconds later we came upon the gruesome remains of their victim. Her head was still attached to the spine; one eye stared into the sky whilst in place of the other were huge canine tooth holes—which must have killed her instantly, or so we hoped. One arm was intact, though half-eaten, as were both legs. The flesh of her thighs had been eaten, and all her ribs were gone. It was really a horrible scene.

We continued our hunt, but we soon gave up the chase because the lion could hear us coming from a long way off and simply retreated farther into the bushes. I asked the chief to form a posse with his young men and try to drive the killers out to where Salum and I would be waiting, but that operation turned out to be just as futile.

I then asked the chief to obtain permission from the victim's family to use the woman's

This is a big male warthog, similar to the one that Salum shot and we tried to use as bait, without success.

remains as bait. Meanwhile I motored into Chunya, some forty miles away, to tell the DC about my plans and get his approval. His words were, "As long as you have the family's permission, you have mine to go ahead. Anything to get rid of these killers."

On the way back I spotted a warthog foraging in a swamp. I told Salum to *piga* (shoot) it for bait. He was an excellent shot and knocked the creature over cleanly with his new .458 rifle.

As we drew close to where the lion were last known to be, we tied the warthog behind the vehicle, cut open its guts, and pulled it slowly behind to a place suitable to hang a bait. I had asked the chief to build a large platform up in some big trees there, overlooking a spot where we hoped the lion would come to feed. It was in place. The villagers had also gathered the human remains and placed them in a sack tied high up in another tree, just in case I had to use them as a last resort.

We hung the warthog from a branch high enough to be almost out of reach for a lion standing on its hind legs. This would keep the predators there, teasing them and perhaps giving us a shot once the spotlight was flashed on them. The chief returned to his village, and I drove back to let Viva know what was happening. Later that day, as I started back to the village, Viva shouted, "Now don't do anything foolish!"

Rashidi, Salum, and I drove back, left the vehicle, and proceeded on foot to the platform that might be our home for the entire night. It was Salum's job to switch on the spotlight once I had given him the signal. Rashidi was to shoot at one lion and I at the other; if we both shot at the same lion, that would be OK, as long as we killed one.

We had dressed warmly, for evenings can get cold, especially if the wind is gusting. Viva had supplied us with Thermos flasks full of coffee and tea, plus chicken sandwiches and biscuits. Well, it turned out to be a fruitless night, except for a couple of hyena that had followed the drag. They couldn't reach the bait, being much shorter than lion, and I didn't chase them away for fear of spooking the lion.

I told the chief that these lion were "*majanja sana*" (very clever), and that they could bury the remains of the old woman. He gave me a dirty look and replied, "*Lakini, Bwana Nyama, sisi waneji nataka wewe kuu tumia hii maiti sababu huyu mama mzee nakuwa Uganaga mkuu. Vilevile. Sisi anajua yeye ta tumia hawa simba kwa bunduki yako.*" (But, Mr. Game, we the locals want you to use the dead body because that old woman was a very good doctor [in witchcraft]. Also we know that she will force the lion to come to your guns.)

Just to keep the peace, we replaced the warthog with the corpse, not a pleasant thing to do. We gave the chief the warthog for food, and the villagers carried it off, singing with delight. Death sometimes means nothing to these people. I believe it is because they see so much of it, out in the bush miles away from medical attention.

As we settled down for another long night on the platform, I was worried that the hyena would return, so I took along my catapult (slingshot), which I often used to scare away animals, and a bag of marbles.

It began to get cold. We had to sit perfectly still; I knew from previous experience that man-eaters rely to a great degree on their cunning to survive. I had told Rashidi that as soon as the light was switched on, he was to shoot at the animal on his left. I would shoot at the lion on the right. If we were lucky, we might kill both.

The only sounds were crickets chirping their nocturnal choruses. Suddenly we heard the crunching of bones. I thought, *Those blasted hyena have returned*, but deep down I had a funny feeling that it was something else.

I lifted my .470 Rigby. This was the signal for Salum to switch on the spotlight. There before us crouched two lion. I fired at the bigger lioness, Rashidi at the other. There were some terrific roars from the "stage" below, and before I could get in another shot, they had vanished into the darkness. Salum said he had heard a bullet hitting something, and he thought I had hit mine, but he couldn't tell where Rashidi's bullet went.

After a few minutes we climbed down and went to check for blood. We soon found several blotches on a nearby bush. At least one of the lion was wounded. We would come back at first light to continue our search.

In the surrounding villages, drums began to beat. I told Salum to go to our car and bring back an old gunnysack into which we would place the meager human remains. Both of my men were reluctant to handle them, so I had to do the honours, not a pleasant job. We headed for the chief's village to tell him what had happened, drop off the gunnysack, and warn that no one must wander about in the bush until the wounded lion was accounted for.

The old chief handed the sack to one of the victim's sons, then turned to me and said, *"Mimi na sema nini?"* (What did I tell you?) He invited us to come and sit by his fire, but we had to get some sleep, for we didn't know what was in store for us tomorrow.

After a restless night's sleep, we had no difficulty in following the lion's path, which soon led us to a small swamp with green grass cropped short by warthog and probably Lichtenstein hartebeest, both of which love to feed in that type of habitat. The blood spoor was getting less and less visible, slowing our progress. We had to keep a wary eye for a charging lion, which could erupt at any time.

Soon we were once again in tall grass, which I detested because it cut our visibility to practically zero. We climbed a huge anthill to look around and were relieved to see fairly open woodland not far ahead.

I decided that this anthill was an excellent lookout position. I would sit here and wait while Salum and Rashidi moved out to try and circle around the lion and drive them in my direction. I set out my plans clearly for them, and before they left I stressed that I would be up on the anthill and they must avoid shooting in my direction. They both nodded and disappeared into the maze of forest and grass. Meanwhile, I settled down where I had a good view for 270 degrees, mostly to my front.

Minutes seemed to turn into hours. Suddenly, not far ahead, a couple of Coqui francolin (a small partridgelike bird) flew up into the air, making their alarm calls. Perhaps the lion were coming my way. I knelt up to get a better view and thought I saw a tawny-coloured "thing" moving very low in the grass some sixty yards away. After some minutes of intense concentration, my knees began to feel my weight, so I relaxed a bit to ease the pain. My nerves and my adrenal glands were working overtime. I pushed off the safety on my Rigby, in readiness for a quick shot.

My strained eyes caught a movement to my right, and to my surprise there was the old lioness crawling along on her belly. She kept looking behind to check if she was being followed; she had no idea where I was. I couldn't see the second lion and presumed that they had split up. Suddenly there came a shot, and another, and again. My heart was pounding, and perspiration poured down my back.

At the shots, the wounded lioness tried to stand up, but her left shoulder was shattered from my shot the night before. She was limping badly when she disappeared into a thicket on the side of another anthill not thirty paces from where I was kneeling. I waited and waited, but no lioness.

I crept down slowly from my vantage point, never taking my eyes off those bushes where I had last seen her. Out of that scrub charged a three-hundred-pound lioness in a murderous mood, a sight never forgotten. I was able to get off both barrels with softnose bullets, which anchored her to the ground, clawing and biting her front foot.

I reloaded and advanced a couple of steps toward her writhing body. She growled and snarled and spat at me, like wild cats do.

Her tail lashed from side to side, and her eyes glared hate at me. I shot her where she crouched, and she rolled over, dead.

After a while, I heard a soft whistle behind me. I turned to see Rashidi and Salum standing atop the anthill I had just vacated. They punched the air with their clenched fists, and I did likewise. I signaled for them to join me—I was anxious to hear their part of the story and to show them the reason this poor lioness had turned to killing people. Her front paws were swollen and infected from hundreds of porcupine quills. Those quills had almost crippled her. She had turned to killing humans, goats, and dogs because she could never have killed a wild animal in her state.

Rashidi told me that they had been charged by the smaller lioness and had managed to get her before she got them. He led me to her body, and we found no bullet holes from the previous night. All three of their shots today had found their mark. I congratulated them and said that now we could face up to the chief and villagers with pride.

We had rid the chief and his villagers of their terror. These two lionesses had killed six humans, plus many goats and dogs. The district commissioner was very happy and congratulated us for our efforts.

"Sable Bulls" *by Mike Ghaui.*

CHAPTER TWELVE
Artus, an Incredible Hound (1990–1992)

I want to tell you a few stories about a fantastic dog that was my hunting companion and true friend whilst I was general manager and senior hunter on one of the largest privately owned game ranches in Namibia. The vast ranch—stretching over some 43,000 hectares (about 105,000 acres)—was owned and operated by Axel Henniges, who hailed from Germany. After years of negotiations and plenty of red tape involving government officials and veterinarians, Henniges brought to his ranch, Ohorongo, two Hanoverian hunting hounds, known in Germany as *Hannoverischer Schweisshund*.

Let me give you a little background. Years earlier, Mr. Henniges was hunting in Germany somewhere when he wounded a stag. He followed and then lost the blood trail. He did not want to leave a wounded animal to die. He had heard of a Dr. Wolf-Eberhard Barth, a senior forest officer, who owned one of these Hanoverian hounds. He had also heard many stories from hunters about how this special breed of dog was excellent at searching for and finding wounded game animals. He contacted Dr. Barth and pleaded with him to bring his dog to help find the stag.

To cut a long story short, the dog soon found the trail and, after a long chase, bayed the wounded stag and barked to call the hunters, who finished it off. The dog impressed Henniges so much that he wanted to buy a pair of them immediately.

This was easier said than done. There was a long waiting list of people who wanted Hanoverian hounds. Even if you were willing to pay enormous sums of money, you had to wait your turn, then prove to a committee that you were a capable hunter, then wait until a dog became available. I believe I am correct in saying that in 1991, there were only 143 Hanoverian hounds in the world. Henniges had to wait three years to obtain a pair.

Dr. Barth, an authority on this special breed, selected a male and female for Henniges, flew with them to Namibia, and introduced them to Ohorongo. He also trained me and my staff on how to handle and work with these dogs. It was fascinating work, to say the least.

The dogs had registered names. The male was Artus von Cerf, the female Aspe von Orbgrund. Artus was allocated to me; Mr. Henniges had Aspe. Henniges gave strict instructions that any animal wounded on Ohorongo could be finished off only by himself or me—not by the hunter. He was aware that in Europe hunters had shot and killed dogs and even other hunters in the excitement of the chase.

Now that you have some background, allow me to relate some of the hunts that Artus made possible.

I clearly recall one particular Frenchman who was supposed to be a fantastic hunter as well as a superb shot. He would tell us stories of his hunts in Zambia or Tanzania and that he had killed fifteen animals with fifteen shots. Everyone around the campfire was impressed. Even his wife vouched that her husband was a fine shot. Well, it was my bad luck to have this so-called crack shot as my client. The events went something like this:

On our first morning, we were looking for a trophy greater kudu. Some monsters roamed the ranch, and I knew a special place where I thought we would find one. My client's two hunter friends went to other areas of the ranch so that there would be no interference with one another's hunting activities.

My driver, Elias, drove us slowly toward my favourite lookout post atop some huge granite rocks. I had spent many hours over the previous couple of years squatting on top of that rocky outcrop and had seen many trophy greater kudu bulls. En route we passed up several shootable bulls, but none was good enough for my client. He and his friends had some behind-the-scenes betting going on to see who would shoot the best trophies.

We arrived at the outcrop just as the sun topped the horizon. At the top, I made certain that everyone knew there was to be no speaking or walking about. Artus was at my heel, as he'd been trained. His tail was wagging—he knew

we were hunting, and he loved nothing better than to chase and bay a wounded animal.

As we scanned the valleys below, Elias spotted a huge kudu bull coming toward us, but about half a mile away. I told Mr. X (that's what I will call him from here on) to get himself positioned and ready just in case the big bull came within shooting range. It took a long time for the bull to meander our way; he was busy nibbling at the new growth on the bushes. Kudu are mainly browsers, not grazers, although they do revert to eating grass when forage is scarce.

Artus had his eyes focused on mine, anxiously awaiting the word to seek. I stroked him to reassure him that all was fine.

After about two hours, the lonesome bull wandered within shooting range, about two hundred yards. Mr. X was shivering, so I told him to relax. We had discussed the size of the kudu's horns. Having been a Rowland Ward measurer for many years, I could tell within an inch how big this fellow would go—easily sixty-three inches, I told him, very high in the record book.

The moment came for our hero to pull the trigger. When the bull was broadside and had stopped to nibble, I touched Mr. X's shoulder, the signal to shoot. I had my binocular focused on the animal when the rifle roared. To my amazement, the kudu stopped eating and looked toward us but didn't run away. I said, "Shoot again, you missed." Mr. X reloaded, but the kudu heard the noise of his bolt working and dashed straight toward where we were perched on top of the outcrop. I whispered for the hunter to wait, and the big bull stopped not eighty yards below us, looking around for the source of the noise. I touched Mr. X's shoulder again, there was another roar, and dust flew below the kudu's stomach.

"Quick, shoot again," I said. Mr. X glared at me and said, "It's impossible for me to miss at this range. I hit him for sure." By this time the lucky kudu was disappearing over the next ridge.

Mr. X maintained that he had hit the animal and insisted that we go down to look for blood, which I knew we wouldn't find. I tried to calm the client down and offered him some schnapps or coffee.

He said, "Why don't you put Artus on the trail so he can locate the wounded animal?"

I told Mr. X there was no blood for Artus to follow and that he had missed both shots. He shook his head and said that we must go back to the rifle range—someone must have knocked or dropped his rifle and put the scope out of alignment.

Back at the vehicle, I radioed the other hunters to say that we were heading back to camp. We went straight to the range, an old dam wall that we used to sight-in the rifles. Actually, we had done this the evening before, and all the clients' rifles appeared to be shooting accurately enough to kill animals.

Mr. X said, "OK, Eric, you shoot my rifle first." I did and centered the bull at 150 yards.

"There you go, Sir," I said. "It's not your rifle."

Artus with an oryx gemsbok wounded by a client. The bullet hole in the neck was Balson's finishing shot. Ohorongo Game Ranch, Namibia, 1990.

199

That was the start of one of the worst safaris I have ever taken out. Even Artus looked sad; he always seemed to smile at other times, especially when he found a wounded animal.

At supper we discussed the next day's hunting. Mr. X remained mostly silent for the entire evening. He wished to try for a gemsbok or oryx the next day. The other hunters had shot a warthog and a springbok, so they elected to hunt for greater kudu and eland.

The early morning was brisk, with dew everywhere; gloves and overcoats were the order of the day. We drove along slowly in anticipation of finding a big gemsbok. Plenty of trophy animals were about, so you had to be ready at all times.

As Elias maneuvered around some rocks, there in front of us stood an enormous blue wildebeest bull, one of the finest I had ever seen. Elias stopped, and I beckoned to Mr. X to shoot. The animal was not more than one hundred yards away and standing half broadside, offering an ideal shot to heart or lungs.

"Take your time," I whispered.

It seemed to take ages for Mr. X to get ready, and when he finally pulled the trigger, I did hear a thud as the bullet hit the beast. Its back legs gave a high kick, and it snorted and took off through the bushes.

"You see, I can shoot, and I know I hit him right here," he said, thumping his chest. "We will find him dead close by." I was not at all sure about that as we went to look for signs of blood. Elias soon found where the animal had been standing, but there was very little blood sign. Artus soon picked up the trail and began his chase. He would bark only when he actually saw the animal and had it bayed, but there was dead silence, and we had already covered a quarter-mile, so I knew Mr. X's shot

had not been too good. Elias shook his head and said that the blood had ceased.

We listened for Artus, but heard nothing. A hushed, negative atmosphere prevailed. Mr. X suddenly broke the silence: "Your bloody dog is useless; he has lost the trail." And he kicked a bush.

"No, Sir, Artus is still chasing your wounded bull and will call us with his barks once he has found the poor beast. We must wait. Elias will drive us to those big rocks, and whilst we have some refreshments, I will scan the countryside for Artus."

During the break I explained that if Artus couldn't find the quarry, he would return to the exact spot where he commenced his chase, and that's why I had left my vest there. These hounds are trained to do this. I also radioed the others to keep their ears open for Artus's barking.

It was long past lunchtime and my backside was getting sore from sitting on those hard rocks when one of the other hunters called to say that they could hear Artus barking not too far from their lunch place. He told me his exact position, and I was astounded—they were fifteen miles away. I told them we were on our way.

It took about half an hour to drive there. Wolf, one of my hunters, pointed. We all listened, and then I heard Artus. He was calling for us to come and put the animal out of its misery.

Elias drove, and I stood on the back seat to try to search for Artus, but the bush was thick and the grass high. Every now and then Elias would stop and switch off the engine, and we were thus able to pinpoint the hound's position. When we were near enough, I told everyone to remain in the vehicle whilst I approached the battle scene.

And a "battle scene" I found. The wounded wildebeest was lying down and Artus was running around it in circles, keeping his distance from the enraged bull. Both were exhausted, frothing at the mouth and panting heavily. The high grass had been flattened in a circle all around the wounded animal, Artus having kept it bayed for several hours. I crept up behind a tree and shot the exhausted animal in the brain.

Artus ran up and jumped into my arms and licked my face. I was so relieved to know that he was safe and pleased that he had done such fantastic work that I didn't worry about all the froth and slime he deposited on my face.

As I was checking to see where Mr. X's bullet had hit, Elias drove the others to the scene. "Look where your shot hit," I said, thumping my backside.

"That's not my shot," Mr. X shouted as he stumbled from the hunting car. "It's impossible for me to shoot like that," and he shook his fist in the air.

"Well, Sir, there are only two bullet holes in this animal; one is yours and the other is mine, and mine certainly didn't hit this poor beast in the buttocks." That shut him up as his wife consoled him.

Then she said, "Mr. Eric, I can't believe that this wonderful dog chased this animal for over fifteen miles and kept it here until we arrived. I will write to Mr. Henniges and tell him what a fantastic dog he has in Artus."

Mr. X finally came to his senses and patted and hugged Artus, saying, "I second what my wife has just said." And he came over to shake my hand and apologize for being such a stupid fool.

During this safari Mr. X shot many animals but wounded each and every one. Artus and I certainly had our work cut out for us. I must have lost ten pounds with all the running I had to do to keep up with that hound.

For example, Mr. X gut-shot his big gemsbok. Artus eagerly gave chase, with me in hot pursuit. I could hear Artus barking bayed, but the bull caught sight of me and took off again, as did Artus.

After about a mile I was completely exhausted, so I collapsed on the ground in some shade. Artus had stopped barking. After a while he appeared in front of me, wagging his tail and panting "ninety to the dozen." He sat down right in front of me, never taking his eyes off mine. I stroked him and told him I was finished and that he must wait for me to get my breath back. He seemed to understand; his eyes smiled, and he lay down next to me. When my breathing eased and I sat up, he also jumped up, wagging his tail. He stared me in the eyes, gave a small whine, and took off into the bush.

A few minutes had passed when I heard his barking not far away. I crept through the thick thorn shrubs and was able to finish the gemsbok off. But what amazed me was how Artus had known where to find me and that he had waited for me to recover before continuing his chase. I shall always remember Artus for that hunt especially.

Mr. X ended a thank-you letter to me with these words: "Please stroke Artus for me. He's such an amazing dog."

I believe that I was the only hunter in Africa to receive a special award from the president of the Der Jagdgebrauchshundundverband for the fifty hunts that Artus did with me. I cherish this bronze medal because it symbolizes the memory of my dear friend and companion, Artus von Cerf.

Another client of mine, also from France, was J. J. Carrier, a fine gentleman, a professional

Artus eyeballing Balson, always waiting for the order to "seek."

hunter, and an author. J. J.'s book, *La Chasse, A La Bécasse*, establishes his special expertise on woodcock, a fine sporting bird.

During one of his three safaris to Ohorongo, J. J. asked me, "Do you think I could shoot two greater kudu bulls with a left and a right?" It took a few moments to figure out what he meant, and then it suddenly clicked. Hunters who seek gamebirds with a double-barreled shotgun occasionally shoot two flying birds at once, one with the left barrel and the other with the right. They refer to this feat as a double, or "a left and a right."

I told J. J. that it was impossible for him to do this with his rifle, which had a single barrel. But I went on to say that if we had the luck to find two greater kudu bulls together, I would allow him to shoot them with two consecutive shots, and we would call this a left and a right.

So it was agreed that he would pay for two greater kudu bulls if the opportunity arose. I asked him why he wanted to shoot two kudu. He said that a friend had asked him to try to shoot a kudu for him, and of course J. J. wanted a good trophy for himself.

It transpired that just before J. J. came to hunt on Ohorongo, I saw four kudu bulls drinking in a sand river, using water holes dug by baboon and warthog to quench their thirst. I told J. J. that we would seek out these four bulls, for two of the four were shootable.

With Elias driving, Artus aboard, and J. J. and me sitting comfortably in the back, we headed for a rocky outcrop that made an ideal outlook post. We sat there for five hours without sighting the four kudu bulls, though we did see some fine singles. On the second day we got lucky—the four bulls appeared, walking in our direction. I loaded two rounds into J. J.'s rifle and told him that if the bulls came within range, I would point out which ones to shoot. Both of us were excited—I because I had never seen a person shoot two magnificent kudu bulls with "a left and a right."

The bulls moved toward us hesitantly— why I don't know, since the wind was in our favour and they hadn't seen us. J. J. was in position, and his breathing had finally slowed to normal. As the bulls fed closer, however, they kept changing places. The biggest was at one time the leader, but then meandered to last place. This concerned me because there was not much space among the four as they traveled our way. But J. J. was an excellent shot, so when the bulls were inside two hundred yards, I told him to shoot at the second animal from the front and then immediately chamber the other round and shoot the one bringing up the rear.

He steadied his rifle on a small sandbag I had positioned as a rest. I didn't look through my field glasses, as I wanted to make sure he fired at the right bulls.

His first shot filled the valley with a tremendous roar, and his bullet struck home with a deep thud; all the bulls stopped in their tracks. "Shoot the last one," I whispered, and his second shot rang out. By this time kudu were jumping and running in all directions. I kept my eyes on the two he had shot at and soon saw the first bull fall over sideways. The second one was limping as it disappeared into a ravine. It never came out the other end, so we presumed it also had succumbed.

We waited a few minutes, and then I shook J. J.'s hand, for I knew he had achieved his

ambition to get "a left and a right." He ordered champagne for dinner that evening.

On that same safari J. J. asked me whether a .22 bullet could kill a large animal. I told him that if he was close enough and hit the animal's eye en route to its brain, the animal would drop in its tracks. He laughed at me. If the opportunity arose, I said, I would prove it to him.

One day as we sat in a hide overlooking a water hole, a very large male springbok strolled in for a drink. J. J. had his .22 in the hide for he wished to shoot a few guinea fowl for the pot. I told him this was an ideal opportunity to use his .22—the buck was no more than fifty yards away. I told him to aim right between its eyes as the animal turned to check out the noise I was about to make. I gave a soft grunt; it turned to look straight at us, J. J. took aim and fired, and it crumpled in its tracks.

It so happened that this was the largest springbok ever shot on Ohorongo during the time I was resident there. Its horns measured 17¾ inches, well up in the record books. Of course, J. J. was as thrilled with his shooting as he was with his fine trophy.

"My friends just won't believe me when I tell them I shot this fantastic specimen with my little .22." He laughed and shook my hand, and we drove back to camp to celebrate.

In the hunting world, as in other modes of life, one comes across all types of human beings. I had one client who wished to shoot only animals with deformed horns. Even if I showed him a fantastic trophy, he would turn it down if its horns were balanced and symmetrical. I told him that we had many animals with abnormal horns, especially greater kudu and gemsbok. This news excited him.

Even so, seeking a sizable deformed kudu or gemsbok during the client's few days of hunting was rather like looking for a needle in a haystack. Well, don't you know, on our second day out I saw a male gemsbok with a fantastically weird set of horns. I couldn't believe our luck. I didn't tell the client until I was absolutely certain it was the bull with the twisted horn that I had spotted some months before. After a few more peeks through my binocular, I told the client that we had found a fine trophy for his collection.

When he saw the animal firsthand, he said, "Eric, whatever we do, we must not let this animal get away from us."

I had to figure out how to approach the herd of about thirty animals without spooking them. Most were females with young, plus a couple of old males. The females were especially wary and protective of their young. But my main concern was that if they took off, the males would follow.

I decided to try a tactic that had often worked before. Elias started the vehicle and drove along slowly. I ordered Artus to *aplegen* (lie down) in the back of the Toyota, which he did. As the vehicle went behind some bushes, I jumped off with the client right behind me. We sat motionless as Elias drove off; the entire herd watched him move around them in a semicircle. This gave us the perfect opportunity to stalk up closer.

The bull we wanted was on the far side of the herd, which made it difficult for the client to get a clean shot. Still, I decided to take the chance; if he could at least hit the animal, Artus would do the rest.

Artus with the abnormal gemsbok.

I positioned him against a tree and pointed out the target animal. He couldn't see the bull through his scope until I physically pointed his rifle directly at the animal. I pointed to my shoulder to indicate where he should place his bullet. He nodded, took aim, and fired. I heard a thud indicating a hit, but God only knew where. The herd scattered in all directions. The wounded bull was nowhere to be seen.

We walked over to check for blood. Sure enough, plenty of frothy pink blotches showed that he had hit the lungs. I signaled for Elias to bring the vehicle—and Artus. Gemsbok are very tenacious of life once wounded, and you must approach a wounded one carefully, for they have sharp horns and have been known to kill their pursuers.

Artus was standing in the vehicle as it approached, staring me directly in the eyes, awaiting his instructions to give chase. I told the client that we should wait twenty minutes or so to let the wounded animal either die or lie down and stiffen up before I set Artus loose, and that he must remain at the vehicle until he heard me shoot. Eventually I set Artus on the trail, and he took off at great speed. I tried to keep up.

It wasn't before long I heard Artus barking bayed. I ran to the place and saw the gemsbok with his behind backed into a bush. He was down on his front knees, facing Artus and trying desperately to hook him with his sharp horns. I couldn't get a good shot, and before I could get into a better position, the gemsbok charged at Artus and then ran off with the dog right at his heels.

It was some time before I heard Artus barking again, far off. I ran toward the sounds and luckily found a rocky outcrop nearby. I scrambled up and peeped over the top. About four hundred yards away, I could see the pair battling, Artus keeping his distance from those sharp horns. I assumed a steady position, confident that my .30-06 was sighted in to shoot at five hundred yards for occasions such as this. I took aim and fired, and the bull took off at a great speed, only to turn a complete somersault after a short distance and lie there kicking. I shouted the "lie-down" command to Artus and awaited the client's arrival. When we reached the dead beast, the client was so thrilled that he shook my hand and kissed Artus, whose wagging tail revealed his delight.

It was a very sad day for me when I had to leave Ohorongo, and Artus. I have never felt so much emotion over an animal. But Viva and I had decided to move to Canada. It was time to leave the land of our birth and start afresh in another country that wasn't plagued by so much turmoil as were many parts of Africa at that time.

Our artist friend Mike Ghaui, drew this sketch of an elephant in just ten minutes with a pencil and inscribed it to Viva and me. Thanks, Mike. I think it makes an excellent way of saying "Kwaheri." (good-bye)

EPILOGUE

The setting sun brushed Kilimanjaro's snowy peak with a deep gold, then a light pink, and finally a dark purple hue, a picture of indescribable magnificence. I sat on my camp chair reminiscing about the good old days on safari with my wife, Viva, our three sons, now grown men, and my dear friend Prince Bernhard of the Netherlands. All around me was beauty and peace—except in my mind, for this would probably be my last night in the *polini* (wilderness) of Africa.

Sadly, the last of the mammoth tuskers, along with the poor black rhinoceros, have succumbed or were wiped out by poachers during the late 1960s and 1970s, and the gene pool to replace them is no longer there. My conscience still pricks me when I think back on how many elephant and buffalo I had to kill in the name of conservation. Today there is heavy pressure for space in which to live and produce food for the survival of the human species, whose world population is said to exceed *six billion*. Mankind looks with covetous eyes upon the national parks, game reserves, and private game sanctuaries for expansion, especially in Africa, where survival of the fittest is the daily norm. It is said that more than half the world's people today are hungry, and just before writing this, I heard on the news that over fourteen million people in the Horn of Africa are on the brink of death.

Much of the earth's surface lies ravaged by war, air pollution, decimated forests, eroded landscapes, and teeming cities. Our lack of foresight, our carelessness, and our failure to nurture the natural world will ultimately result in the decline, decimation, or complete extinction of this planet's fauna and flora.

As I sit in my study writing, I am surrounded by oil paintings that have a special place in my heart. One of my uncles, an accomplished artist, kindly left us £10,000 in his will when he died at the age of ninety-three. But back when Viva and I were married in 1956, this same uncle asked what we would like for a wedding present. We asked him to paint us a picture of some elephant walking with Kilimanjaro in the background.

"Why?" he asked.

I told him that when I was small, my family traveled through Tanganyika to visit some of my parent's friends in Arusha. My father wanted to use an old track that he knew across the Ngasarai plains, and the road was very dusty. We had an open, box-body car with tarpaulin blinds that were useless at keeping out the clouds of fine lava dust, and before long we were suffocating

Prince Bernhard of the Netherlands, with one of his dogs, saying "Salute!"

In 1935, when Balson was five years old, he saw a herd of elephants crossing in front of Mt. Kilimanjaro. The scene stayed in his memory ever after. This painting represents that very scene.

from both the dust and the heat. My mother told my dad to stop at a small stream flowing down from Mount Meru. Whilst we washed our faces and had some lunch, my father said, "Look over there." A herd of elephant was walking across our front. I vividly remember that scene—it was the first time we had seen elephant in the wild or seen Kilimanjaro[1] so close.

Well, Viva and I waited thirty-six years for our wedding present, and when the painting eventually arrived, we were so disappointed with it that we decided to use the £10,000 to commission an artist friend of ours, Yvan Dushmanitch, to render ten special paintings for us. The one you see here depicts the very scene from my boyhood, and the other paintings stir special feelings in both Viva and me.

As Prince Bernhard would say, "Salute." I wish all those who read this book "*Kwaheri, Allah bilkheri,*" a Swahili salutation meaning "Goodbye, God prosper you."

1. Mount Kilimanjaro is the highest mountain in Africa and the ninth highest in the world at 19,340 feet. It was originally part of British East Africa, but Queen Victoria (1819–1901), queen of Great Britain and Empire, gave it to Kaiser William II (1859–1941), king of Prussia and German emperor, as a gift because, it is said, he had no high, snow-clad mountain in his empire. Today it is in the country of Tanzania, formerly German East African (Tanganyika).

AFTERWORD

I was as excited as a young boy when, in 1998, I was invited to go on a hunting safari in my beloved Tanzania. Twenty-six years had gone by since Viva and I had finally packed our bags and left Africa with broken hearts, heading for new pastures. It was a strange feeling for me to return to my old stomping grounds as a professional hunter rather than my old role as a senior game warden.

A friend of mine, Danny McCallum, asked if I could please help him out—he had four overseas clients coming and only three professional hunters. Of course I snapped up the opportunity and made my way to Arusha, where Danny's operation was based. I was happy to find that some of my old friends still lived in or around that once-delightful little town. But my heart was saddened to see how much it had deteriorated in the years I had been gone.

Thousands of people had built shanties on the outskirts of the town. The roads, once excellent, were now strewn with deep potholes, and the town itself needed a complete overhaul—every single house I saw needed to be painted. What a shock to my pleasant memories of my once-beautiful Arusha.

The shocks continued as we drove the few hundred miles to Danny's concessions in the Chunya District. Once, many years ago, it was "*inchi yangu*" (my domain). Now the roads were so corrugated that it was a wonder the vehicles weren't rattled to bits. Hundreds of people had moved to the roadsides and built houses, cutting down the once-fantastic woodlands in the process. This was a good example of the infamous slash-and-burn agriculture method: Cut down the trees and brush, burn them, then cultivate the land for a couple of years, never fertilizing, exhausting all the nutrients; then move to the next piece of land and repeat the process. It is a never-ending cycle of destruction.

As we drove along, I once again had to face the frightening reality that the accelerating rate of destruction of the fauna and flora is steadily leading to an ecological disaster. If humankind, in its ignorance and financial greed, continues to destroy the environment in this manner, it could mean our ultimate demise.

However, I believe that it is not too late to reverse man's negative influences on his environment. Given the innovations of modern technology combined with enormous international assistance, there exist great possibilities to reverse the downward trend and improve the living standards of the poorer peoples of this world.

The ultimate objective should be to educate all people to live in partnership with nature and its ecosystems. The general populations of most Third World countries must be taught to see that their wildlife, forests, rivers, lakes, and oceans must be preserved rather than wantonly exploited. I am perhaps biased in overstressing the ecological implications; however, I also know that human advancement cannot be achieved without some sort of disruption of the environment. But minimal impact must be the linchpin. Sadly, there is precious little time left to meet these objectives.

210